VEILED THREATS

Representing 'the Muslim woman' in UK public policy discourses

Naaz Rashid

First published in Great Britain in 2016 by

Policy Press
University of Bristol
1-9 Old Park Hill
Bristol
BS2 8BB
UK
+44 (0)117 954 5940
pp-info@bristol.ac.uk
www.policypress.co.uk

North America office:
Policy Press
c/o The University of Chicago Press
1427 East 60th Street
Chicago, IL 60637, USA
t: +1 773 702 7700
f: +1 773 702 9756
sales@press.uchicago.edu
www.press.uchicago.edu

British Library Cataloguing in Publication Data
A catalogue record for this book is available from the British Library

Library of Congress Cataloging-in-Publication Data
A catalog record for this book has been requested

ISBN 978-1-4473-2517-8 hardcover
ISBN 978-1-4473-2519-2 ePub
ISBN 978-1-4473-2520-8 Mobi

Policy Press works to counter discrimination on grounds of gender, race, disability, age and sexuality.

Cover design by Policy Press
Front cover image: Ernesto Costanzo
Printed and bound in Great Britain by CPI Group (UK) Ltd, Croydon, CR0 4YY
Policy Press uses environmentally responsible print partners

Contents

Acknowledgements

Many people have been involved in supporting me through the research process and the eventual publication of this book. First and foremost I am grateful to the research participants for their time and generosity. I admire many of them for the work they do with such passion and commitment and hope they will not find this book too critical. Many thanks to Laura Vickers and the staff at Policy Press; and thanks also to Ernesto Costanzo for producing the cover design which was adapted from an original image by Sam McDonald.

I would like to thank Suki Ali for her support, enthusiasm and guidance throughout the doctoral process and LSE for providing research studentships which helped fund my studies. I am also grateful to Claire Alexander for her unstinting generosity in supporting early career academics working in the field of 'race'. Thanks also to my PhD examiners Avtar Brah and John Solomos for their positive feedback and encouragement. I am also deeply grateful to the anonymous reviewer for their enthusiastic comments about this book.

I have benefitted greatly from being part of various early career academic networks such as REPS and NYLON with colleagues at LSE and Goldsmiths. Academic comradeship and camaraderie has come from Des Fitzgerald, Ajmal Hussain, Malcolm James, Hannah Jones, Helen Kim, Christy Kulz, Sanjiv Lingayah, Manal Massalha, Nabila Munawar, Victoria Redclift and Christine Scharff. Special thanks go to Malcolm James for sharing the everyday conviviality and angst of PhD student life. At the University of Manchester I would like to thank Wendy Bottero, Vallu Sivamohan, Bethan Harries and Katy Sian for making the commute worthwhile. I am grateful to the Department of Sociology at the University of Sussex for making it possible to finish this book. I would also like to thank the MSc 'ladies' (not all of whom were) at Birkbeck College. Discussions with Kalpana Wilson, Joelle Maulguet, Monique Charles and Christine Ru Pert-em-Hru felt like coming home. I would like to extend particular thanks to Yasmeen Narayan for encouraging me to embark on doctoral studies; the thought had genuinely never occurred to me previously. For intellectual sparring beyond the academy, many thanks to Michael Thomas, Hardip Begol and Sergio Palacios who, despite our many disagreements, have helped keep my mind keen and alert through our many protracted but always stimulating debates. I would also like to thank my students, particularly those at LSE, for their interest in my work.

Much love goes to Howard Doble for his unwavering practical, intellectual, and emotional support throughout every stage of the process. Words alone cannot do justice but I am grateful to him (and our feline friends) for keeping our home a place of comfort and calm during otherwise difficult times. Finally, I would like to dedicate this book to the memory of my much loved and deeply missed parents, Anowara Begum and Mohammad Abdur Rashid. I hope you would have been proud.

About the author

Dr Naaz Rashid is currently a Teaching Fellow at the School of Law, Politics and Sociology at the University of Sussex. She previously worked in central government and has held positions as a Research Associate in the Sociology Department at the University of Manchester and as a Graduate Teaching Assistant at the London School of Economics and Political Science, where she completed her PhD in 2013. She has also previously studied at Birkbeck College and SOAS at the University of London and at the University of Cambridge. Her research interests include 'race', gender, religion, urban studies, and social policy. She has had her work published in *Ethnic and Racial Studies*, as well as in *Open Democracy* and *The Guardian*.

PROLOGUE

Veiled threats?

I was standing in the courtyard garden of the V&A with a group of school girls. They were from a girls' school in east London and had been taken there as part of a local authority funded project. I had met the organiser, Sophia, through one of my research interviewees. She was a member of the Three Faiths Forum, an organisation set up in 1997 to encourage friendship, goodwill and understanding between people of different faiths (Judaism, Christianity and Islam). The girls had done their morning's activities, a worksheet that needed to be completed whilst looking at the exhibits, and were outside having their lunch. It was a beautiful sunny day and they were glad to be outside. As we sat on the grass, I chatted to one of the volunteers and around me the girls made the most of a day off school. Boisterous, although not rowdy by any means, they drew attention from other visitors to the museum, principally, I imagined, as all the girls were dressed in their school uniform of black *jilbabs*.[1] Suddenly, someone in the group suggested that they should all have their photo taken. The group assembled in makeshift lines. As the designated photographer shouted 'cheese', a number of the girls struck flamboyant cat walk poses. As various girls held their arms and legs akimbo and balanced precariously on the grass, brightly coloured trainers and jeans could be seen beneath, their scuffed Adidas bags slipping off their shoulders.

The poses were perhaps unsurprising given that the school trip was part of a project called Faith and Fashion. As exuberant as the girls were, as much as they appeared to enjoy the day, and as passionate as the organisers were about the value of what they were doing, the question nonetheless remained. What could an event looking at Faith and Fashion possibly have to do with combating terrorism?

In January 2008, Hazel Blears, Secretary of State for the Department for Communities and Local Government (DCLG) under the Labour administration, announced initiatives to empower Muslim women. She encouraged Local Authorities to use some of the £70m funding they had been given to 'prevent violent extremism' to 'empower Muslim women'. The Preventing Violent Extremism or 'Prevent' agenda was a policy response to the London bombings of 2005 and the threat of 'home-grown' Islamist terrorism.

In addition to these initiatives at the level of local government, a National Muslim Women's Advisory Group (NMWAG) was established to advise central government. This advisory board comprised 19 Muslim women from a wide spectrum of communities, professions and traditions and was, at least in principle, supposed to advise the government on issues affecting Muslim women. This number was subsequently extended to 25 after an open application process.

NMWAG was specifically tasked with overseeing three work streams. The first was a role modelling project designed to raise the aspirations of Muslim girls. Its focus was to present Muslim women who had achieved success in atypical careers as role models. There were six regional road shows which were accompanied by the publication of a booklet featuring 12 successful women and a website was launched called Our Choices.[2] Secondly, there was a project aimed at improving the religious understanding of Muslim women in society as part of a wider project on 'Faith Capacity' focused on 'theological disclosure' or 'theological interpretation'. Thirdly, there was a campaign to increase the civic participation of Muslim women through training and mentoring which was linked to a Councillors' Commission project to increase the number of black and minority ethnic (BME) women representatives more generally.

The acronym EMW ('Empowering Muslim Women') will be used to refer to the broad policy initiative which includes the three work streams within NMWAG's remit, as well as local authority projects funded through Prevent which were focused on Muslim women and girls. The EMW initiatives, in conjunction with parallel initiatives for youth under the remit of the Young Muslims Advisory Group (YMAG), were part of an agenda to 'give the silent majority a stronger voice' (Winnett 2008:1).

These initiatives were introduced against a particular landscape of community cohesion policies and the broader securitisation agenda. In this context, the initiatives and associated policy narratives raise issues about how Muslims, and Muslim women specifically, are discursively produced at a particular historical juncture. On one level, this book examines the process by which social problems are made; the shared common sense understandings through which they are articulated. It explores how 'the Muslim woman' is socially constructed through an analysis of contemporary UK racialised and gendered policy discourses and narratives. It examines the emergence of 'the Muslim woman' through analysis of the policy agenda associated with the UK's War on Terror. In addition, however, by using original empirical material, this book also looks at how Muslim women who were themselves directly involved or affected by these initiatives navigated and negotiated these top-down policy narratives. It looks at the way in which these ideas were conformed to, resisted or disrupted by policy practitioners. Through in-depth study of a small scale initiative the book manages to capture a range of alternative perspectives regarding the way social policy works in practice.

There is a great deal of both popular and policy fascination with 'the Muslim woman' and there is extensive literature available for both public and academic consumption. In such a broad field it is important to specify what this book covers and perhaps more importantly what it is *not* about. Specifically, I want to define the research remit in terms of its historicity, what claims it seeks to make and which broader debates it contributes to. Firstly, this book is about the *representation* of 'the Muslim woman' within the context of a particular policy paradigm during a particular time period and in a particular place, the UK. This is at both the level of political representation and at the level of discursive representation. The specific focus is the EMW initiatives and the Prevent agenda. As the relationship between empowering Muslim women and combating terrorism is, however, never explained explicitly, the analysis needs to consider the wider policy landscape in order to make the narrative intelligible. This includes issues which are implicitly or explicitly associated with Muslim women, such as forced marriage, honour killings, and FGM. Although such conflations regularly dominate media discourses, these associations are explicitly made in both policy and political discourse which legitimise the more populist variants.

This book is primarily about the UK, however, it cannot be denied that what happened in the UK following 7/7 was very much influenced by the repercussions of 9/11 more globally. As the next chapter shows, the global war on terror has instrumentalised feminism as justification for military interventions and this is reflected at the level of national policy, sometimes explicitly, sometimes more subtly. Although the focus of this book remains the UK, it necessarily acknowledges the impact of globalisation and transnationalism; what happens globally, influences and is influenced by what happens more locally. The analytical approach set out in the book therefore remains pertinent beyond the scope of the historical and geopolitical specificities of the topic.

Chapter 1 sets out the wider policy landscape associated with the EMW initiatives and looks at the narratives which emerge in the policy documentation around the subject of empowering Muslim women to combat terrorism.

Chapter 2 is based primarily on documentary research and analyses the EMW initiatives and the wider Prevent agenda in the context of Huntington's Clash of Civilisations thesis. Despite the rhetoric that the War on Terror was not a war against Islam, I show how the language of Prevent is imbued with the language of Huntington's polemic; Islam as an ideology is blamed and the responsibility for preventing terrorism is collectivised to all Muslims. I describe how these discourses are gendered and argue that the intelligibility of the EMW initiatives relies on constructing a homogeneous 'Muslim community' as problematic, particularly vis a vis the perceived position of women in it. As the EMW projects cannot be evaluated in terms of success against their stated objectives of preventing violent extremism, instead I analyse what work these discourses do.

Chapter 3 highlights the way particular local circumstances affect how policy initiatives are received and implemented and that, within these geographic variations, issues such as class, ethnicity and citizenship status are also important, intersecting with gender and religious identity. The chapter reflects on the importance of recognising diversity *within* diversity. In particular it compares policy delivery in local areas where Muslims constitute the only minority population (and are broadly from one ethnic or social class background) with policy delivery in areas where the Muslim population constitutes a more diverse category (in terms of ethnic origin, citizenship status and class, for example), and where they are not the only minority ethnic group in a local area. It will suggest that the Prevent agenda is problematic in both because religious identity is privileged at the expense of other axes of identity. As such it removes opportunities for solidarity with other disadvantaged groups.

Chapter 4 examines the success of one of the objectives of EMW which was to 'give the silent majority a stronger voice'. Firstly, it questions the idea that Muslim women were absent from the political arena and needed the state's intervention in the form of such initiatives to be empowered. It explores interviewees' understandings of Muslim women's alleged silence in relation to those suggested by policy discourse, considering the ways in which the state's attempt to 'give voice' worked in practice. It is focused on the establishment of NMWAG and the way in which NMWAG operated in practice. I argue that the operation of such initiatives worked instead to constrain Muslim women's voices, restricting 'voice' to a narrow range of speakers, speaking about a narrow range of issues.

Chapters 5 and 6 address the way in which respondents conceptualised 'empowerment' in relation to Muslim women. Empowerment is simultaneously both individualised and collectivised. Chapter 5 illustrates how empowerment, as envisaged in the context of the role models road show, is seen as part of an individualistic, aspirational, neoliberal project in which education and employment combine to provide access to consumer citizenship. It introduces the idea of 'cultural barriers' to individualised empowerment and illustrates how the discourse of empowerment rests heavily on the trope of mothering.

Chapter 6 develops the theme of collective 'cultural barriers'. It analyses research participants' views regarding Islam as both a source of disadvantage, as well as a potential source of empowerment. It focuses on the theological interpretation work stream of the EMW initiatives, examining how it worked in practice. Muslim women's empowerment acts as a proxy for integrating what is assumed to be a culturally homogeneous yet inassimilable community. The chapter discusses the consequences of this privileging of religion to the exclusion of other salient factors, focusing on experiences of religious discrimination and the impact of such privileging on solidarity with other BME women's organisations. What might be considered collective but 'secular' forms of oppression, arising from different class positions, are instead considered as individual challenges which need to be overcome. In this way, important structural inequalities which are not based on religion which impact on (some) Muslim women's lives are written out of the analysis.

The conclusion draws together the research findings and analyses them in the context of the themes raised in Chapter 1. No sociological research is carried out in a vacuum and this research is historically located. Any decisions about establishing a cut-off point for my research were taken out of my hands. In early 2010 there was a Select Committee enquiry into the whole Prevent agenda which was very critical of it. As the second year of my PhD (and my interviews) drew to a close there was also a General Election and New Labour was replaced by a coalition of the Conservatives and the Liberal Democrats. At that point it was not clear what the new government proposed, although a review had been planned. In the epilogue I explore some of the most pertinent developments which have taken place since 2010.

Overall, the book argues that policy focused on 'Muslim women' collates together all women who are Muslim, a disparate and multiply-differentiated group and de facto attributes any problematic issues to religious affiliation. According to the last census there are 2.7 million Muslims in the UK. This includes a range of women from various ethnicities and different religious traditions and sects as well as converts or 'reverts'. Diversity at this level is explicitly recognised. Equally, if not more importantly, this figure includes Muslim women based in different parts of UK, from varying socio-economic backgrounds and with different citizenship statuses. These variations are, however, not explicitly recognised. What emerges in the EMW discourse is that Muslim women are discursively produced within the wider policy landscape as in need of empowerment as victims of oppression. At the same time (some) Muslim women emerge as potential agents of change. Whilst clearly there *are* women who are both Muslim and marginalised, these efforts to engage them do so solely in relation to them as Muslim women via advocates who may or may not adequately represent them. Consequently, other aspects of their multidimensional identities, on both subjective and structural levels (Brah 1992; 1996), are ignored. The idea of empowering 'Muslim women' presents Muslim women's lives as removed from class, ethnicity, region, age, sexuality and race. This research project is therefore arguably a 'historically rooted and forward looking consideration of intersectionality' (Brah and Phoenix 2004:83). As well as perpetuating anti-Muslim racist stereotypes, such policy discourses, focused on religious affiliation alone, also obscure continuities with earlier racisms, as well as other axes of social division in society, such as class and regional inequalities which also affect non-Muslims. This engagement, which is restrictive and externally prescribed, and the underlying discourses represent a form of colonisation which 'implies a structural domination and a suppression – often violent- of the heterogeneity of the subject(s) in question' (Mohanty 2003:18).

Notes

1 Full length outer garments often covering head and hands.

2 Available at www.ourchoices.org.uk and featuring 12 role models from non-traditional careers (including a scientist, a civil engineer and the first Muslim woman to play rugby for England).

ONE

'Muslim women: your country needs you!' Gendering the UK's 'War on Terror'

On one level, initiatives designed to 'empower' Muslim women are difficult to criticise. They are nonetheless also deeply problematic when framed in the context of the UK's counterterrorism agenda. This is not because the presence of marginalised Muslim women in the UK who may be in need of empowerment is under question (although equally, that is not to suggest that *all* Muslim women are marginalised or in need of empowerment). Nor is there any doubt that the UK is subject to Islamist terrorist threats. The issue is, however, one of understanding the relationship between the two: how is the empowerment of Muslim women causally related, or even connected, to preventing violent extremism?

This book analyses the narratives around the relationship between 'violent extremism' and Muslim women's empowerment. It is based on research which analysed relevant policy documents, including parliamentary debates and political speeches, exploring 'a group of statements which provide a language for talking about a particular topic at a particular historical moment' (Hall 1997: 44); in this case, 'Muslim women' in the UK in a post 7/7 context. Furthermore, 'in consequence of being so classified, individual women and their experiences of themselves are changed by being so classified' (Hacking 1999: 11). Consequently, the research also entailed interviews with policy actors, predominantly Muslim women, involved in these initiatives at a range of different levels of the policy chain. Documents analysed date from between 2005 and 2010; interviews were conducted between January 2009 and July 2010. The objectives of the research were twofold; to deconstruct the idea of the Muslim woman which emerges in the policy discourse through analysing the policy narratives and to explore the way Muslim women engaged with the narratives themselves. This deconstruction contributes to a process of 'disalienation', that is, 'the unmaking of racialized bodies and their restoration to properly human modes of being in the world' (Fanon cited in Gilroy 2004: 45). Further, as Errol Lawrence argues, the relationship between such '... common-sense notions, like common-sense ideologies generally, are not just carried round in people's heads. They are embedded within actual material practices' (Lawrence 1982: 76). One of the themes that this book looks at therefore is the impact that Prevent funding has had on Muslim women's organisations and their relationship with other black and minority ethnic (BME) women's groups.

The following section sets out the key themes that foreground the discursive production of 'the Muslim woman' in relation to the policy landscape of the War on Terror, both globally and nationally, including debates on the relationship between multiculturalism and multi-faithism and feminism; as well as historical and parallel global perspectives on Muslim women.

Prevent

The 2005 London bombings prompted a broad range of policy responses from the New Labour government. One of these was the Preventing Violent Extremism agenda (or 'Prevent'). Prevent itself was part of the Home Office's counter-terrorism strategy which consisted of the 'Four Ps': Pursue (to stop terrorist attacks), Prevent (to stop people from becoming terrorists or supporting violent extremism), Protect (to strengthen our protection against terror attack) and Prepare (where an attack cannot be stopped, to mitigate its impact).

The Prevent Strategy itself consisted of five key strands which were as follows: *Challenging* the violent extremist ideology and supporting mainstream voices; *Disrupting* those who promote violent extremism and supporting the institutions where they are active; *Supporting* individuals who are being targeted and recruited to the cause of violent extremism; *Increasing* the resilience of communities to violent extremism; and *Addressing* the grievances that ideologues are exploiting. By the time the Empowering Muslim Women (EMW) initiatives were launched, the Prevent agenda was already being criticised on a variety of levels: for demonising the Muslim population as a whole, in particular through creating and perpetuating anti-Muslim racist stereotypes; for securitising the race equality agenda and for inadvertently supporting extremist groups.

Local Authorities and the police were granted funding to work with local communities in order 'to build resilience' against extremism (HM Government 2008: 13); one of the things they were encouraged to do was to give 'the silent majority a stronger voice in their communities'. Both women and young people were seen as part of the 'silent majority' and two working groups were set up focused on them. There was, however, a clear overlap since a key initiative directed at 'Muslim women' was in fact directed at Muslim girls, highlighting the fact that often when we refer to 'youth' it is a gender neutral way of referring to boys and young men rather than young people of both sexes. The Prevent agenda (and the counterterrorism agenda more generally) is undoubtedly gendered in that it was, albeit implicitly, predominantly focused on young men, yet there was very little explicit discussion in the policy arena regarding this.

The Prevent agenda, as part of a wider counter terrorism strategy, forms part of the UK's 'War on Terror'. It emphasised the battle for 'hearts and minds' and addressed (non-violent) extremism in individuals before they could become radicalised and drawn into committing acts of terrorism. As Kundnani (2014) argues, however, the relationship between extremism, radicalisation and the propensity to commit acts of terrorism is by no means clear (see Chapter 2). Khan describes how 'the transnationalised governmentality of the "war on terror" has become inflected within the discursive vocabulary of racism' (2006: 184). This racism is both gendered and sexualised (Bhattacharyya 2008; Razack 2008). In consequence, mainstream liberal feminism has found a strange bedfellow in neoliberal imperialist projects throughout the Muslim world.[1] Feminism has been instrumentalised such that 'Western sexual freedoms are strategically deployed in order to support notions of civilisation and superiority' (McRobbie 2009: 1). In this book I am specifically interested in how feminism, or at least a particular variety of feminism, may be implicated in the process of racialising Muslims in the UK. More importantly, this *faux feminism* 'displaces possible solidarities, with a reinstated hierarchy of civilisation and modernity' (McRobbie 2009: 27).

Community cohesion

Prior to Prevent, the UK's race equality agenda was dominated by the community cohesion policy paradigm. Multiculturalism had been strongly critiqued for allegedly leading to communities living 'parallel lives' (Cantle 2001) and a society 'sleep-walking into segregation' (Trevor Phillips, Chair of CRE 2005). Even the 'progressive' left had pronounced the death of multiculturalism in its infamous edition of Prospect magazine (2009). As a result, since the urban disturbances in the north of England in 2001, policies focused on 'community cohesion' emerged as the dominant paradigm of 'race relations' governmental policy and practice (Solomos 2003; Kundnani 2002a). Although on one level talking about 'communities' enables language to be deracialised (Worley 2005), in practice, however, it often refers to talking exclusively about Muslim communities[2] and, particularly following the 7/7 bombings in 2005, is imbricated with the desire to manage the risk of terrorism rather than any explicit desire to address racial inequality (McGhee 2005). More generally, as Fortier has argued, the cohesion agenda 'fails to recognise any claims to difference...as political...in terms of the relational, material, symbolic and cultural variations and power relations that position people and groups differentially in terms of access to, and uses of, resources' (Fortier 2010: 27). As discussed in this book this is a fundamental omission, further exacerbated since 2008 by the politics of austerity which foreground the more specific community or counterterrorist focused policy initiatives.

As Jones argues, analysing the community cohesion agenda highlights 'the importance of shifting and unstable meanings in policy,' and the complicated nuanced meanings that circulate at different areas of putting policy into practice in different places (2013: 1). This is equally relevant in the case of Prevent. Embedded within it are various underlying suppositions which may or may not be true. Nonetheless, despite this slipperiness and the possibilities of more nuanced negotiation in terms of practice, at the level of top down policy discourses, the Prevent agenda and community cohesion policy are inherently contradictory (Husband and Alam 2011). On the one hand, community cohesion is a policy imperative whose raison d'être is to overcome the alleged boundaries purported to exist between different 'communities', that is, to make sure everyone gets along[3]. On the other hand, the Prevent strategy is ostensibly focused on communities deemed to be at risk of extremism, that is, an imagined Muslim community. Both agendas are, however, framed by broader questions about multiculturalism. As a concept or policy ideal 'multiculturalism', despite the fluidity in its definition, has been called into question at a variety of levels. First it has been accused of undermining national unity; second it has been suggested that it has been superseded by 'multifaithism'; and thirdly multiculturalism has been deemed to be incompatible with feminism.

The death of multiculturalism...

...and Britishness

The 7/7 London bombings and concerns about 'home-grown' terrorism were widely framed in terms of the presence of ethnic and religious diversity. As a result, they stimulated debates about Britishness and in the immediate aftermath in particular there were (and continue to be) increasing government appeals to foster 'Britishness' to counter future terrorist acts and there was a resurgence in the idea of nationalism as a cohesive force (Brown 2006). Within this new nationalism different 'others' are constructed thus allowing Britishness to be negatively defined by focusing on what (or who) needs to be integrated or assimilated. This imagining of a national community (Anderson 2006) or nation building project is gendered (Anthias and Davis 1992). Scharff (2011) for example shows how gender constructions of white British (and German) women are formed in opposition to 'disempowered' Muslim women. (Chapter 2 explores this in more detail through documentary analysis).

EMW policy initiatives therefore form part of a broader imperative to define national (and European) borders against a background of racism and post-colonial guilt, rather than 'women's liberation' per se.[4] In addition, given that culture is perceived to be located within the private and domestic arenas of home and family (Worley 2005), women are perceived as being primarily responsible for cultural reproduction. The book seeks to analyse how, in the contemporary geopolitical climate, the idea of 'the Muslim woman' is used as a marker of difference between 'the West and the rest', signifying the inherent incompatibility of Muslim 'culture' with Britishness.

...and the rise of multifaithism

The demise of multiculturalism is also viewed in terms of a process of 'de-secularisation'; it has been suggested that we are moving from multiculturalism to multifaithism[5] and that civil society is becoming increasingly de-secularised (Patel 2008; Yuval-Davis 2009; Dhaliwal and Yuval-Davis 2014). Patel (2008) has argued that the entrenchment of faith communities represents a particular threat for women and I discuss this in more depth below. These issues are also examined in more depth in Chapter 6. Such developments, frequently associated with the Rushdie affair, have often been characterised as a 'shift away from *demands for equality* on the basis of race/ethnicity to *demands for special treatment* on the basis of religion' (Macey 2010: 39) (author's emphasis). This was specifically with reference to demands about extending blasphemy laws to accommodate non Church of England religions.

This move towards de-secularisation is frequently presented as relatively recent. Furbey et al (2006), for example, suggest that formal recognition of faith communities and their organisations in public policy was first reflected in the Inner Cities Religious Council (ICRC), established in 1992. This, however, ignores the long history of links between the state and church in the UK and the normative position of the Church of England. The presumption that Britain is 'secular' is brought into question by the fact that religion has an 'established' position in the structure of the state (Modood 1997); many of the normative ideas about the British nation have religious underpinnings for example, the fact that the monarch is both the head of state and the head of the Church of England, the existence of voluntary aided (Church funded) schools, and Christian acts of worship in schools. One consequence of this 'Anglican privilege' may be that there is no system of formally recognising that 'other faiths' exist (McLoughlin and Cesari 2005). Requests for accommodation by members of minority religions might therefore represent a desire for 'equality' rather than 'special privileges'.[6] Furthermore there are a variety of interpretations of what constitutes 'secularism'; the alternative to religious fundamentalism is not necessarily fundamentalism of the secular sort (Al-Ali 2014).

Despite this suggestion that religion is superseding (ethnic) 'culture', it is worth noting that many Muslim (and other religious) 'communities' continue to be organised around ethnicity. There are of course sectarian divergences within the Muslim population, between Sunnis, Shias, Ismailis and Sufis, for example, and mosques follow these distinctions. In addition, although there are mosques which serve very diverse ethnic minority communities, historically in the UK they have largely been established by particular ethnicities in specific geographic locations. For example, there are 10 or more different mosques in Southwark alone organised by ethnicity – Somali, Nigerian and Ivorian, as well as the longer established Turkish, Pakistani and Bangladeshi mosques. This suggests that the separation between 'faith' and 'culture' (based on common sense understandings of these terms) is rather more complex. If religion has supplanted 'culture' then why are mosques organised like this? Arguably, language, the geographical concentration of those with a shared ethnic heritage often as a result of particular migratory trajectories, and access to resources, seem equally, if not more, influential. The increasingly diversified composition of the UK's 'Muslim community' and how this needs to be taken into account is discussed in greater detail in Chapter 3.

The problem with multiculturalism...and feminism

Within feminist political theory there has been much theoretical debate about the compatibility or otherwise of multiculturalism and feminism. In her polemic article *Is Multiculturalism bad for Women?* Okin (1999) argues that the two are fundamentally opposed and that granting 'group rights' fosters cultural relativism. Okin's work uses a range of examples predominantly from France, yet the rationale for her position applies in the UK and is best exemplified by the work of Beckett and Macey (2001) and Macey (2009) who argue that some cultural and religious 'traditions' are in direct conflict with the struggle for justice and equality. Their presentation of domestic and homophobic violence as a 'cultural practice' which is particular to Muslims is problematic since describing them as such implies that they 'are normal and widely endorsed behaviours in minority communities' (Dustin and Phillips 2008: 419).[7] Quite clearly, however, occurrence does not mean endorsement.

Both Okin (1999) and Macey (2010) can be criticised for the problematic way in which they characterise multiculturalism and the way in which minority women might suffer in that context. The emphasis on inter group differences at the expense of intra group differences is problematic (Sassen 1999). Other women's lives are seen primarily in relation to their belonging to minority communities and 'culture' is invoked for anything that happens to Third world or immigrant women (Mohanty 2003). The asymmetrical ascription of culture assumes that 'other' cultures are regarded as frozen static entities (Narayan 1997 cited in Volpp 2001: 1190).[8] In this sense women are only seen as subject to patriarchy from within their communities rather than subject to gender discrimination more widely and racism, anti-Muslim or otherwise.

As Meetoo and Mirza have suggested, however, 'within the discourse of multiculturalism, women "fall between the cracks"', arguing that 'race' and ethnicity are prioritised as gender differences and inequalities are rendered invisible (2007: 197).[9] The debate about 'multiculturalism vs feminism' creates a false dichotomy in which we are asked to choose between prioritising either gender or 'race' equality. This is not in fact a choice at all since it presupposes that all black people are men and that all women are white, that is, that neither racism nor patriarchy are issues which affect black women. In spite of the extensive work that has been done by black and postcolonial feminists to highlight this thorny issue (both in terms of the academy and activism), mainstream understandings continue to position the two separately. As Anne Phillips has argued, 'multiculturalism can be made compatible with the pursuit of gender equality and women's rights so long as it dispenses with an essentialist understanding of culture' (2007: 9). One way to dispense with such essentialism is to write *against* culture (Abu-Lughod 2013), that is to emphasise the wider geopolitical and socio historical contexts within which such phenomena occur.

Something old, something new: colonial antecedents

In talking about how 'the Muslim woman' is discursively produced at a particular historical moment, it is important to attend to the continuities and discontinuities with both earlier and concurrent gendered racisms. It 'is necessary to analyse the social processes through which gender differences have been constructed and reproduced against the background of colonialism and imperialism' (Brah 1992: 68). The way in which the Muslim community is constructed in policy narratives draws on Orientalist ideas, in which communities are fixed in a timeless present (Childs and Williams 1997) and where members are constructed as childlike, requiring guidance from their Western superiors (Fanon 1968; Nandy 1988). In the context of the Prevent agenda, the 'Muslim community' as a whole is infantilised and Muslim women are infantilised even further (Brown 2011).

Historically (and specifically in the British context), South Asian women have played a key role in the production of difference between the West and the Rest (Hall 1992; Puwar and Raghuram 2003; McLintock 1995). Furthermore, the language of feminism and the 'liberation of women' has been used by colonialists to define a boundary between the liberated West and the barbaric East[10] and it can be argued that melodrama marks the place of South Asian women in popular, official and academic discourses (Puwar 2003). Colonial justifications for social policy interventions included bringing universalist Enlightenment values to the 'dark continents', and there are clear parallels with contemporary humanitarian interventions (Chandler 2002), as well as in domestic policy discourses. As Spivak (1988: 297) has articulated, there is a long tradition of 'white men saving brown women from brown men' and comparisons can be drawn with social interventions in relation to South Asian women.[11] Spivak's oft-quoted phrase could be extended to include 'white women' alongside white men; there is a growing body of literature on the role of discourse and gender in the colonial era and the impact of colonialism on the development of first wave feminism (Sangari and Vaid 1989; Jayawardena 1995; Levine 2004; Powell and Lambert-Hurley 2005; Midgley 2007).[12]

In more recent history, the theme of the Asian woman disadvantaging her children has characterised how Asian women in post-war Britain have been perceived. Pratibha Parmar writes, for example, how Asian women are problematically conceptualised as:

> ...non-working wives and mothers, whose problems are that they do not speak English, hardly ever leave the house, and find British norms and values ever more threatening as their children become more 'integrated' into the new surroundings. Their lives are limited to the kitchen, the children and the religious rituals, and they are both emotionally and economically dependent upon their husbands. (1982: 250)

This passage remains salient, over thirty years on, particularly if the term 'Asian' is replaced with 'Muslim'.[13]

Islam and Feminism

Even within the category South Asian, Muslim women are positioned as being in particular need of empowerment. The role of religious fundamentalism in supporting patriarchy in a number of religious communities has been documented (Sahgal and Yuval-Davis 1992; WLUML 2001; Dhaliwal & Yuval-Davis 2014). There is, however, a particularly prevalent discourse about Islam and gender equality more generally (Razak 2007; Fernandez 2009; Kumar 2012). As Abu-Lugod argues, 'gendered orientalism has taken on a new life and new forms in our feminist twenty-first century' (2013: 202). This discourse is widely established in the broadsheet liberal media (Toynbee 2001; Hari 2008; Burchill 2010). As Afshar writes, 'feminism...is hailed as the ultimate weapon of the British middle class hegemony and is at its most pernicious where Muslim women are concerned' (1994: 145). There is also a large body of popular literature, which Donohoue Clyne (2002) calls 'airport fiction', on the themes of oppressed Muslim women and generalised Muslim misogyny (in Muslim countries) that has allowed much vitriol to be cast on Islam from 'within' (Darwish 2006; Hirsi Ali 2006; 2007; 2010) and 'without' (Fallaci 2002).

The theme of empowering Muslim women to combat terrorism therefore resonates because of prevalent discourses around the insurmountable incompatibility of Islam and feminism and the incompatibility of feminism and multiculturalism. This idea of empowerment is seductive, feeding into common-sense understandings since it additionally builds on the racist stereotypes of South Asian women in the British postcolonial context. As such, the EMW initiatives and wider initiatives are conducted in a fairly narrow framework of empowerment 'within the community' rather than in the context of society at large.

Empowerment

Despite being a 'buzzword', the term 'empowerment' lacks explicit and conclusive definitions (Ette 2007). Feminist perspectives on empowerment, while not homogeneous, include more layered and multi-dimensional approaches that depart from perceiving empowerment as part of a liberal atomistic privatized form of citizenship (Honig 1999) which is inseparable from individualism and consumerism (Rowlands 1997). Instead, feminist interpretations emphasise collective empowerment, or 'power-with' (Rowlands 1995) and psychological forms of empowerment, or 'power-from-within' (Stacki and Monkman 2003), and are more concerned with the social context of power. Empowerment requires the challenging of patriarchal power relations that result in women having less control over material assets and intellectual resources (Batliwala 1994).

Empowerment is not therefore a process that can be 'done to or for women' (Afshar 1997: 4); it must emerge from women themselves. Although ostensibly the EMW initiatives were overseen by Muslim women, 'empowerment' is only sought in so far as it relates to the Prevent agenda. There were parallel initiatives about increasing the number of Muslim (and other BME) women councillors. Even these approaches, though, continue to position 'Other' women almost exclusively within the framework of 'community' politics; they appear to be motivated more by a desire to change who is seen to represent 'the Muslim community' rather than Muslim women being seen as credible representatives of wider non-Muslim political constituencies. In this sense, these initiatives conform to the very multicultural policy paradigm New Labour purported to want to move away from. Muslim women are engaged with as women in Muslim communities rather than as Muslims living in a particular borough, city, the UK, or as women in a patriarchal *society* (not just community) or as insecure citizens in a world with ever increasingly policed borders.

Feminism in the context of the EMW initiatives therefore emerges as part of a civilisationist discourse in which it is positioned as part of a modernising mission. This perspective claims ownership of and responsibility for feminism as a Western value, thus ignoring a whole history of black feminist critiques of white Western feminism and also the existence of 'native feminisms'. As a feminist I am concerned at the way in which feminism, albeit a liberal individualistic variant of it, has been appropriated to this end.

(Mis)representing Muslim Women

> Reflection on how social phenomena get defined as problems in need of explanation in the first place quickly reveals that there is no such thing as a problem without a person (or groups of them) who have this problem: a problem is always a problem for someone or other (Harding 1987: 6)

The visibility of Muslims in both academia and the policy arena is unequivocal if highly problematic. The relatively recent focus on 'Muslims' as a category in sociological research reflects political developments both nationally and globally. As Alexander has argued, '[t]he conceptual mapping of "the Muslim menace" which links suicide bombers with extremist Muslim clerics and recent "riots", articulates a very specific imagination of "the Muslim community" in Britain – one which is marked by both gendered and generational difference' (2003: 3, cited in McGhee 2005).

Back et al refer to the 'penumbral regions that link mainstream social science to social policy design, think tanks and journalism' (2009: 2) and there is unquestionably an iterative relationship between policy and research. Research informs policy but equally, policy steers research, particularly since it is often accompanied by funding. In the case of research on Muslims, the current political climate, both nationally and globally, means that there is much governmental interest in funding research around radicalisation and counter terrorism. To give a sense of the volume of literature dedicated to the radicalisation thesis, according to Kundnani, by 2010 one hundred articles per year were being published in peer reviewed journals (2014: 119). Unsurprisingly therefore there remains 'widespread popular fascination with Muslim masculinity' (Archer 2003: 1) in academia since it is men who are considered to be most susceptible to radicalisation, although this too is changing as I will discuss in the epilogue. This mirrors broader policy concerns about Muslim masculinity specifically (as opposed to masculinity more generally) following the 2001 urban disturbances and 7/7 bombings (Lewis 2007; Choudhury 2007). Muslim male youth emerge as contemporary folk devils (Salgado-Pottier 2008). By contrast Muslim women are presented rather differently. There is a greater focus on education and employment (as though Muslim boys do not experience any ethnic penalty in education or more importantly at the point of entry into the labour market). Women's relationship to religion also features prominently and religion is dichotomously, or even simultaneously imagined as either empowerment or oppression (Afshar et al 2005; Ameli and Merali 2006; Werbner 2007). Religion as a form of social capital can be used differently by young British Muslim men and women (Ramji 2007) and for some Muslim women the formation of an articulated 'Islamic' identity in the public and private spheres enables them to negotiate and acquire rights in new and transformative ways (Dwyer 1999a; Brown 2006b).

Against this background in both academic and policy domains I experienced ethical concerns regarding undertaking research in this field and personally contributing to reinscribing 'new racist ideologies of essential cultural difference' (Alexander 1996: 13–14) in the production of anti-Muslim rhetoric. Undertaking this research, both in terms of the topic itself and the manner in which it was conducted, was therefore 'an expressly political project aimed at creating knowledge about the social relations and practices of domination, white supremacy, and exploitation for the purposes of challenging and changing these systems' (Hughes 2005: 205). The book scrutinises these social relations empirically and in so doing constitutes feminist research since it offers '...alternative origins of problematics, explanatory hypotheses and evidence, alternative purposes of enquiry, and a new prescription for the appropriate relationship between the inquirer and his/her subject of inquiry' (Harding 1987: vii).

As Jones argues, the unstable meanings within policy '[create] space to engage with larger themes including the nature of society, identity, equality, migration and belonging' (2013: 1). This is why the study looks both at documentary and interview material as a way of understanding the dynamics of discursive racial formations of 'the Muslim woman' in the narratives and practice of policy. As Deborah Cameron argues, '...names are a culture's way of fixing what will actually count as reality in a universe of overwhelming, chaotic sensations, all pregnant with a multitude of possible meanings' (2001: 12). Discourse therefore represents a site of struggle where forces of social (re)production and contestation are played out (Lazar 2005). Otherwise '...to detach language from its historical, cultural, and social roots, to think of it as outside individual and societal control, is a certain route to political quietism – a sense that nothing can really be changed' (Cameron 2001: 19). To demonstrate how women are represented and constructed in and by language is therefore a political act (Zalewski 2000).

It would be difficult to deny the systematic (mis)representation of Muslims and Islam in the press (Said 1997; Richardson 2004; Poole and Richardson 2006). I chose, however, to focus attention on discourse in the political arena because of the ways in which political or elite racism validates or legitimates 'popular' racism. While arguably the media is more pervasive, it is not, however, necessarily the more influential of the two; political discourse derives considerable power from both its scope and legitimacy and is a key constituent of elite racism (van Tijk 2008). Moreover, there is clearly a relationship between the state and the media and the two doubtlessly interact; it is certainly true that many people's understanding of political discourse is negotiated via the media. Within the media, however, politicians have preferential access relative to the public more widely. Not only is what politicians say widely reported on, politicians themselves occasionally take on the role of columnists, both in the broadsheets and the tabloids (Brown 2004; 2009; Blair 2007; Blunkett 2009; Cable 2010). In addition, as the Leveson enquiry illustrated, the relationship between politicians and the media is far from innocent, and as Butler argues, in the post 9/11 climate there has been a growing acceptance of censorship in the press: while the media 'report the "voice" of the government for us... [their]...proximity to that voice rests on an alliance or identification with that voice' (2004: 1).

More fundamentally, government policy establishes a framework within which individuals and 'communities' operate in terms of political engagement; it therefore *produces* them as subjects of social policy. Rather than simplistically compare the language of political discourse with that used in 'everyday life', this book looks at how discourse *constitutes* everyday practice. It builds on the idea that 'the relationship between discourse and the social is a dialectical one, in which discourse constitutes, and is constituted by, social situations, institutions and structures' (Howarth and Stavrakakis 2000: 11). 'It is not simply the documents and official definitions of community cohesion that are important in understanding how community cohesion works; it is also the way these documents are understood, interpreted and reacted against' (Jones 2013: 5).

This project is therefore not about language alone. It is about the way that policy operates and is practiced and has real effects and consequences. As demonstrated in the following chapters, changes in policy language are not a question of mere semantics; such changes influence and affect how people can access resources. This analysis draws attention to the role of government in creating, perpetuating and reifying particular racial categorisations. It is not a policy evaluation in the sense of measuring outcomes, principally because there are no 'outcomes', at least none that are easily quantifiable. Instead, I analyse how the policy works at a symbolic level.

My intervention into this arena was an effort to analyse how this 'Muslim menace' has been constructed at the level of policy discourse and specifically how it is gendered. I also wanted to look at the experiences of Muslim women involved in this policy area and explore the problems associated with the privileging of religious affiliation particularly for those defined within the 'Muslim as problem' paradigm.

Being Muslim

> Knowing is not so much about the assemblage of existing knowledge as it is about recognizing our constitution as 'ourselves' within the fragments that we process as knowledge; 'hailing' and being 'hailed' within the discourses that produce us and the narratives we spin. (Brah 1999)

While wary of overanalysing the importance of positionality, as Harding notes, 'introducing this 'subjective' element into the analysis in fact increases the objectivity of the research and decreases the "objectivism" which hides this kind of evidence from the public' (1987: 9). As an 'ethnicised'[14] woman who has gone from being hailed as merely '(South) Asian' to 'Bangladeshi' to appearing as 'Muslim' in policy discourses, these taxonomical changes are imbued with personal relevance. The very fact that these categorisations vary illustrates the historical and political specificity of particular racial categories; it is not the case that 'racial divisions… [are] anterior to politics' (Gilroy 2004: 35). Furthermore, this curiosity is not merely a simple case of narcissism; the reality is that such representations inspired unsettling feelings of dissonance. Despite the pervasive power of images of 'the Muslim woman' and the virulence with which such caricatures have proliferated, I have been unable to recognise either myself or anyone else of my acquaintance in these depictions. In saying this, however, I am certainly not claiming that I have any more authority or authenticity as a result of my Muslimness, only that my research questions, findings and analysis are produced through this lens.

This book does not claim to be an evaluation of the policy. Nor is it an intervention into the debate about the empowering effects of religion; nor a commentary on whether Muslim women need empowering. It is based on a small scale study analysing pertinent texts and using in-depth interviews with different people at various levels of the policy chain. Not only were the initiatives on a small scale, I interviewed a wide range of disparate people. As such the book provides a detailed snap shot of a policy in action; it situates it in a wider policy landscape and examines the relationship between policy discourse and policy practitioners.

The key document was a Department for Communities and Local Government (DCLG) publication called *Empowering Muslim Women: Case Studies* (DCLG 2008). This was the outcome from the Preventing Violent Extremism Action Plan (DCLG 2007) in which the Government committed itself to the publication of a document on effective initiatives to strengthen the role that Muslim women play in their communities. The booklet provided a snapshot of projects involving initiatives to empower Muslim women to play a role in their communities and society more widely. The projects fall into a number of categories, reflecting the routes through which it is imagined that Muslim women may be empowered: economic participation, education, civic participation and arts, culture and sports. In addition, it includes a number of projects that are underway which allegedly directly support women in playing a pro-active role in preventing violent extremism. I analysed this in the context of other documents where women were referred to. These included press releases, articles by politicians, as well as related policy documents. I also looked at transcripts of speeches given by politicians.

EMW is positioned within a broader social policy framework. Policies targeted at Muslim women are situated within wider debates on immigration, community cohesion, integration and nationalism. This demanded consideration of a broader range of texts, highlighting the importance of 'intertextuality' in analysing discourse; that is, recognition that all text and talk is situated within a complex of other texts. Talbot defines intertextuality as that which 'expresses a sense of blurred boundaries, a sense of a text as a bundle of points of intersection with other texts' (2005: 168). Such an analysis is clearly important if one accepts that 'a political project will attempt to weave together different strands of discourse....to...organise a field of meaning so as to fix the identities of objects and practices in a particular way' (Howarth and Stavrakakis 2000: 3).

In total, I undertook 25 interviews between 2009 and 2010. I was able to interview five members of the National Muslim Women's Advisory Group (NMWAG), two anonymously. In addition, I interviewed a range of people indirectly or directly involved in the policy initiatives: local authority Community Cohesion Officers, Community Police Officers, civil servants and journalists as well as activists and third sector workers from BME women's groups (secular and Muslim). In March 2009 I also attended an Equalities and Human Rights Commission conference (in Birmingham as it was organised by the West Midlands

Regional Office). Its objective was to recognise Muslim women's roles and contributions to society to mark International Women's Day. The conference was part of a programme to promote 'new voices' and the Commission's work to empower the unheard or marginalised. I attended the quarterly NMWAG meeting on 22 February 2010 which was followed by a networking lunch for the members of both NMWAG and YMAG. Between January and March 2009 I attended three of the six road shows set up 'to empower Muslim girls'. This allowed me to meet a number of role models and members of the partner organisations delivering the road show in different places. I attended a Prevent conference in December 2009 in Birmingham at which John Denham MP spoke and which included workshops focused on good practice. Gaining access to some of the other work streams was harder (and not only for me; one of my interviewees complained about not being able to get access to what she described as the 'sexier' topics such as theological interpretation). I also attended one of the workshops and school trips funded by Prevent that had been organised by the Three Faiths Forum. The project was called Faith and Fashion; I attended the workshop at the school and the school trip to the Victoria and Albert Museum exploring ideas about modesty in a historical context. My interviews and observation took place in London (Newham, Brent, Ealing and Westminster), Bristol, Cardiff, Birmingham, Bradford and Manchester.

Letherby (2003) highlights the importance of reflexivity and emotion as sources of insight. The research, involving in-depth semi structured qualitative interviews with a range of people across the policy trajectory, meant that the relationship between me as the researcher and the researched varied. Such variations were an integral part of the research process and highlight how knowledge was constructed in this particular research project. As Ali has argued 'criticisms of "subjectivity" obscure the complex relationship between subjects, epistemology, politics and research' whereas '"being reflexive" means not only reflecting on one's own identity, but reflecting on how one's identity relates to issues of power, and impacts on research and respondents' (2006: 476).

Despite not wanting to perpetuate the obsession with what Muslim women wear, it was difficult to escape the fact that the veil has become an 'over determined marker of difference' for the identity of young British Muslim women (Dwyer 1999a: 5). As well as being a dominant theme that came up in policy, in interviews and in the media during the research period, the issue of how I presented myself to others, in terms of what I wore, was also a theme in the research process.[15] Given the 'whole constellation of meanings' attached to wearing 'Asian' clothes or English clothes (Dwyer 2000: 478) I chose to dress differently with different interviewees. Although initially concerned at my contrivance, I eventually concluded that it was no different to what I and most people do every day. I cannot know whether any of my interviewees even noticed or were remotely bothered by how I was dressed.

Given my own preoccupation with the way the Muslim women are represented, there are ethical concerns for me in how I represent research participants' voices. Letherby (2003) emphasises the authority of the researcher in selecting and rejecting data at the different stages of the research. Obviously, I have respected requests for anonymity but I have been concerned about including particular comments and statements which I have found uncomfortable. Are the representations of Muslim women which others will see in my book any more valid than the representations I am purporting to critique?

Within this policy arena there are strong opinions, informed by experience and emotion and some of this felt difficult. Many of my interviewees were quite keen to seek my opinion. Given the political nature of the topic and the controversy that had surrounded it, I found it difficult to answer questions relating to my opinion of the work they were involved in. Some were keen to find out my opinion on the work of NMWAG. I was also aware that my own particular view of anti-Muslim racism and the imperative to decode and deconstruct was not shared by many of my respondents for various reasons. Some, for example, felt that anti-Muslim racism was 'just like any other racism' and should not be identified separately as it detracted from other racisms. Also many respondents were very passionate about what they did and did not necessarily see or were not interested in the bigger picture that I was trying to assess, that is, the unintended consequences of Prevent. There were people who shared my discomfort with the Prevent agenda, but for different reasons, and had no qualms about reifying or in fact genuinely believing in the idea of a universally oppressed Muslim community.

Notes

1. See Abu-Lughod (2002) for a critique of the role of anthropology in this.
2. The urban disturbances in the northern cities of Oldham, Blackburn and Bradford involved clashes between predominantly Muslim male youth against the police and white male youth.
3. Interestingly I have also seen the term 'community cohesion' invoked to refer to something very different, in fact, the opposite of the way it is used in policy language. In a souvenir brochure marking the granting by OFCOM of the first 24 hour licence for a Bengali language radio station in Europe, *Betar Bangla*, the term was used to suggest that 'community cohesion' was about cohesion *within*

the Bengali language community, demonstrating the ambiguity in the term (Jones 2013)

[4] See Joan Scott (2007) in relation to the veil debate in France, for example.

[5] Omoniyi & Fishman (2010) define multifaithism as the 'institutional recognition of multiple faiths by the state and the granting of equal rights and protection to devotees by law.'

[6] Moreover, the history of the Muslim presence in the UK is much longer than is often recognised. The first Muslims date from early as the 12th century with the first English convert in the 16th century and the first purpose built mosque (in Woking) established in 1889 (Ansari 2004).

[7] See Bawer (2006) who uses the issue of gay rights in an Islamophobic invective (while at the same time acting as an apologist for US Christian fundamentalist homophobia).

[8] Volpp also highlights that African-American 'communities' are seen to be dominated by women and are pathologised for not being patriarchal enough.

[9] It is also perhaps disingenuous to cite cultural sensitivity when, as Razack (2008) argues, the invisibility of violence against minority women is in fact an illustration of racism in service provision and authorities' racist tendency to naturalise violence against South Asian women.

[10] Notwithstanding the considerable variations within the potentially totalising discourse of the West and the rest.

[11] Mani (1998) has, for example, considered the way in which women were in fact marginal to the debate on *sati* and that the British imperative to abolish it stemmed more from the moral civilising claims of a colonial power and a negotiation with patriarchal Brahmin Hindu elites.

[12] Ahmed (1992) and Lazreg (1994) explore these themes in colonial feminisms in the Egyptian and Algerian contexts respectively. Given the increasingly diverse composition of Britain's Muslim population, which now includes non-South Asian migrant heritage Muslims, these other histories of feminism and colonialism have resonance.

[13] See also 'The common sense image of the Asian mother is similar. She is isolated from the beneficial effects of English culture because her movements are circumscribed by custom, and she therefore invariably fails to learn English. She is viewed as particularly prone to superstitious beliefs and, being more traditional than the other members of her family, is also more 'neurotic' in her new urban setting...it is worth noting here how the Asian mother is presented...as the main barrier to the integration of her children into the 'wider British society'' (Lawrence 1982: 78).

[14] I am using this term as defined by Meetoo and Mirza (2007) to emphasise the *process* of racial objectification. 'Thus *being* or *becoming* 'ethnicised' brings into play the power relations that inform and structure the gaze of the 'other' which, we suggest frames the women's experience' (2007: 2)

[15] For example, there were various discussions in relation to legislating against the niqab and burka in Belgium, Italy and France during this period as well as parallel discussions here (BBC 2010a; BBC 2010b; Ruggeri 2011).

TWO

Gendered nationalisms: the 'true' clash of civilisations?

> Ascribing the violence of one's adversaries to their culture is self-serving: it goes a long way towards absolving oneself of any responsibility. (Mamdani 2005b:148)

> ... the cultural fault line that divides the West and the Muslim world is not about democracy but sex. (Inglehart and Norris 2003:63)

Introduction

On 15 January 2009, just before the Bush administration was set to leave the White House, David Miliband, then UK Foreign Secretary, claimed that the use of the term 'war on terror' following the September 11 attacks had been a mistake, possibly causing more harm than good. In the UK the term had begun to fall out of favour in the Foreign Office as early as mid-2006; by 2007 the Engaging with the Islamic World Unit in the Foreign Office was advising the rest of the UK government to stop using the term 'war on terror'. By contrast, in the US there was widespread support for the phrase throughout the duration of Bush's government. At the most basic level this reflects wider tensions between the US and UK governments in their approaches to global terrorism as well as different levels of public support for the military interventions in Afghanistan and Iraq in each country. Specifically, however, as a Foreign Office spokesman said, the UK government wanted to 'avoid reinforcing and giving succour to the terrorists' narrative by using language that, taken out of context, could be counterproductive' (Burke 2010). Furthermore the shift in language encapsulated the British belief that 'we cannot win by military means alone, and because this isn't us against one organized enemy with a clear identity and a coherent set of objectives'.[1]

This conscious shift in terminology and the associated discussion acknowledged the importance of language and its 'potent persuasiveness' (Steuter and Wills 2008: 4). Despite this acknowledgement, however, this chapter shows how the language used continued to perpetuate a discourse of a clash of civilisations (Huntington 1993) even if policy actors shied away from specifically using the term 'war on terror'.

By definition, the efficacy of a project designed to 'prevent violent extremism' is difficult to assess in any meaningful way. There are too many other variables to consider in determining whether such government initiatives have been successful. Even if measuring success were possible, ascertaining the reasons for such success would be little more than speculation. Determining the specific role played by women in this endeavour would be almost impossible. This chapter does not provide any evaluation of the Prevent agenda or Empowering Muslim Women (EMW) initiatives; instead, it considers the 'work' done by the discourse or the policy narrative of both. Adopting an intertextual approach, it analyses the symbolic power of the discourse used in relevant policy documentation as well as politicians' interventions in these and related fields. In doing so it examines the rationale underlying the intelligibility of the initiatives. As previously highlighted, social problems are always problems *for* someone. It could therefore be argued that social problems and the objects of social policy interventions are constructed through the very process of policy development and implementation itself. The intelligibility of a social problem relies on a shared narrative and a shared understanding of the vocabulary which is used to articulate it. In the case of EMW and Prevent, the policy objective is to 'prevent violent extremism' and, while the vocabulary of extremism, radicalisation and terrorism has entered the everyday lexicon of common sense political debate, the meaning given to these terms is neither fixed nor universally agreed upon. Through consideration of specific and associated policy texts, I analyse how we are to understand the rationale of Prevent and the EMW initiatives through contextualising the language used. Specifically, how can we make sense of the idea that these initiatives, allegedly focused on empowering Muslim women, could 'stop people wanting to become terrorists'?[2]

The first section focuses on how, despite emphatic disavowals, the Prevent agenda remains inflected with the wider global discourse of Samuel Huntington's 'clash of civilisations'. As such it positions the Prevent agenda in terms of global politics, related national policies around terrorism and immigration, and debates around multiculturalism and Britishness. It explores the way in which the concept of 'culture' is invoked and implicitly (and sometimes explicitly) defined. For example, I look at the way that both Al Qaida inspired and far-right extremism are discussed in parallel, yet attempts to highlight their similarities only serve to demonise the 'Muslim community' more acutely. This is partly done through the 'asymmetric ascription of culture' (Narayan 1997 cited in Volpp 2001:1190); the causes of far right extremism are not attributed to 'culture', whereas Islamist terrorism almost always is. Furthermore, these policy discourses are by their very nature gendered. The risk of terrorist activity is principally located in young disaffected men, yet the bodies and rights of Muslim women are a crucial defining feature in the quest for 'shared values' and the much vaunted 'battle for hearts and minds'.

The second section of this chapter focuses on the articulation of gender within nationalist discourses in the UK by addressing the way in which 'the Muslim woman' is constructed in social policy discourses in the post 7/7 era. This process is multi-layered and complex. In the criss-crossing of various social policy initiatives she emerges as a symbol of all that is wrong with Britain's ill-begotten multicultural experiment, lacking in agency and unable or unwilling to inculcate the right values in her progeny. This section looks at the way in which the involvement of women in the Prevent agenda is made sense of. I consider the role of 'culture talk' (Mamdani 2005b) and the explicit way it is gendered in UK social policy discourse and how this is affected by the contemporary geopolitical landscape. I show how emphasising or privileging ahistorical decontextualized 'culture talk' allows for the conflation of different phenomena (which are either associated with Muslim communities or attributed to or seen as integral to 'Islamic' or 'Muslim culture'). I analyse how they work to produce a gendered, racialised group within the body politic of the UK at a particular historical juncture.

A clash of civilisations: creating the enemy within

> This is the problem with unedifying labels like Islam and the West; they mislead and confuse the mind, which is trying to make sense of a disorderly reality that won't be pigeonholed or strapped down as easily as all that. (Said 2001)

Huntington's infamous article 'The Clash of Civilisations?' (1993[3]) has been a controversial yet highly influential framing of post-Cold War global politics. In the aftermath of the Cold War Huntington suggested that there would be a 'revival' of religion in providing 'a basis for identity and commitment that transcends national boundaries and unites civilisations' (1993: 26) and by implication would pose a threat to national boundaries. Huntington suggested that the fundamental source of conflict in a post-Communist era would be 'cultural' rather than primarily ideological or economic (1993: 22).[4] Moreover, although he mentions up to eight different civilisations, Huntington's focus is on Islam as the civilisation against which the West must do principal battle.

The underlying rationale for the Prevent agenda was set out in the Department for Communities and Local Government (DCLG) document *Winning Hearts and Minds* (DCLG 2007) and it begins by categorically stating that this 'is not about a clash of civilisations or a struggle between Islam and "the West"' (DCLG 2007: 4).[5] Despite frequent and emphatic denials, however, the pervasiveness of Huntington's discourse can clearly be seen in the UK government's responses to the 7/7 bombings (and in response to subsequent terrorist threats as I discuss in the epilogue). It can be seen in the following: that religious diversity was deemed responsible for the 7/7 attacks; that Muslims are collectively responsible for the terrorism committed in the name of Islam; that being Muslim is sufficient risk in itself of radicalisation or terrorism; that Islamist terrorism is treated in different ways relative to other types of extremism; and that religious interpretation is emphasised as both an explanation and a solution to Islamist terrorist threats.

The Muslim problem; creating the enemy within

At a global level, 'defending civilisation' was quickly established at the core of the 'war on terror' (Vertigans 2010). For example, in an article entitled 'A battle for global values' for the journal Foreign Affairs (Blair 2007b), which was published at around the same time as *Winning Hearts and Minds,* Tony Blair sets out his position on what he believes are 'the roots of extremism'. He characterises the struggle not as a clash *of* civilisations, rather it is a clash *about* civilisation. He states: 'It is an age old battle between progress and reaction, between those who embrace the modern world and those who reject its existence – between optimism and hope, on the one hand, and pessimism and fear on the other'. This statement is explicitly couched in Orientalist terms which characterise discussions of the West and the rest (Hall 1997). References to 'an age old battle' that has been in evidence since time immemorial allude to historical confrontations, such as the Crusades. In this way, Blair echoes Huntington by turning 'civilisations' into 'shut-down, sealed off entities that have been purged of the myriad currents and counter currents that animate human history', thus ignoring histories of 'exchange, cross-fertilization and sharing' (Said 2001). The way in which the term 'difference' is invoked suggests a static and decontextualized difference where others occupy hermetically sealed 'cultures'; it ignores the shifting dynamic understandings of what constitutes difference in different contexts. Such characterisations also ignore the fact that battles between secularism and religion occur *within* civilisations not just between them (Yuval-Davis 2011), and that there are significant rifts within religions between reformist, orthodox, fundamentalist and progressive strands.

Moreover, despite the clear echoes of Huntington, the rephrasing to suggest that the war on terror is in fact a battle *for* civilisation itself is more far reaching than Huntington's thesis, since it suggests that the alternative cannot even be considered civilisation. It is less than civilised; it is barbaric. And as the second section of this chapter will explore, nowhere is this more apparent than in discussions about the position of women in Muslim communities.

The 7/7 bombings were described as '....the most horrific manifestation on British soil of a complex Al Qaida inspired threat to our security' (DCLG 2007:4). The attacks were deemed to be particularly shocking as the perpetrators were British born. Diversity itself was identified as the problem. In Gordon Brown's keynote speech on 'The Future of Britishness' at a Fabian Society conference in 2006, he stated that '...terrorism in our midst means that debates ...about Britishness and our model of integration clearly now have a new urgency.' He went on to say that:

> ...we have to face uncomfortable facts that there were British citizens, British born, apparently integrated into our communities, who were prepared to maim and kill fellow British citizens, irrespective of their religion – and this must lead us to ask how successful we have been in balancing the need for diversity with the obvious requirements of integration in our society. (Brown 2006: 250)

Similarly, Tony Blair (2006) also made an explicit link between terrorism, the alleged failures of multiculturalism and the duty to integrate stating that:

> ..it [the 7/7/bombings] has thrown into sharp relief, the nature of what we have called, with approval, 'multicultural Britain'. We like our diversity. But how do we react when that 'difference' leads to separation and alienation from the values that define what we hold in common? For the first time in a generation there is an unease, an anxiety, even at points a resentment that our very openness, our willingness

> to welcome difference, our pride in being home to many cultures, is being used against us; abused, indeed, in order to harm us.

With its allusions to Frisch's Firestarters[6], this passage clearly illustrates a powerful host/guest metaphor which has historically characterised immigration and race relations policy in the UK (Solomos 1993). It suggests that the 7/7 bombers are guests who have abused their hosts' hospitality, rather than British citizens engaged in acts of (political) violence or criminal activity.

It was not, however, merely the presence of diversity itself; it was the presence of a particular type of diversity that is, religious and cultural diversity as opposed to ethnic diversity. These attacks were conceptualised as the unfortunate outcome of the competing politics of belonging whereby the bombers' allegiance to Britain was seen as being in conflict with their religious allegiances (Yuval-Davis 2011). So it was as British-born Muslims that they were problematised. Accordingly, just as Huntington isolated Islam as the principal civilisation with which the West must do battle, so too was the Prevent agenda focused on Muslims.

The Prevent agenda is founded on the idea that, '...while a security response is vital, it will not, on its own, be enough...winning hearts and minds...is also crucial.' (DCLG 2007: 4). Tony Blair (2007a: 79) explains how 'we could have chosen security as the battleground but we did not. We chose values'. He went on to say that 'you cannot defeat a fanatical ideology just by imprisoning or killing its leaders; you have to defeat its ideas.' Although clearly 'imprisoning' and 'killing' are not off the agenda, the priority is a far more righteous endeavour, the battle for values, the battle for hearts and minds. The use of the term 'hearts and minds' instils the idea of Muslims' collective responsibility for terrorist attacks committed in the name of Islam. The term itself is an emotive expression with a long and contested history, having been used differently in different historic contexts, for example in relation to the US and UK responses in Vietnam and Malaysia respectively (Dixon 2009). In general, however, the term has been used in relation to counterrevolutionary or counterinsurgency measures rather than counterterrorism. Counterrevolutionary or counterinsurgency measures are invoked when there is perceived to be substantial popular support among the wider population (Dixon 2009). The frequent references to the term 'hearts and minds' therefore supports the idea that the Prevent agenda is less about counter terrorism (that is, its more overt security measures) and more about counterinsurgency (that is, affecting people's values and by extension their supposed support for terrorism). As such, despite the acknowledgment that radicalisation only refers to a small minority, the Prevent Strategy assumes the entire Muslim community to be a suspect community since it is deemed to be tacitly supportive of violent extremism and terrorist activities. The Prevent strategy therefore symbolised an expression of Huntington's 'clash of civilisations' on 'home soil'[7] reflecting his assertion about the revival of religion as a basis for identity which transcends and therefore endangers national boundaries.

The Prevent strategy was not seemingly based on calculated security risks nor on any particular intelligence. The Prevent Strategy literature referred to a figure of potentially 2000 'radicalised' individuals (HMG 2008:5) although the strategy itself included no explicit explanation of what the term 'radicalised' meant. Despite such small numbers relative to the numbers of Muslims in the UK, the Prevent strategy was focused on the entire Muslim population and areas with large Muslim populations were automatically seen as being at greater risk and therefore eligible for Prevent funding. The eligible areas mapped almost directly onto those areas which had hitherto been the subject of community cohesion initiatives (Husband and Alam 2011). Furthermore, in response to controversies about potentially engaging with and funding 'extremist' groups, the Prevent strategy focused its attention on moderate and non-extremist Muslim community groups and organisations. While possibly an astute decision at a presentational level, these were also the very organisations with the least capacity to effect any influence over anyone who was at risk of 'radicalisation' or likely to be involved in terrorism. Not only was such a strategy likely to be ineffective it also was counterproductive in its contribution to demonising an entire 'community'.

Having isolated and identified all Muslims as potentially suspect, the narrative of the Prevent agenda is also inflected with a strong sense of 'us and them', which had been a key theme of George Bush's framing of the war on terror. It can be seen particularly in the Preventing Violent Extremism (PVE or Prevent) policy literature when comparisons are drawn between Islamist extremism and other types of extremism. This juxtaposition of far right extremism and Islamist terrorism supports the idea of the West versus Islam. Far right extremism is positioned as 'our' problem; Al Qaida extremism is 'theirs'. Far right extremism has allegedly been successfully 'isolated'. This success is attributable to the armaments of 'the battle for hearts and minds' which are: promoting shared values; supporting local solutions, building civic capacity and leadership; and strengthening the role of faith institutions and leaders

(DCLG 2007: 5). The logic suggests that as these mechanisms have successfully been used to help 'us' deal with 'our' extremism, 'we' are going to help you with yours.

Despite the optimistic claims that far right extremism had been isolated, in 2009, two years after the Prevent agenda was introduced, it was in fact expanded to incorporate domestic terrorism from far left, far right and animal extremists. The impetus for this widening was in response to criticism of the Muslim-centric emphasis of Prevent. The inclusion of far right extremism suggests that either far right extremism was not in fact 'isolated' as previously suggested, or that the alleged success in isolating it had not worked sufficiently to prevent it re-emerging. More problematically, however, this effort to widen the agenda in fact served to further highlight the differences in the way Islamist extremism and far right extremism in particular are perceived. Even though acknowledging other types of extremism might have been intended to reduce the focus on Muslims, in reality the differential approaches in fact served to achieve the opposite.

This can be seen in a number of ways. For example, far right extremism is not predicated on the idea of a problematic community. If far right extremism and Al Qaida inspired extremism were seen as equivalent, 'moderate' racists would have been recruited to assist in its eradication, and women and young people would have been targeted or assisted to develop a stronger voice to counter it. Similarly, when Christians engage in acts of violence in support of these views (for example bombing abortion clinics in the US) this is not homogenised to the global 'Christian community'.

By contrast, radical or even socially conservative views among Muslims are automatically associated with a terrorist threat and these are extrapolated to the 'Muslim community' as a whole, who are seen as responsible by default. This logic is not applied in the case of mass murderers such as Anders Breivik. Indeed they are not even described as 'terrorists'. Instead responses have been detailed in depth psychological analyses of Breivik's motivations which focus on him as a 'Lone Wolf' (Kellner 2012).There is little discussion of the ideology which underlies these other forms of terrorism and heterosexual, white, nominally Christian men are not seen as potentially susceptible to the same type of extremism. The fact that there are right-wing Christians who are homophobic or anti-abortion, or Christians who are against the ordination of women or gay marriage and civil partnerships, is not seen as an indication of 'radicalisation', extremism and therefore an indication of potential terrorist activity.

The Muslim Solution

Having created a suspect community the response embedded within the Prevent narrative is to focus on Muslim communities collectively and on Islam as a religion for a solution. This logic is reliant on the presumption of a pathologised Muslim community which needs to 'get its house in order' and relies on 'good Muslims' to assist the state in dealing with the 'bad Muslims' (Mamdani 2005). It is evidenced in the following statement: 'Many individuals and organisations have a role to play in defeating terrorism – but voices from within the Muslim communities and the actions of Muslim organisations can be more powerful than most'. (DCLG 2007: 9)

These 'voices from within the Muslim communities' which might be considered 'more powerful' are identified as the voices of young people and women. The reasons why this may be the case are not explicitly discussed. They are only inferred. It is possibly that young people are themselves most at risk; that they could be susceptible to the process of being radicalised or may know people who are. (Notably here the fact that it is young men rather than women who are presumed to be most 'at risk' is not explicitly acknowledged). Equally, the emphasis on young people may also be a result of the enduring stereotype of Asian youths caught up in a 'culture clash', and in particular that young men are rebelling against being represented by 'elders' who are out of touch with their realities of unemployment and racism (Burlet and Reid 1998).

By contrast the logic of why women need to be involved is different. Simplistically, the fact that the perpetrators of 7/7 were men, and that women are not widely considered to be potential terrorists means that they are automatically presumed to be moderate or mainstream. Women are seen to be incorruptible and moreover, while youth are potentially corruptible, they can be 'saved' as a result of the greater influence of women who will enable greater state surveillance. This logic is flawed, however, in that on the one hand it suggests women and young people are potentially more powerful, and on the other it stresses that they also need the support of the Government to be heard. The inclusion of women nonetheless remains a powerful symbolic gesture capitalising on gendered Orientalism post 9/11 (Abu-Lughod 2014) which I explore in the second half of the chapter.

Furthermore, while government Ministers and officials were clear not to lay the blame at Islam's door per se, the fault was instead attributed to a perversion of Islam. Such extremist ideologies were then deemed to be the necessary target of government intervention. Religion is seen therefore as both the cause of Islamist terrorism as well as a source of hope for its eradication. For example, the literature states that work needs to be focused more specifically 'on undermining the distortion of the Islamic faith by violent extremists' (DCLG 2007: 5). It continues by saying that the government wants to ensure the most effective use of the education system in promoting faith understanding and that, in order to confound those who seek to exploit a lack of understanding of Islam, the government needs to provide access to 'trusted high quality learning about faith and Islam in Britain today'. The clear goal is to work 'particularly with Muslim communities to undermine the myths and half-truths being peddled by violent extremists and to equip communities with a counter narrative' (HM Government 2008: 18). It is argued that these strands of work are important in undermining the ideology of division and conflict.

Positing Islam as a solution can also be seen in the fact that one of the clear objectives of the Prevent agenda was to 'promote a stronger understanding of faith, culture and history' through using opportunities in the school curriculum, and in colleges, universities and elsewhere, to convey a deeper understanding of faith, history and culture: 'We need to develop a stronger understanding of Islam and Islamic culture, society and history across all communities, breaking down the suspicion and misunderstanding that can result from ignorance' (HM Government 2008: 16).

Although at first glance it might appear that this refers to 'the suspicion and misunderstanding that can result from ignorance' among non-Muslims about Islam following the 7/7 bombings, if read in the context of other policy literature, however, it is clear that the focus is not in fact on educating non-Muslims about Islam, but rather it is about educating Muslims themselves. More broadly, the policy discourse emphasises the need to work 'particularly with the Muslim community to help strengthen religious understanding among young people and in particular support an understanding of citizenship in an Islamic context' (HM Government 2008: 18) There are calls to broaden the provision of citizenship education in supplementary schools and *madrassahs* which should be designed to demonstrate how Islamic values are entirely consistent with 'core British values' (DCLG 2007: 5). [8]

Such references to 'equipping communities with a counter narrative' and the frequency with which they are deployed imply that a 'distorted' view of theology is of itself a necessary and sufficient condition for acts of terrorist violence. By extrapolation, therefore, promoting the right type of Islam ensures that you can prevent acts of violence committed in its name. This is clearly simplistic. The radicalisation thesis (Kundnani 2014), which presumes that exposure to extremist ideas is causally related to terrorism, has become a foundational myth in this debate, such that consideration of any other explanatory factors has come to be regarded as 'apologism'. (I will consider this in more depth in the epilogue). That is not to suggest that people's religious beliefs and interpretations do not have any role to play in why certain people are drawn to involvement in terrorist activities. Rather, the issue is the emphasis given to this relative to or excluding other factors which may also play a contributory role.

Principally, this emphasis on religious text, interpretation and ideology de-contextualises extremist violence from any political motivations. Such a view ignores that there are a range of other factors which may equally be necessary to instigate such violence (Butler 2004). In addition, it removes any analysis of the causes of radicalisation from material and structural factors. Instead the language perpetuates the idea of a homogenous but wayward community that does not fully understand its own religion and which needs to be brought back into the fold.

The policy response in the UK to concerns about religious belief, as evinced through the Prevent narrative, has not been focused on removing the visibility of religion from civic society, as in France, through a quest for an ideal secular republic. Instead, the debate has centred on promulgating the 'right type' of non-radical or progressive Islam. It represents an attempt to codify and fix a particular interpretation of Islam. Historically such initiatives are predated by policies in colonial India which attempted to understand two of the main religions (Islam and Hinduism) in an alleged effort to ensure that 'native sensibilities' were not inadvertently offended thus destabilising colonial rule. (Such policies were often connected to uprisings that had taken place, for example, the 1857 rebellion or 'mutiny'). Furthermore, colonial efforts to codify religion in India relied on narrow interpretations of only small sections of the community and in fact curtailed indigenous syncretism, leaving entrenched fault lines between different religious groups, sects and regions (Misra 2007) in a clear case of divide and rule.

At its most basic level the Prevent agenda is premised on an 'us and them' paradigm. This is done through making an imaginary monolithic 'Muslim community' simultaneously the primary focus of suspicion as well as responsible for eradicating violent extremism. Religion remains the prism through which the Prevent agenda and violent extremism is understood. What is conspicuous by its absence, however, is the failure to acknowledge foreign policy as a grievance (as opposed to a justification) that might need to be addressed, even though clearly it too is a factor frequently 'exploited' by extremists. As Butler writes, 'Our own acts of violence do not receive graphic coverage in the press, and so they remain acts that are justified in the name of self defense, but by a noble cause... the rooting out of terrorism' (2004: 6).

The Prevent narrative is only intelligible through a wider policy discourse in which an imagined Muslim community is pathologised as part of a locally inflected 'clash of civilisations'. Seen in the context of wider debates on Britishness these debates are clearly racialised. Furthermore, as Yuval Davis and Anthias (1989) make clear, the construction of national boundaries are not only racialised, they are gendered; the threats represented by Muslim women and men are different. While Muslim men are presented as dangerous for their radical ideologies and their potential for political violence arising from disaffection, the Muslim woman, by contrast, as the next section explores, has come to symbolise the dangerous consequences of 'too much multiculturalism'.

The Funeral Pyre of Multiculturalism

Ongoing critiques of multiculturalism, from a variety of political perspectives, have often centred on Okin's thesis that multiculturalism is bad for women since it supports cultural relativism in relation to the issue of women's rights (see Chapter 1 for more detail). Explicit discussion of gender as a variable is absent from the UK's counterterrorism agenda; women are barely mentioned unless in relation to specific women-only initiatives and gender neutral text implicitly refers to men. Given the interrelatedness of different policy discourses, however, the rationale for EMW initiatives draws on these pre-existing characterisations of the Muslim community as particularly problematic and uniquely patriarchal (Kumar 2012). The discursive production of 'the Muslim woman' in the Prevent agenda shows the pathology of the wider Muslim community as a whole through both the patriarchy of Muslim men and the victimhood of Muslim women. The picture is, however, more complex and ambivalent as I will explore. In addition to symbolising all that is wrong with the Muslim community (as victims of its patriarchy and misogyny) Muslim women simultaneously symbolise the alleged separateness or self-segregation of the Muslim community, particularly in relation to veiling.

Saving Muslim women

The association between empowerment and Muslim women has a common sense appeal because of two factors: the perceived status of women in Islam and secondly, given that the majority of Muslims in the UK are of South Asian origin, (post)colonial constructions of the 'submissive Asian woman'. These powerful discourses support the idea that Muslims constitute a problematic community and that part of their danger comes from being 'backward'. One expression of this backwardness is the perceived generalised status of women as oppressed or marginalised within Muslim communities. That status alone, that is, marginalisation by Muslim men rather than their status in wider society (by virtue of their ethnicity, class, geographic location, citizenship status), is considered responsible for their social positioning. This generalised patriarchy is most acutely expressed in discussions of what are described as 'barbaric cultural practices'; the process of pathologisation is complete.

The press release accompanying the launch of NMWAG, in explaining its role stated that: 'They [that is, NMWAG] will discuss issues and concerns that affect Muslim women, for example education, employment, access for women to mosques and their management committees and *cultural barriers* including issues around forced marriages' (my emphasis).

Here, the issues and concerns that 'affect Muslim women' are being defined. There are a number of problematic assumptions embedded within this. For example, the only issue which applies *exclusively* to Muslim women is access to mosques. The document states that 'Mosques are community hubs' and that the 'Government's dialogue with Muslim women has shown that access to Mosque life is vital for them to engage effectively in the community'.[9] (DCLG 2007: 10). Tony Blair even referred to 'their [Muslim women's] frustration at being debarred even from entering certain mosques' (2006). There have undoubtedly been women-led campaigns about access to mosques (Brown 2008), but the issue of the state's engagement with Muslim women's struggles to gain access to mosques is problematic. As Katherine Brown has suggested, 'the instrumental use of gender by government has had the impact of relegating Muslim women's political activism to a sideshow' (2008: 487). More importantly perhaps is that Muslim women's engagement here is narrowly defined in that it is focused on women's attendance at mosques. As a result it is Muslim women who attend the mosque who are the Muslim women that the government feel should be engaged with and who can and should have a say in community matters. It therefore perpetuates, reifies or ossifies a particular community structure rather than widening the basis, scope or criteria for seeking Muslim women's engagement. The discourse emulates or reinforces particular characterisations of Muslim women, not one which all Muslim women are necessarily comfortable with (as discussed in Chapter 4).

The statement above also refers to forced marriage as a 'cultural barrier.' This is possibly even more concerning in the context of EMW. First, it particularises forced marriage to Muslims despite the fact that such crimes occur among non-Muslims. Second, it is not clear how talking about forced marriage is connected to terrorism, other than if we accept that both are indicators of a 'failed community' or are somehow condoned by Islam. Its inclusion as part of the EMW initiatives in this statement exemplifies the way that social policy discourses related to the Prevent agenda are characterised by the conflation of what are conceptually distinctive policy concerns (such as immigration, forced marriage and terrorism). The securitisation of the policy landscape means that potentially any issues which fall within the social policy cluster relating to Muslims can then be targeted. In relation to women, these conflations are particularly striking.

A cursory analysis of policy literature on preventing violent extremism shows the frequency of references to what are referred to as 'cultural practices'. Tony Blair's 'duty to integrate' speech included reference to 'cultural practices' such as forced marriage which he claimed contradicted British belief in standing 'emphatically at all times for equality of respect and treatment for all citizens'. Blair (2006) noted 'that in many religions the treatment of women differs from that of men' (yet he omitted to mention that gender differences and imbalances are normalised in wider secular society too and that many secular organisations do not reflect women's voices as a proportion of the population – the House of Commons being a prime example). Furthermore, during a talk about Prevent entitled 'Many Voices; understanding the debate about preventing violent extremism', Hazel Blears also included numerous references to forced marriage, female genital mutilation and homophobia, and made various references to 'respect for women' and 'violence against women' (Blears 2009).

This conflation can also be seen in the slippage between other policy discourses. A House of Lords debate on honour killings which took place shortly after the London bombings, as well as racialising such crimes exclusively to Muslims, made links with both immigration and terrorism. Lord Russell-Johnston stated that while he may be 'soft on those seeking asylum from persecution...[he was] not soft on the importation of barbarism' (Hansard 2005: 1421). During the same debate, Lord Parekh uses the expression 'domestic terrorism' to discuss a 'man who has disposed of his daughter' and suggests that 'he does not see himself as a criminal; nor does his community see him as a criminal – he is a martyr'. Lord Parekh then goes so far as to compare the situation as 'like that of a suicide bomber' concluding that 'if a man does not fear death or pain, the law has no sanctions to impose on him'. The invocation of the term 'terror' is striking in this context and is no doubt connected to the timing of the debate, a few months after the 7/7 London bombings.

Similarly, such policy conflations allow policy solutions directed at one area of policy to be extrapolated to other policy areas. This can be seen in the way in which the issue of forced marriage has been instrumentalised in order to enact immigration laws which limit citizenship rights. In 2007, for example, as part of an announcement on crime, security and justice, the Labour government proposed to raise the minimum age at which foreign nationals can receive marriage visas to enter Britain. It was raised from 18 to 21 in an effort 'to crack down' on forced marriages.[10] The rationale for this move is to 'allow the young people involved to have completed their education as well as allowing them to gain in maturity and possess adequate life skills' (BBC 2007). Yet in the UK it is possible to get married at 16 with parental consent, a fact which illustrates the racist assumptions underlying the policy. The state is now 'using the demand for women's rights in minority communities to impose immigration controls and justify a racist agenda' even though there is little evidence that such changes have benefitted abused women (Siddiqui 2005: 273). For example, changes in immigration law only protect British women, whereas conversely foreign national brides who experience problems are at risk of being deported (Anitha 2008). To be clear, forced marriage is a social problem which occurs and which needs to be tackled, but it is its policy positioning as a specifically Muslim concern which is problematic.

Similarly, the 'cultural practice' of gender segregation followed by some Muslims has been associated with extremism. In 2009, another New Labour politician made some interventions, drawing on the theme of women, segregation and extremism. Jim Fitzpatrick was MP for Poplar and Canning Town at the time (and since 2010, MP for Poplar and Limehouse) and made a high profile intervention in this area when he declined to stay at a wedding which had been segregated by the couple who had invited him to attend 'out of respect for the elders attending'. He said that he did not want to sit separately from his wife and explained that he had left the wedding so as not to cause offence. Later, however, in an interview, Fitzpatrick claimed he was concerned that this was an indication of the increasing influence of the IFE (Islamic Forum in Europe) in Tower Hamlets (although in the same interview he claims this is only the second time in ten years he has observed a segregated wedding) (BBC 2009). Segregation in itself was assumed to imply extremism. Sex segregation exists in wider society of course and is largely uncontroversial (for example, single sex schools, bathroom facilities and changing rooms). Where it does arouse controversy, for example gentlemen's clubs which bar women, this is not articulated as 'extremism'. Rather it is regarded as old fashioned, antiquated or anachronistic. In the case of segregated weddings, however, given that it is something that some Muslims do, it becomes associated with extremism.

Combined, these policy conflations link the prevention of violent extremism to a variety of issues and concerns, all of which rely on a rescue paradigm and which construct Muslim women as victims of their 'culture'. The process is, however, more nuanced and the figure of the Muslim woman is also symbolic of the self-segregation of which Muslim communities are accused. This is most clearly seen in policy discourses about the veil. While the EMW initiatives steered clear of explicitly referring to the veil, a number of politicians have made some very public interventions on it which form a backdrop to the Prevent narrative.

'Veiled threats'?

In the EMW literature itself there is only one reference to the veil. In her ministerial foreword to Empowering Muslim Women: Case Studies Blears writes, 'we pay too much attention to Muslim women's appearance – with perennial debate about headscarves and veils – and too little to what they say and do' (DCLG 2008: 2). While this statement is in itself uncontroversial and was echoed by the research participants, it draws attention to the issue of the veil (and in fact the majority of the photos in the EMW brochure are of hijab-wearing Muslim women). No other garment of clothing has sparked so much debate. In the UK there have been no initiatives to ban the burka or prohibit schoolgirls from wearing the hijab as there have been in France, Belgium and Italy. Jack Straw (Labour MP), however, notoriously triggered a national debate by writing about the subject in his weekly column in a local paper in his constituency in October 2006. In this column he described his feelings about niqab-wearing women who came to see him in his Lancashire constituency. He explained that although the particular encounter which provoked these thoughts had been 'polite and respectful', it apparently made him uncomfortable that he could not see what he described as the 'lady' who was exercising her democratic right to come and see her Member for Parliament. He argued that the conversation would have been of greater value if the woman had taken the covering from her face. He then explained how he always asked niqab-ed women to remove their veils, even claiming, despite any apparent supporting evidence, that 'most...seem relieved' that he did so and that in one case 'the veil came off almost as soon as...[he]...opened...[his]...mouth' (Lancashire Telegraph October 2006).

This is despite the fact that even Jack Straw admits they appeared to be wearing the niqab from personal choice rather than at the behest of fathers, brothers or husbands, thus differing considerably from the French position where it is automatically assumed to be a symbol of Muslim patriarchy. An alternative interpretation might be that these were articulate assertive women who had come to seek advice or assistance from him, a well-known politician, on a constituency matter, and that they felt obliged to remove their veils given his vociferousness on the matter. In that encounter Jack Straw clearly had power to help or not help, listen or not listen to his constituents. Despite the furore, with a wide range of politicians and media commentators wading into the debate, there is tellingly little sign of the voices of the women at the centre of this debate themselves; how did *they* experience being asked by their representative in Parliament to remove their niqabs? They may well have been relieved as Jack Straw suggests, or alternatively, they may have felt humiliated or exploited. In the absence of the voices of the women he is referring to, it is more probable that his assumptions are projections reflecting his own discomfort and justifications for his actions.

Media responses to Straw's intervention illustrate how Muslim difference is conceptualised according to accounts of i) Britishness and national identity, ii) citizenship and social cohesion, and iii) matters of gender and violence (Meer, Dyer and Modood 2010). In his 'duty to integrate' speech, Blair also mentions the veil, lending support to Jack Straw's inopportune interventions.[11] Interestingly, he caveats his comments by saying that he knows ' ...it is not sensible to conduct this debate as if the only issue is this very hot and sensitive one of the veil. For one thing, the extremism we face is usually from men not women'.

This implies that if women did represent a threat, then their clothing could be an indicator of possible extremism. In contrast to ongoing debates in Europe and elsewhere (Turkey, Tunisia and Malaysia, as Blair is keen to highlight)[12] where the emphasis has been on the veil as a symbol of the oppression of women, political discourse on the veil in the UK has been more nuanced. While the theme of the 'oppressed Muslim woman' permeates the discourse, its relevance is also accounted for by its role as a very visible marker of difference and self-segregation. The veil, therefore, has an ambivalent position in UK political discourse; on one level it signifies self-segregation, yet on another level it symbolises a certain kind of militancy and empowerment through religion for Muslim women. For example, there have been a number of high profile cases (Dustin and Phillips, 2008) where women have fought for the right to wear the veil and been accused of both militancy or succumbing to patriarchal wishes.[13] And as I discuss in the epilogue, as the number of Muslim women and girls who join ISIS increases, no doubt its symbolism as an indicator of possible 'extremism' will gain further momentum.

Having demonstrated how 'the Muslim community' emerges as a uniquely problematic group in the wider policy landscape of the UK, particularly in relation to the role of Muslim women, I now return to the key question of how the relationship between 'empowering Muslim women' and preventing violent extremism can be made intelligible.

Empowering Muslim women to combat terrorism

In the policy literature Muslim women, along with young people, are positioned as being uniquely placed to combat terrorism. There is, however, very little clarity as to the raison d'être for this. In the introduction to the report 'Women's Role in Peaceful Coexistence Tackling Violent Extremism and Promoting Community Cohesion Faith',[14] Meg Munn highlights the way that 'Women suffer disproportionately as victims of violent extremism unleashed by conflict, especially in countries where rape has been used as a weapon of war'. In the report, women with experiences from Ghana, Bosnia Herzegovina and the UK (including Northern Ireland) are brought together. This is consistent with long standing feminist critiques of militarism and references the potential for cross border solidarities between women. Comparing the experience of civilian women in the UK with women from Bosnia Herzegovina who have experienced ethnic cleansing, however, trivialises the experiences of the latter. Nor are there any references to women who might be affected by wars in which the UK has long been embroiled. What this juxtaposition achieves, however, is the tentative suggestion that there is a broader case for the involvement of women in preventing violent extremism.

The most explicit discussion in the policy literature of any possible direct association between empowering Muslim women and preventing violent extremism, however, is put forward by Sadiq Khan (Labour MP for Tooting, assistant government whip at the time, and the Minister for Communities & Local Government). Khan writes:

> But it (women's rights) also has serious *consequences* for preventing extremism, given that the majority of the extremist and radical ideologies that lead young men to turn themselves into human bombs are also deeply misogynist. The Taliban and their barbaric laws towards the women are a good example of this misogyny.' Sadiq Khan MP (Khan, Katwala, Jameson 2008: 41) (my emphasis)

Although Khan states that women's rights have consequences for preventing extremism, he does not identify an explicit *causal* relationship between misogyny and radical/terrorist political activity. It appears to be enough, seemingly, to refer to both in the same sentence and a meaning can be inferred, suggesting that by dealing with one, you make inroads into the other.

An initial cursory reading of Sadiq Khan's statement suggests that, beyond the coincidence of misogyny and terrorism, Muslim women were somehow responsible for misogyny, or at least collude in it. His statement intimates that if only Muslim women were empowered, then Islamic radicals would not be misogynists, and if they were not misogynists, then they would not become terrorists. Although a rather cynical interpretation, it appears to be vindicated by a later speech by Khan which he gave to a group of Muslim women and in which he implied that women have almost brought patriarchy on to themselves: 'Misogyny is an integral part of their (extremists') ideology....By being the best you can be – as professionals, as citizens, as proud Brits and Muslims, as hope-givers – British Muslim women can prove the hatemongers wrong and weak in the face of strength' (Khan 2009).

In these interpretations, while ostensibly framed in feminist terms, the possibility that Muslim women might have the potential to be politicised or express their grievances in similar ways to those anticipated from young men was not even entertained.[15] There are no references to women and girls having the potential to be radicalised despite research which suggest that women's emancipation may *increase* the number of women terrorists (Oliverio and Lauderdale 2005).[16] In the epilogue I consider these earlier assumptions in the light of the increasing number of British Muslims girls leaving the UK to join ISIS.

At the level of public life, Muslim women are seen to be powerless and in need of state assistance. Conversely they are deemed to have power in the narrow environment of the home. The main way in which women are engaged with is therefore through their role in the family, or as at 'the heart of the community', and in their relationship to young people. For example,

> these individuals and groups should reflect the diversity of Muslim communities, including Muslim women and young people. Women can be a particularly effective voice as they are at the heart not only of their communities but also of their families...It is important to reach beyond would-be gatekeepers to the community when seeking strong community voices. (HMG 2008: 17)

This statement highlights the paradox of the logic of empowering 'strong community voices'; clearly, if they require external assistance to be heard over 'would-be gatekeepers to the community', they are not so strong. As Brown (2011) argues, the frequent references to women and young people together is infantilising. In addition it resonates with discourses around protecting 'womenandchildren' (Enloe 1990).[17]

Just as in development discourses, where women are presumed to hold the key to successful economic development, Muslim women are presumed to be moderate and 'good Muslims' and able to positively affect the community. What is implied is that if women have a stronger voice and are able to influence members of the community more widely then it will necessarily be for the good of 'the community'. The implicit presumption is that women are never at risk of becoming radicalised and that they would never be supportive of or sympathetic to expressions of violent extremist ideology or terrorist acts.

In the Prevent literature a number of documents were published which sought to highlight existing good practice. The aim of these was to inspire and guide those third sector organisations who intended to seek local authority Prevent funding. Very few of these original 'Pathfinder' projects were specifically focused on women, however. The Pathfinder projects specifically related to women are included in a section about 'Building the resilience of communities to resist violent extremism' (DCLG 2009). Resilience is never explicitly defined, however, and the closest definition is:'...help them (communities and community groups) actively reject and condemn violent extremism'(DCLG 2009: 4). It suggests that resilience is almost akin to immunity; that women's empowerment represents a vaccine for the community against violent extremism and radicalism and that women are the carriers of that immunity.

Only one case study was solely focused on Muslim women. It was an e-safety awareness course in Harrow (DCLG 2009: 14–17) and was provided for Muslim women who had children or worked with young people. According to the brochure, 'the training encompassed the potential issues that can arise from use and misuse of available digital technologies.' Having said that, the literature is clear in its message that the aim of the project was to consider *all* aspects of 'e-safeguarding' (for example, cyber bullying, chat rooms, pornography and grooming as well as 'radicalising' materials from groups promoting violent extremism) and the user website was aimed at different audiences, not just Muslims (DCLG 2009: 14). The project worked with local mosques and community groups, especially women's organisations, to promote and encourage key target groups to participate. Muslim women were the clear targets or focus of the project, yet the themes were much more broadly applicable to a wider audience, not just women or Muslims, but parents and other people working with young children more generally. Harrow Central Mosque Ladies' Committee helped to promote the event, encouraging women to participate. The project '...reinforced the key messages of safeguarding and mainstreamed Prevent into another initiatives for safeguarding young people' (DCLG 2009: 15). One of the stated outcomes was that, 'by receiving e-safety training, mothers and teachers understand how and why young people can become susceptible to *radicalisation and other dangers* through information available online and via other digital media if their usage of these information sources were to remain unmonitored.' (my emphasis) (DCLG 2009: 15).

The fact that the only project which is overtly focused on women concerns e-safeguarding validates observations about Prevent, that it was fundamentally about spying and surveillance, a criticism which was levelled at the initiatives primarily focused on young people (Kundnani 2009). This suggests that the EMW initiatives within Prevent were about teaching mothers and sisters to spy on their sons and brothers. If this is read in the context of John Reid's speech (made in East London in 2006), the message that mothers should spy on their children is even more transparent. In that address he is quoted as saying that:

> 'There is no nice way of saying this... these fanatics are looking to groom and brainwash children, including your

> children, for suicide bombings. Grooming them to kill themselves in order to murder others.'
>
> He added: 'Look for the tell-tale signs now and talk to them before their hatred grows and you risk losing them forever. In protecting our families, we are protecting our community.' (Batty 2006; Travis 2006)

Conclusion

The language of the debate ensuing from 7/7 clearly emphasised the 'otherness' of the perpetrators through their religious affiliation and as a result the 'Muslim community' became positioned as 'the enemy within'. The Prevent agenda emphasised religious ideology as *the* principal explanation for Islamist terrorism to the exclusion of any other potentially relevant factors. Furthermore it was only Muslims who were positioned as being uniquely conflicted by the assumed contradiction between their religious and civic duties, caught within the competing politics of belonging (Yuval-Davis 2011). This could clearly be seen when the Prevent agenda was tasked with dealing with other forms of extremism such as that of the far right. Ironically the remit was widened in response to criticisms of the exclusive focus on Muslims. This new remit, however, which led to frequent comparisons with far right extremism, only served to highlight the singular pathologisation of Muslims inherent in the Prevent agenda. Only Muslims are reduced to their religious affiliation ('religious essentialism') despite the complexities and contestations inherent within such a categorisation. As such, the Prevent narrative reflects the principal themes of Huntington's 'clash of civilisations' thesis (Huntington 1993). I have also shown how these discourses are gendered and argued that the intelligibility of the EMW initiatives relies partially on constructing as problematic the position of women within a homogeneous 'Muslim community'; policy literature is imbued with these discourses either explicitly or implicitly.

In this chapter I have therefore also analysed the policy discourse of the war on terror as it relates to Muslim women in the UK. This wider discourse of 'them and us', a failed community, the wrong type of Islam and the role of women paves the way for the securitisation agenda, the dehumanising, and the end of tolerance (Kundnani 2007). Feminism in the context of the EMW initiatives emerges as part of a civilisationist discourse in which it is positioned as part of modernising mission. This perspective claims ownership of and responsibility for feminism as a Western value, thus ignoring a whole history of black feminist critiques of white Western feminism and also the existence of 'native feminisms', for example, Islamic feminisms. Liberal feminism ends up becoming equated with the West and is thus even less likely to be accepted by those for whom the West represents the source of neocolonial and imperial exploitation. Associating counterterrorism measures with the issue of women's rights becomes another way of delineating the line between 'them and us'. This resonates with Inglehart and Norris citing Polly Toynbee: 'What binds together a globalized force of some extremists from many continents is a united hatred of Western values that seems to them to spring from Judeo-Christianity' (2003: 65).

On its own, the EMW agenda does not do this. It works in tandem within the context of a wider policy landscape. My argument is that the EMW is an overt expression of the way in which Muslim women are viewed solely in relation to their communities. The themes raised in this chapter will be revisited in subsequent chapters as I trace the way in which these ideas permeate, circulate or mutate in the context of policy in practice. The very fact that the objectives of Prevent are untestable arguably lends credence to the idea that the agenda is, at best, presentational (that the government is at least being seen to be doing something); at worst, it is tantamount to anti-Muslim racist propaganda.

Notes

1. Hilary Benn cited in NBC news (Associated Press 2007). Although notably Gordon Brown continued using the term (Afshar 2012)
2. As set out in the Prevent Strategy
3. Foreign Affairs is the Journal of the Council on Foreign Relations whose Board of Directors includes Madeline Albright, Colin Powell and Fouad Ajami, all of whom form part of the Bush circle that framed the response to 9/11 according to Joseph Power (theorist of soft power) cited in Kumar (2012)
4. Huntington suggests the 'great divisions among humankind and the dominating source of conflict will be cultural'. He explicitly links culture and civilisation, describing the latter as 'a cultural entity'.
5. See also John Reid speech where he repeats this and clarifies that 'It's not Muslims versus the rest of us' (Reid 2006)
6. Frisch's *Fire Starters* or *Biedermann und die Brandstifter* (1986) is a play in which two characters disguised as hawkers talk their way into people's homes and settle down in the attic, whereupon they set about the destruction of the house. The play was written in the immediate post-second world war period as a metaphor for Nazism and fascism, showing how ordinary citizens could be taken in by evil. The central character is a businessman called Biedermann. The first 'hawker' talks his way into spending the night in the attic through a mixture of intimidation and persuasion. Later a second arsonist appears, and before Biedermann can do anything to stop it, his attic is piled high with oil drums full of petrol. He even helps them to measure

the detonating fuse and gives them matches, refusing to acknowledge the terror of what is happening and becoming an accomplice in his own destruction.

[7] Bawer (2006) writing in the US uses similar metaphors, describing the ticking time bomb of increasing Muslim 'immigrants' as Europe's 'Weimar moment' (alluding to the Weimar Republic's weakness in the face of the rise of Hitler and the rest of Europe's appeasement).

[8] Vron Ware at The New Muslims conference on 8 March 2013 at The University of Manchester explained how the British Army's imam had issued statements making clear that nationalism and patriotism were compatible with Islamic beliefs.

[9] Given the way in which the majority of mosques have developed in the UK this could also be connected to lack of space and funding to expand rather than the explicit bar that Blair's comments suggest.

[10] This follows in the footsteps of Denmark where the age has been raised to 24 for overseas spouses.

[11] The timing of Blair's speech was not long after Jack Straw's remarks for which the latter has since apologised in a politically opportunistic moment prior to the 2010 general election (Walker 2010).

[12] By which he simultaneously invokes solidarity with these other countries but also conveniently ignores that these are Muslim majority countries in which the timbre of the debates are distinctly different.

[13] Afshar (2012) discussing a more European wide fascination with the veil associates it directly to a fear of terrorism.

[14] Women's Role in Peaceful Coexistence Tackling Violent Extremism and Promoting Community Cohesion, Faith Regen Foundation Conference Report 2008 (16–18 June 2008).

[15] Stephen Timms MP was attacked by Roshonara Choudhary, a 21year old hijab-wearing woman of Bangladeshi heritage, during a constituency surgery in east London. The way the attack was originally reported was interesting. Some blogs and discussion boards have noted the reluctance of some of the media to refer to her ethnicity, faith or background as part of a diatribe against PC, but I interpreted it as a discomfort about representing a Muslim woman who had done something unusual and unexpected; I cannot help thinking about how the incident might have been portrayed if the perpetrator had been male. Later reports which came out after her trial suggest that Roshonara Choudhry carried out the stabbing because she held Timms personally accountable for voting in favour of the Iraq war. Her concern over the war drove her to seek out a website such as RevolutionMuslim and to subsequently download Anwar al-Awlaki lectures which allegedly 'radicalised' her. See Githens-Mazer (2010).

[16] The Prevent agenda discourse focuses on 'radicalisation' and 'violent extremism' and 'empowerment' (rather than 'terrorism' and 'emancipation' to which Oliverio and Lauderdale (2005) refer).

[17] In Chapter 5, I explore in greater detail how many of the references to Muslim women are as 'mothers and grandmothers'.

THREE

Tales of the city: diversity in diversity, working between and within local differences

> '...on a micro and macro level, you are needed. Muslim women are needed to fulfil your own fullest potential for your own individual benefit, for the benefit of your family, for the benefit of your local community, for your region or city. Of course, our country (and it is our country) needs all of us to maximise our potential and especially some of the untapped talent of British Muslim women. And frankly our planet needs you.' Sadiq Khan MP, 10 Jan 2009

Introduction

Since Muslims as objects of research tend to be concentrated in specific urban locations, much of the research is frequently as much about the places in which the research is undertaken. This can be seen in the focus on East London and Bradford, for example. While individually the place-specific research takes into account local factors, the findings are frequently homogenised and extrapolated to the Muslim population as a whole, a point which many research respondents noted. In the opening quote, Sadiq Khan highlights the various different levels of society at which Muslim women might be engaged with. He makes clear reference to 'region' and 'city' and there is seemingly some recognition of the different levels at which individuals operate. Later, he also exhorts Muslim women to 'be good neighbours, good citizens – both local and global'. The members of NMWAG (the National Muslim Women's Advisory Group) were described as '...ambassadors for the grass roots, speaking direct to the heart of government' (DCLG 2008a). The policy literature therefore clearly refers to 'region' and 'city'. Practically speaking too, there is the fact that local authorities who were granted Prevent funding were able to allocate that funding according to particular local circumstances. A central argument of this book, however, is that the EMW (Empowering Muslim Women) initiatives prioritise religious affiliation, identity and heritage at the expense of other salient aspects of 'identity'. This chapter argues that differences that might exist between Muslim women's experiences because of where they are located geographically in the UK are not taken into account in any meaningful way. It also looks at the ways in which 'the local' matters in practice and the relationship between the national and the local.

The research on which this book is based took me to a number of different places and I was regularly reminded of the variety of ways in which quite a small initiative varied in different sites of research. Using predominantly interview data (as well as some ethnographic observation) compiled in different urban contexts, this chapter highlights the importance of acknowledging diversity within diversity and drawing attention to local specificities in policy delivery and reception. In focusing on geographical diversity it considers how UK-wide social policy initiatives to 'empower Muslim women' varied in practice, both between and within different localities. I explore how other axes of identity emerged through interviews with respondents and during the course of fieldwork, and how these varied from place to place. In doing so it (re)emphasises the point that different dimensions of social life cannot be separated out into discrete and pure strands and consist instead of complex, varied and variable effects when multiple axes of differentiation intersect in historically specific contexts (Brah and Phoenix 2004).

It could be argued that the urban unrest in 2001 in the northern mill towns instigated changes (or at least accelerated changes) in the policy landscape in relation to multiculturalism. The trigger points in Oldham, Burnley and Bradford may well have been different. The official policy story, however, suggested that the underlying causes of the unrest stemmed from allegedly 'self-segregated communities' living parallel lives, and that the heart of the problem lay the cultural incommensurability between different communities. The emphasis of the policy responses was therefore on the perpetrators themselves and not on the conditions within which the disturbances occurred; people rather than problem centric. Yet as Khan (2006) argues, 'policy responses to issues affecting young Muslims [and presumably any other "group"] should be based on the detail of their lives rather than on political imperatives reacting to events' (cited in Khan 2010: 86).

As well as the causes of the 2001 riots being over determined by 'culturalist' explanations, it is also worth explicitly noting that the policy responses to these disturbances, which were based in three specific places, have been rolled out across the whole of the UK, irrespective of local variations. While the suggestion that Bradford was 'bicultural' rather than multicultural (Webster 2003) is problematic, since this supports the idea of bounded internally homogeneous ethnicities (Modood 1992), it at least draws attention to the idea that not all 'diverse' places are 'diverse' in the same way. There is diversity in diversity.

Researching these initiatives further emphasises the importance of acknowledging this diversity within diversity. Following the initiatives themselves, the data is drawn from areas with substantive populations of Muslims. All are medium to large conurbations with ethnically 'diverse' populations. Yet the extent of diversity and the composition of these diverse populations necessarily varies. Specifically, research was conducted in three different boroughs in London (Ealing, Brent and Newham) as well as in Manchester, Cardiff, Bradford and Bristol. Despite superficial parallels between these sites, given that they are all home to 'diverse communities' (including Muslims), they are of course very different. Within these places, for example, there were areas which had long-established predominantly South Asian migrant heritage communities, such as cities like Bradford in West Yorkshire. On the other hand, there were areas in London which might be described as 'hyper diverse', areas such as Brent and Ealing, which have historically had a varied population encompassing both long established 'ethnic minority' communities, as well as newer migrants from A8 countries and varied (and internally diverse) refugee populations.

This chapter analyses the theme of 'the national to the local' in two ways. This is partly determined by the initiatives themselves which operated at both national and local levels. First, the Empowering Muslim Women initiatives were inspired by a nationally devised Prevent strategy, driven by a central government department, the Department for Communities and Local Government (DCLG), and overseen by NMWAG. Even though both DCLG and NMWAG had national remits, the national initiatives were of course locally delivered. One of the projects funded by DCLG and delivered by NMWAG was a role models road show which visited six different cities in England and Wales.

Second, at a local level, Local Authorities had been encouraged to use Prevent funding to 'empower' Muslim women locally. The Prevent agenda has been instituted almost in place of the community cohesion agenda in areas with substantial Muslim populations.[1] In fact it was implemented wherever there were Muslim populations, irrespective of their circumstances and internal diversity, or any analysis of susceptibility to radicalisation or 'violent extremism' (assuming that this was something that could be determined with any degree of certainty);

to have a sizeable Muslim population was sufficient qualification. Here therefore there was scope for local variety in how this played out. The research, which comprised interviews with a range of policy actors spread throughout the country, necessarily encountered a cross section of projects funded via Prevent in which such local differences emerged. Although local variations were not originally a key concern of the research, as I embarked on the interviews they emerged as an ever present salient theme.

The Prevent agenda is a paradoxical development following the community cohesion agenda (Husband and Alam 2011). This is because the latter is at least nominally focused on 'bringing communities together', whereas the former is predicated explicitly on a particular problematic community. Given this contradiction it is important to consider the way in which the Prevent agenda has impacted on intracommunity relations. This impact is a thread which runs through this chapter. As well as arousing criticism from those concerned at the impact on 'Muslim communities' (Kundnani 2009), the Prevent strategy was also critiqued by those for whom such funding represented 'too few rewards for good behaviour and too little punishment for bad behaviour' (Maher and Frampton 2009:7; Briggs and Birdwell 2009). In this chapter therefore other communities' responses to Prevent are also discussed. As Flint and Robinson point out, local areas have been given 'considerable autonomy to define their own 'community cohesion' problems (or lack of them) and implement local solutions' (2008: 5). It is not surprising, therefore, that responses to the community cohesion and Prevent agendas have varied accordingly. I suggest that these responses must necessarily vary from place to place depending not only on the composition of the population, but also the local circumstances, histories and trajectories of migration and local politics.

The community cohesion agenda is a racialised discourse in which social cohesion is prioritised at the expense of dealing with underlying deeper structural issues. As Flint and Robinson note, this agenda has enabled prioritisation of certain types of cohesion in order to problematise particular groups. For example, racial and religious 'cohesion' are privileged over gender and class as the focus of policy initiatives (2008). Further, they argue that although the community cohesion agenda built on the work of Kearns and Forrest (2000) it did so with important omissions. In lieu of a recognition of the importance of reducing wealth inequalities, a hollow concept of 'equality of opportunity' is referred to which indicates a 'reticence of the community cohesion agenda to acknowledge and address structural inequalities rooted in economic processes' (Flint and Robinson 2008:

4–5). Furthermore, it is important to note, such structural inequalities are regionally inflected.

This chapter looks at how the Prevent agenda worked in areas with populations comprising Muslims and non-Muslims, coming as it did in the wake of the community cohesion agenda. Much has been written about how multiculturalism or multiculturalist policies have led to a 'white backlash', observable in a variety of contexts, and the way this has fed into support for the BNP (Hewitt 2005; Garner et al 2009; Rhodes 2010). Comparatively less, however, has been written about the effect on other BME (black and minority ethnic) communities or intercommunity relations. The second half of the chapter explores this theme and tries to contextualise the discussion in terms of geographical diversity in the composition of Muslim and non-Muslim BME communities in the different sites of research (both in terms of ethno-national categories as well as socio-economic diversity). The significance of spatial location, geographical concentration, BME (ethno-religious) diversity and local politics are all variously taken into account.

I will look at the way in which these national and local projects varied between and within different places. Rather than consider local particularities as inconvenient 'white noise', it analyses the variations arising from local events and contexts which means that even cities with similar demographic structures can develop different types of political interaction (Stroschein 2007). The following section considers the idea of the national to the local in the context of the nationally devised, yet locally implemented role models road shows.

Local inflections in delivering a national initiative

The role models road show, *Our Choices*, was one of three initiatives overseen by NMWAG, and took place in early 2010. *Our Choices* went to six places: London, Manchester, Cardiff, Dudley, Rotherham and Middlesbrough. The issue of local variation was immediately apparent in the way the road shows were organised, received and experienced which prompted an analysis of the way in which the delivery of a national initiative was locally inflected. This section starts by reflecting on three of the road shows. It then sets out how the initiative was locally inflected in terms of its rationale, its composition and its reception. It discusses how and why the six particular sites were chosen, how the organisers tried to ensure that each of the road shows was locally pertinent and also some of the problems encountered in different places. In doing so, this section highlights differences between and within the different road shows by also reflecting on other contrasts between and among both the attendees and the participants.

A tale of three cities

Fieldwork was undertaken at the road shows in London, Manchester and Cardiff. Despite all being large conurbations the road shows in each of these cities were very different. The London event, in particular, had a very different ambience to the others. Although it was the road show for the capital, it was in fact the most intimate event of the three attended, centred as it was on just one school. It took place at Little Ilford School in the London Borough of Newham and was targeted solely at pupils attending that school. As such, it was very much a Little Ilford School event and had a 'community' feel to it; everyone, staff and students, seemed to know one another. In contrast to the other events and possibly because it took place in a school, it was held outside of school time on a Saturday morning. Although the event was principally directed at Muslim girls attending the school, there were a number of non-Muslim girls present, as well as some boys and a number of the girls' parents. The latter had been specifically encouraged to attend and those that did were mainly mothers.

By contrast, the other two road shows in Cardiff and Manchester were on a far larger scale, with a more corporate feel to them. These events, as with the other non-London workshops, had girls from more than one school in attendance (although all had been invited, haphazardly or otherwise). The Manchester event was a plush and slightly controversial one, characterised by 'politics'. Helen Wollaston, Director of Equal to the Occasion, the organisation recruited by NMWAG to deliver the road shows, explained that there were "political (political with a small 'p') concerns that it wasn't a strategy that the local authority as a whole" necessarily supported. Also in particular, one of the schools invited to attend was an independent (that is, fee-paying) Islamic girls' school so "it was a bit of an issue for somebody to say, why has the Council sponsored something when half the audience are from a private girls' school?" The policy for selecting schools to attend the road shows was clearly quite arbitrary. (It emerged that the independent girls' school had been selected because one of the local role models appearing at the Manchester roadshow had previously attended that school).

As well as municipal politics in Manchester, issues around party politics also emerged. One of the role models, who had been invited to attend the Manchester event specifically to make it more 'local', was the Labour candidate at the time for Bury North, Maryam Khan.[2]

Her presence and presentation caused a minor controversy. In trying to inspire the girls to become politically empowered she suggested they come and help her in her electioneering work, stuffing envelopes and canvassing, for example. Unsurprisingly, since this was a barely disguised invitation to volunteer for the Labour Party, this was not well received by some Council attendees, even if the girls themselves appeared largely oblivious to this.

The Cardiff event was well supported by the National Assembly with Assembly representatives illustrating clear commitment to the project.[3] This event was the most mixed in terms of ethnic background and, rather than 'politics', the event was characterised by celebrity. The girls were clearly delighted and impressed that Almeena Ahmed (one of the national role models), a journalist/newsreader, originally from Cardiff, who regularly appears on the BBC, had come to speak to them. Most of the closing session questions were directed at her, for example. The lure of celebrity at the Cardiff event was most apparent, however, in an incident which occurred at the tail end of the day.

During a breakout session, I was sat at a conference table along with a couple of role models and around ten girls from Year 10. One of the role models was a West London based GP (also originally from Cardiff). She was asked, given that she was based in London, whether she had any famous patients. She revealed that a band member from a popular boy band was one of her patients. The response was astounding. There were shrieks of excitement from around the table and I gradually realised the ripple was spreading throughout the entire auditorium as friends at other tables were messaged. There was such hysteria it was as though the artist himself had turned up to the road show. The organisers, unaware of rising tide Beatlesque mania, appealed for calm from the main stage. Eventually, as some semblance of calm was restored, one of the girls passed a billet-doux to the doctor for her to pass on to the singer when he next popped into the surgery. I had not expected hijab-wearing school girls to turn into shrieking teenage wrecks at the mention of a boy band, but it served as a vivid reminder that 'Muslim teenage girls' are after all also just teenage girls who are Muslim.[4]

The next section contextualises these reflections in terms of the logistics of delivering a national road show highlighting how 'the local' was taken into account in practice. It starts by looking at how the different sites and role models were selected.

(not) The Usual Suspects

The role models initiative was established by NMWAG in association with civil servants at DCLG (although one of the members of NMWAG had implied that the road show was "a done deal"). As far as implementation went, four members of NMWAG formed a steering group to manage delivery of the road shows. This in itself was not uncontroversial since many of the members of NMWAG had told me separately that they expected to be primarily involved in an influencing and advisory capacity, rather than directly involved in project delivery. The steering group recruited a consultancy agency, Equal to the Occasion, to deliver the road shows nationally. The agency worked with local authorities, schools and other stakeholders at a local level to design and run the events at each of the six different locations.

The road show evaluation report, produced by Equal to the Occasion for NMWAG and DCLG, outlined how for each road show the relevant local authority was involved in establishing a planning group of local partners. In Middlesbrough it was principally the Council, whereas in Rotherham it was the Police and Youth Service; in Dudley, the local Muslim forum; in Cardiff, the National Assembly Government and Race Equality First. Manchester City Council provided funding via a grant to Inspired Sisters who organised the event, and Newham Council paid towards Little Ilford School's costs in holding the event. The issue of place was therefore built into delivery of the road show initiative and there was an explicit recognition that circumstances in the various places were different. (Although this recognition did not go so far as to undermine the assumed homogeneity of 'Muslim women' and girls and what they needed, underlying the entire initiative.)

This had not, however, been the original plan. Shaista, one of the members of NMWAG I interviewed, told me that the plan had initially been to hold a "London-centric two-day event" aimed at Muslim women rather than girls. She told me that she had objected strongly to this idea, and thought that:

> you want to inspire girls at school, right? …A better project would be that we do a road show in schools; that way you cover more areas, you go into schools which means you reach the right target audience and you have a variety of professions… (Shaista)

She maintained that it was the result of her vociferous objections to the original idea that led to the eventual format of the road show.

In the end the project enlisted twelve women as role models for the overall (national) campaign. These included a scientist, a rugby player, a journalist, a nurse, a union rep, and an artist. A glossy brochure was produced detailing their personal stories and a website was set up to further broaden the audience base.

The budget allocated by DCLG allowed for six road shows to take place. The six sites clearly needed to have a significant Muslim population to warrant hosting a road show. These six sites, however, included a number of less obvious places, not automatically associated with Muslim communities in the public and policy imaginary. According to the evaluation report of the project (Equal to the Occasion 2010) these choices stemmed from a strategic decision by NMWAG to include local authority areas with smaller Muslim communities. Rotherham, Dudley and Middlesbrough were chosen specifically because they were not the obvious choices. Adeeba, who was a member of the Steering Group, told me:

> For Yorkshire, we decided to go for Rotherham because everybody thinks, 'come to Bradford or Leeds'. But I was very keen to look at areas that, well if you looked at the six areas, some were obvious and some were not that obvious; I think it's important to get that mix. Because, why should it be the obvious ones that get it all the time? (Adeeba)

Helen Wollaston, Director of Equal to the Occasion, felt that those less obvious places were chosen because they were:

> where people would have had fewer opportunities to see role models which was a good decision … I think, you know, it was really appreciated particularly in those areas which I would say were Middlesbrough and Rotherham, Dudley where the communities are a bit smaller and are not used to having things for Muslim women and they were really appreciative (Helen)

Adeeba added:

> And, you know if you just look at Rotherham for example, the first one, there was an excellent turnout, you know we had a number of mothers there as well, the children had turned up, the teachers had turned up, community people, employers had turned up, you know we had a good, over

> a hundred and twenty people there. For Rotherham, it's pretty good going… (Adeeba)

This greater appreciation in the less obvious places was, however, matched by disappointment from some of the more obvious places which had expected to be involved. Adeeba acknowledged that this strategy was always "going to upset people" but told me that what all the authorities which were eventually involved had in common was a commitment to the road shows because:

> the concept was to get the local authority to get very much involved, because the NMWAG can't do that, so in terms of getting the ownership, in terms of it being embedded to some extent into what the local authorities were already doing, it was very important that we had local authorities that were supporting us. And we did, right across the board… (Adeeba)

This was also reflected in the role models who were invited to attend particular road show events. A decision was made that a couple of the national role models would attend each road show and this would be supplemented by local role models recommended by the local partners. As Helen explained, both she and NMWAG had learned from the experience:

> that you have to work with the local context, you know… You can't impose a national project on local areas when you rely on that local engagement so it takes time. It probably took longer than I envisaged to build those relationships (Helen)

Not all of the local authorities were unequivocal in their support and this was partly associated with how other (minority) communities might perceive the events or be affected. In this way, the reception to the road show was contingent on pre-existing histories of tension or competition for resources. The evaluation report, for example, refers generically to initial reluctance on the part of some local authorities to participate in the initiative, given tensions between the road show project and local strategies around community cohesion, educational achievement or employability. Muslim girls and women were not necessarily regarded as a strategic priority at a local level for increased attention; there were other categories of (young) people whose needs were deemed to be more pressing. As a result, local authorities expressed concern about targeting Muslim girls specifically for special attention. Helen told me that at least one authority (Kirklees) had not got involved for that reason because "they wanted to target *all* people not just Muslim girls".

Furthermore, even where the local authority was comfortable with the remit and ethos of the Our Choices road show, some of the schools which were involved or were invited to get involved were not. Helen explained how in Rotherham, for example, the schools were worried about a backlash if they were to send only girls to the road show. She explained that this reticence arose partly as a result of earlier experiences doing projects with the police which had been for girls only (not just Muslim girls). Additionally she explained that Rotherham:

> was an area where the Muslim population is concentrated in two or three wards so there's quite a lot of mono-cultural wards, there's a white working class...there's definitely far right quite active so all those things are there and therefore the schools and the colleges were worried about a backlash, both on gender with it being only women, from boys and men and on the Muslim/ethnicity, 'what about the white boys and about the white working class?' you know those kind of issues...(Helen)

At the same time there was clearly feedback from attendees, pupils and parents, who appreciated being targeted and attended the events because they were targeted at them. As such it reflects respondents' beliefs, discussed in greater depth in Chapter 5, that mainstream services fail to provide services to Muslim girls and women ('institutional Islamophobia'[5]); or that there is a general failure in delivering careers services to pupils from the 'wrong' class, gender, ethnicity or religion. The impact of such initiatives on other non-Muslim communities or 'intercommunity relations' is examined in more detail in the second half of this chapter.

One question that remained at the forefront of my mind throughout the fieldwork was how the girls attending the Our Choices road shows would perceive the role models. At the London event, held in Newham, which was the first road show I attended, I recall feeling quite conscious of the potential (social) distance between the role models and the girls in the audience. Although the school itself is doing well (according to OFSTED reports at the time), it is in a very deprived part of Newham according to a range of social indicators. As I watched a sleekly bobbed, suited and stiletto-heeled corporate lawyer take to the stage, I had wondered to what extent the pupils, predominantly of Bangladeshi heritage and wearing hijabs, would relate to her. This had clearly been a concern of the road show organisers who tried to 'localise' the events by including local as well as national role models. Shaista told me that "the idea of picking local ones was to pick *real* women they could relate to."

The feedback the girls gave following the road shows gave some indication of whether they 'related to' the role models. Even though there was no negative feedback about specific role models, there was markedly positive feedback for particular role models. At the Newham event, for example, in addition to the corporate lawyer, one of the local road show role models was a British Bangladeshi writer, Kia Abdullah[6]. She had grown up in Stepney and was very well received by the girls in East London as "a proper East London Bengali".[7] She was someone who had grown up in the same kind of area as them, come from the same kind of family they had, and had experienced (or at least was familiar with) some of the deprivation/marginalisation they had grown up with. She also seemed genuinely delighted at being in a position to give back to "her community".

Similarly, in the context of Cardiff, Almeena, who was also one of the twelve national role models, was very well received as a 'local girl' and because of her celebrity status, as mentioned previously. In the case of Almeena, who I was also able to interview, the appreciation was reciprocal. Her eventual decision to get involved was because one of the road shows was going to be held in Cardiff. Almeena explained that she had initially been reluctant to participate because of the project's association with Prevent. She told me that as a journalist she had been well aware of the controversies associated with the Prevent strategy. She claims that for her, as a "Cardiff girl" it was the lure of coming to Cardiff which was the deciding factor in getting involved. Local role models mattered to the girls and being local mattered to the role models.

All for one and one for all

As well as recognising the importance of the local differences between the different events, there is the issue of difference within the individual road shows in terms of, for example, the different role models and their respective experiences. How effective was the exercise of 'localising' the role models when there were clear differences between the role models themselves in terms of their own class positioning? When asked whether the target audience could necessarily relate to the role models, Shaista told me:

> in the Dudley one I think we did alright because we had a nurse there from up north and she was from a working class background. She said you know my dad didn't want me to be a nurse and whatever… and the other one was a firefighter…she comes from a working class background errm so that was OK… I think the rest that were featured in the Dudley role model road show I think we had the grassroots people there… (Shaista)

The fact that other cleavages of difference distinguished the different role models struck most starkly in Cardiff. Despite her local connection and clear attachment to Cardiff and the objectives of the role model road show, Almeena herself had not experienced any of the issues the road show was designed to address. She explained that her parents had always been incredibly supportive of her and her early ambition to go into journalism. She had done well academically and studied at Cambridge. It was through her mother that she had first got a summer job at BBC Wales, which kickstarted her career. I was therefore interested to know what had inspired her to get involved with the role model road show since clearly that had not been her own personal experience. Her immediate family had not shown any reticence or hostility to her academic success or to her pursuing a 'non-traditional' career. She told me that she was motivated to get involved and felt qualified to do so because she had done "a lot of mentoring in Tower Hamlets and Poplar and I know what the issues are".

During my conversation with Almeena there was little acknowledgement of the distance between her own experiences and those of the girls to whom she was a role model (either in East London or in Cardiff). She had not needed a role model to achieve her ambitions; her own account suggested that she had always wanted to do something in the media. Fortuitous and judicious use of social networks and cultural capital on the part of her mother had facilitated her entry into the profession, a notoriously difficult sector to get into without such connections (Granovetter 1973; Franzen and Hangartner 2006). Her local affiliation was paramount for her decision to be involved in the road shows and seemingly sufficient qualification for her to be a role model.[8]

By contrast, Zainab, one of the local role models in Cardiff, made what seemed to me to be quite pointed remarks in her address to the girls about how she might be "just a teacher", but that she had struggled to get where she had. If the rationale for the road shows was to assist girls who were being held back or were unsupported by their parents (as was strongly implied), she probably gave one of the most inspiring presentations. Her parents had not been supportive of her academic endeavours; she had struggled to get the opportunity to be educated beyond the age of sixteen. Zainab told a story of negotiation, persuasion and her own agency in spite of all the odds (deprived community, intractable parents) which she used to eventually get her A levels, a degree and then to do a PGCE (Postgraduate Certificate in Education). If there were others girls in the audience who were experiencing similar issues, her story would have been most useful in terms of practical help. They could be inspired to do the same as her even if they were not as well connected as some of the other role models were. Helen told me that Shahien Taj, the Cardiff NMWAG contact, had specifically wanted Zainab because she:

> came from a very traditional background, had been kept home in early adulthood and had then gone on and persuaded and brought the family with her and she felt, Shahien, knowing the community and the culture in Cardiff, that there would be a lot of girls who can identify with that situation, more so than they would if she'd been to Oxford and in a way that Cardiff one was unusual because the two role models who spoke nationally were very high achievers… (Helen)

Although Helen refers to "*the* community and culture" in Cardiff in the singular, the experiences of these two role models Almeena and Zainab, both from Cardiff, illustrate how much internal diversity there is within the imagined 'Muslim community in Cardiff': the contrast between the two role models could not have been greater. This highlights the diversity in class and cultural capital between and among 'Muslim women' and hints at a tension between high flying national role models and those who have overcome everyday struggles to do 'traditional' or 'mundane' everyday jobs, but who might have more in common with some of the girls to whom such projects were ostensibly directed.

This section has focused on the way in which a national initiative was locally inflected. The road show project worked both across and within local differences. There was an overarching initiative which had been devised in Whitehall by members of NMWAG and civil servants. The experience of the road show illustrates the importance of local factors in influencing how each of the events was delivered in practice. Local contacts were instrumental at an operational and administrative level and local networks were important in delivering the road shows. In addition, the presence of local role models was also significant. How the different road shows were received and their impact was felt differently in different places. This depended on local histories and experiences, as well as the composition and diversity of Muslim populations in these different areas. In addition to differences between the different road shows there were differences within them. This was most clearly shown in the variety of experiences among the role models; the issues of class and cultural, social and economic capital clearly had had an impact upon each of them.

The second half of this chapter, therefore, explores the theme of 'between and within' through looking at how Prevent funding at the level of local authority funding was received, and particularly in relation to the EMW initiatives and NMWAG. It discusses how different local contexts affected how Prevent operated, focusing on diversity between different areas, as well as diversity within particular locations, and looks at the relationship between 'the Muslim community' and others, in particular non-Muslim BME groups.

Local Contradictions and Useful Fictions

> The very process of competing for resources encouraged a language of homogeneous and opposing identities... Furthermore, even when factions united around..[an].. ideological divide they shared the same concerns – racial discrimination, housing, education, unemployment – and pursued similar strategies by using the local political arena and seeking to influence the powerful decision-makers. (Eade and Garbin 2002:147)

Pragna, one of the Directors of Southall Black Sisters (SBS), explained how in 2008 SBS had their funding by Ealing Council withdrawn, allegedly in the interests of community cohesion. Ealing Council originally argued that funding a separate black women's organisation went against the aims of its community cohesion policy.[9] Ealing Council's reaction was consistent with the logic of community cohesion to the extent that, according to such objectives, the Council should not support initiatives which promoted difference or segregation. By contrast, as SBS was being threatened with having its funding withdrawn, Ealing Council, according to Pragna, were simultaneously being encouraged to fund Muslim women's groups specifically as part of their Prevent agenda.

The irony of this was not lost on Pragna. She alleged that in Southall, Muslim women's organisations were in effect being set up principally in order to achieve Prevent funding. I was quite surprised at her comment; I had already interviewed representatives of long established Muslim women's organisations elsewhere and saw no immediate reason why this might not have been the case in Ealing. On reflection, however, this initial discomfort provided the impetus to reconcile her comments with the range of experiences encountered during fieldwork. Addressing the effects on other communities required contextualising EMW in terms of local factors, such as historical and contemporary geographical concentrations of different populations, as well as the composition of ethnic minority populations in particular areas.[10]

The section begins, however, by theorising the possible impact of diversity within diversity through analysing the impact of the Prevent agenda in Bradford and Bristol, two cities in which the composition of the Muslim population varies dramatically. I choose these two places as exemplars of two ends of the spectrum of *diversity within diversity*. Bradford's BME population is largely Muslim and of South Asian origin. By contrast, Bristol's Muslim population, although proportionately smaller than that of Bradford, is relatively more diverse and this is reflected in intra-community hostilities. As a result, the impact of Prevent and EMW is different in these places, but it is problematic in both because religious identity is privileged at the expense of addressing materially differential experiences and building potential solidarities with other disadvantaged groups.

What's in a place?

It is not uncommon for research conducted in a specific place to be generalised more widely. The following is indicative of the type of claims which are often made about research. Dhaliwal et al, writing about Metroborough (the anonymised name for a hyper diverse part of London) suggest that 'some of the findings are likely to be echoed in other boroughs' and that, 'concerns raised within this report are an indication of what could be taking place on a wider scale and on a more regular basis in other boroughs and regions within England, particularly those characterised by stronger racial segregation and strong religious leadership' (2006: 83–84).

While in some contexts such extrapolations are useful and pragmatic, they can also be problematic. Hopkins' (2008) analysis of Pakistanis in Scotland tries to pinpoint the 'crucial discontinuities and disjunctures' between the Scottish and UK contexts referring to the '...diversity, distribution and structure of minority ethnic groups' as well as the particularities of Scottish politics and associated constructions of national identities (2008:122).[11]

Bradford: 'the quintessential expression of the problematic presence of Islam in Britain'[12]

Some of the respondents (Humera and Adeeba) complained about the way in which research conducted in a particular part of the UK became emblematic of 'the Muslim community'. Bradford, for one had become synonymous with problematic Muslim communities in the UK. Whether remembering the Rushdie affair or the riots of 2001, Bradford conjures up images of all that is regarded as wrong with multiculturalism in Britain. It has probably been over-researched as a result, and that research is often almost unquestioningly seamlessly extrapolated to the UK's other Muslim communities. As noted by Husband and Alam, Bradford represents a 'simplistic iconographic representation of Islam in Britain, being used in news, film and television drama as the quintessential expression of the problematic presence of Islam in Britain' (2011: 6–7).

In Bradford I had interviewed Adeeba. She had sat in an advisory capacity on a number of boards across a range of policy areas working with different government departments. On one level her comments echoed Pragna's:

> I'm not saying that there aren't groups out there who are not doing good work 'cause there are, but... is it being (Prevent) funding led or is it actually being led because the people do realise that there is an issue here [that needs funding]? (Adeeba)

She was very clear that, as far as she was concerned, in Bradford specifically, there had not been demands from Muslims as Muslims. I asked her whether, given that her organisation QED Foundation was focused on education, training and employment, there was any value in talking about it serving 'a Muslim community' specifically.

> I think there is now...I don't think it was that the group [Muslims] asked for it, I think it just happened to them unfortunately because of everything that happened... I don't think they were set out to, 'oh, you know, we are the Muslim community and this is what's happening. (Adeeba)

I would argue that this stems from the composition of Bradford's BME community. Bradford currently has a Muslim population of around 17% and Bradford's Muslims are predominantly of South Asian origin. Bradford's BME community consists principally of Pakistani origin communities, as well as small numbers of Bangladeshis and Indians.[13] Without disputing diversity within Bradford's Muslim population in terms of ethnicity, class, region, migrant status and gender, Bradford's principally Muslim BME population is relatively homogeneous compared to some of the other areas studied. As such, any multiculturalist/anti-racist policies from the 1980s onwards would have been directed principally at Bradford's Muslim population. It did not have to compete with other BME groups that may have had class advantages relative to it or experienced different trajectories of migration. (That is not to suggest, however, that within Bradford there would not have been class, language and gender differences which were reflected in internal struggles for local funding).

Adeeba told me that she thought "the Muslim problem" in Bradford was "mainly about Pakistanis" and that Bradford's Indian Muslim and Bangladeshi communities were "just quietly getting on with what they get on with". She even suggested that there was some resentment from Indian Muslims, in particular, at the negative attention focused on Bradford's Muslims. Her emphasis was therefore on Bradford's Pakistani population rather than Muslims per se, and to some extent her comments about Bradford's Pakistanis aligned with the emblematic status of Bradford's Pakistani Muslims in academic and policy discourse.

Despite this, however, Adeeba's reasoning remained nuanced, attending to the particular circumstances of inner-city Bradford in which economic conditions and socio economic indicators show the concentration of relative poverty among Pakistani and Bangladeshi populations in those areas (Webster 2003). She referred, for example, to the high geographic concentration of (some) Pakistanis in some of the more deprived wards of the city which led to very tight knit, closed communities where the kids "are very isolated in their communities". She also contextualised this, however, by referring to Bradford's position in the UK more generally, suggesting that it would be interesting to research the factors which "advance" the Pakistani community in

London, for example, and compare them with the factors in Bradford and see how they differed.

Furthermore, Adeeba also recognised that many of the issues which affected the lives of inner city Pakistanis equally affected those from non-Muslim communities in those areas, particularly when compared to London. For example, when we discussed the effects of the Prevent agenda on the 'white working class' she acknowledged that it was important to recognise "whether it's white working class people or Pakistanis (whichever group it is) it's about what is it that's been put up in front of them that's not made them feel part of the community" which needs to be taken into account. In their detailed exploration of the Bradford 2001 riots, Bujra and Pearce (2011) contextualise the immediate triggers in terms of a collective failure, both locally and nationally, to deal with structural inequality and marginalisation against a backdrop of long term economic decline. Speaking about the region more widely, Webster argues that long term economic decline of the textile industry was responsible for 'generating a community discourse of nostalgia and cultural decline' (2003: 96), adding that fear, risk and insecurity are geographically concentrated.

Given the relatively homogeneous composition of Bradford's Muslim community, BME organisations in Bradford were de facto 'Muslim' ones. As a result, in Bradford at least, the policy shifts from multiculturalism to community cohesion to Prevent did not provide any incentives for strategic opportunism or pragmatism to emphasise Muslimness, as Pragna suggested had occurred in Ealing. Furthermore, although there were clearly effects and repercussions in terms of relations with the 'white working class community,' there is no reason why this was any worse than that which had existed previously prior to the arrival of Prevent. By contrast, Bristol offers an interesting case of a very different scenario. With its greater diversity and dynamic demographics the impact of Prevent and EMW has necessarily been different.

Bristol: 'similar [to London] but on a small scale'

Bristol is a very different proposition from Bradford. According to the Bristol council website 2% of Bristol's population is Muslim compared to Bradford's 17% (with 0.2 % Sikh and 0.3% Hindu). Bristol is also historically more associated with African-Caribbean populations (Pryce 1979) and areas such as St Paul's are infamous for urban unrest in the 1980s, as well as more recently in 2011.[14] In Bristol I interviewed Kalsoom, a member of NMWAG who was also a community cohesion officer and later a Prevent officer in Bristol Council. I asked Kalsoom about the demographic makeup of Bristol's Muslim population. She described how much Bristol had changed even in the time that she had been there:

> Well, over the last fifteen years it's changed quite considerably, when I came to Bristol just over twenty years ago, your main community would have been Pakistani or Bangladeshi, obviously Afro Caribbean but in terms of the Muslim community it was Pakistani and Bangladeshi...But, very gradually now the Somali community has become the largest Muslim community so the demographics of Bristol have changed quite a lot.... (Kalsoom)

During our interview, we discussed the particularities of 'the Muslim community' in Bristol. As in London and many other cities, the situation was complex and constantly changing. The demographics and the relations between different groups were constantly in flux. Clearly the Prevent agenda had brought all Muslims together under one banner despite their very different experiences and positions. We discussed the various antagonisms and hostilities, both within the Muslim community as well as with other BME communities. She told me that the increase in hijab and niqab wearing was attributed to the arrival of other non-South Asian Muslims.

> Well, there are a lot of hijab-wearing women and I think again that particularly started with the Somali community as well, and we have had more international students and workers here that come from Arab countries where wearing hijab is very much a cultural part of faith and perhaps the Bangladeshis and Pakistanis didn't wear it but they've been told it's unIslamic ...and there's definitely that sort of resentment here that you know it's been imposed like that, so there's a very judgemental attitude...so that exists between the different communities, if you like (Kalsoom)

In Bristol I also spoke to three police officers (all of whom were white English) involved in delivering the Prevent agenda. They reflected on the fact that Bristol had similarities to London regarding its diversity, with Sarah describing it as "similar but on a smaller scale". They too all mentioned that there was a "very big Somali community" in Bristol which was also "the newest". They suggested that it was more segregated than London which was "very multicultural wherever you go" telling me that,

> Easton which is across the road from where we are this.... area is predominantly Muslim whereas in some other, certain areas – would you agree? – that are predominantly white... I've not got any figures or anything (Sarah)

They explained that this was the community with which they had the most engagement in terms of Prevent. This was not always easy and in fact in Bristol the name Prevent had been changed to 'Building the Bridge'. For example, they told me that there had been quite a few complaints "from Somali people travelling through Bristol airport and saying that they were getting stopped and searched under the Terrorism Act". Luke explained that this stemmed from those being searched thinking they were being stopped under the Terrorism Act when in fact it was for drug related offences. Luke, who had himself been involved in stop and search operations, understood why there had been fears that Somalis were being targeted. This echoes the way in which Sara Ahmed has described how 'fear sticks to these bodies' (2004b: 79) and the figure of the international terrorist has been mobilised in close proximity to the figure of the asylum seeker. Luke also thought this was to do with the spatial concentration of communities. He told me that having these powers could be difficult and that he knew

> you need to use it proportionately and wisely but if you're working in a certain area, as my colleague Rebecca explained earlier... whereas in London if a Police officer went out and stopped ten people in central London the ethnicities and cultural backgrounds would be totally random...whereas if you do it in Easton it's not going to be ...it's educated guesswork, isn't it? Now if that happened half a dozen times in a day in one area it may be all one ethnicity or one cultural background; do it in another area and it'll be different. So there is a disproportionate percentage when you look at population versus stop check; it's acknowledged that it looks a little bit abnormal but all I can say in ten years of being a Police officer it's not... I've never been with a Police officer who has stopped somebody because of the colour of their skin (Luke)

They also explained how as a force they learned from other forces around England "in areas that have got denser populations" of Muslims, suggesting that such forces were "at a more advanced stage now". Although Luke told me he thought "Bristol is reasonably well-up when it comes to these things", by contrast the West Midlands, the Met and Manchester will have encountered "these problems earlier than us" and so they could learn from them through mechanisms for sharing good practice (and placements in other police forces).

Although the police officers used the term 'Muslims' in the context of our discussion, it was also clear that they were often talking principally about Somalis. This raised the issue of the relationship between different Muslim communities within Bristol. Kalsoom spoke to me about the way that wider media discourses around immigration affected the relationship between more established Muslim communities and more recent Muslim migrants. She suggested that Pakistani and Bangladeshi people in Bristol felt insecure because their own position was made precarious by the arrival of newer migrants. Often members of these communities adopted the same stereotypes promulgated by the media. She told me about a social event she attended with very middle class Pakistani women where she heard what she described as "blatant racism and prejudice about the Somali community". When I probed further she told me:

> This was exactly the Daily Mail, 'they're taking our housing', 'they're claiming the benefits', 'they haven't got their husbands', 'their husbands come over and impregnate them every year'– those were the sorts of comments that were being made...you could have been on a white working class estate actually and the comments would have pretty much been the same (Kalsoom)

In addition, regarding the impact of Prevent and EMW initiatives on inter-community relations, I asked Kalsoom what response there had been from Bristol's other BME communities:

> I mean definitely I think, you know I had a lot of antagonism towards this funding from members of the city's Sikh community, that said 'actually, you know, before we used to work together as Asian women, now it's very much Muslim women's groups and we think this funding should be to bring us together' (Kalsoom)

She suggested that the current policy framework focused on Muslims fostered a certain type of pragmatism on the part of third sector Muslim community organisations in order to secure funding for projects. Although such pragmatism is understandable, it also illustrates how previous alliances have been disrupted and potential solidarities displaced as a consequence.

Moreover, even within different 'ethnic groups' there were sometimes further 'cultural differences' to contend with. Kalsoom, for example, told me about two Somali women who refused to work together because of what they described as 'clan' issues. This potentially de-historicises and thereby essentialises such differences ignoring the possibility that their particular geo-political trajectories (including migration to Europe and the UK) may have influenced their relationship.[15] Such a focus obscures other axes of identity which might hold the potential for more far reaching solidarities, between both other Muslims and non-Muslims.

Muslim women's organisations; grass roots or pragmatic opportunism?

This section considers whether the suggestion that Muslim women's organisations were effectively created to secure Prevent/EMW funding is a valid one which applies outside Ealing (the borough within which Southall is situated). Southall, as with many places, holds a particular place in the postwar postcolonial ethnicised imaginary, tied to its own stories of South Asian (mixed) migration, settlement and employment patterns (Baumann 1996; Brah 1999). Similarly, it has become iconic of a particular juncture in the history of anti-racist political mobilisations in the UK (Shukra 1998).

Just as Southall has a particular history and context, so too does Brent and that has influenced the way in which An-Nisa was established. Khalida and Humera are two sisters who founded and continue to run the An-Nisa Society. As their website describes, 'An-Nisa Society was established in May 1985 by a group of young British Muslim women, in response to the needs of Muslim women and their families.' I discussed with Khalida in detail what had provided the rationale for An-Nisa. Khalida told me that despite working in a multicultural London borough where the authority was committed to anti-racism, "Muslim groups were coming out worse off in everything". She expanded:

> because I was working on the race relations unit, I saw that actually the anti-racist things that were being done, you

> know, all the initiatives that were being done, were actually bypassing Muslims and actually we'd see Muslim families in great distress in my work ...I saw all these appalling things happening and there was nothing being provided and it wasn't just me, and it was like a few of the others because we were like, most of us, the core group, were working in the system and we thought: wow, what's going on with Muslims is terrible (Khalida)

She explained that this was:

> because they weren't looking at faith, they were looking at ethnicities, they were bypassing Muslims. So for example, everything I went to, I never saw Muslims anywhere, never saw Muslims accessing funding; Muslims, you know, weren't getting resources. The Hindu community, the East African Asians that came in the 70s and 80s, they had been much better [at accessing resources] (Khalida)

Khalida herself confuses faith and "ethnicities" by disregarding that the "East African Asians" she refers to were not all Hindu and some might have been Muslim[16]. Nonetheless she says this was the impetus for establishing their organisation, focused on Muslim women specifically, as well as a long standing justification to lobby central government against religious discrimination. Khalida and Humera's experience of working in 'race relations' in Brent in the 1980s clearly affected their decision to establish An-Nisa even though the whole faith agenda had not yet emerged as an influential force in the UK social policy landscape. They also explained that they had experienced difficulties securing funding for anything that was faith based. For example, one of the first things they wanted funding for was a Muslim nursery where Muslim children "would be taught...'Bismillah' when you eat, going to the toilet that you wash, and eat with your right hand and that sort of thing...appropriate for Muslim children" (Khalida). She told me that they were "astonished at the hostility" that they received "from all sections of the community" and Humera said it was "like you know, we weren't fitting ... we were supposed to be Asian, they kept saying 'You're Asian, you're Asian... and Asian this and so why do you want another Asian group?"

Clearly for organisations like An-Nisa, the impetus for their formation arose from dissatisfaction with the existing framework and the way multiculturalist policies operated at that particular historical moment in the context of Brent. Arguably there was nothing strategic or opportunistic about establishing An-Nisa at that moment, although it could be suggested that the emerging faith agenda was a response to such initiatives and that subsequently the faith agenda (and later the Prevent agenda) has helped facilitate other similar initiatives in other localities. This is in stark contrast to Adeeba's experiences in Bradford where she argues that demands for assistance had not been made by Muslims *as* Muslims.

The previous chapter argued that forced marriage and honour-related violence have become particularised to 'Muslim communities'. While the role of discourse in that process is clearly important, I would also argue that the institutional framework and funding arrangements have helped to facilitate this in practice. As local authorities have been encouraged to fund projects that 'empower Muslim women' it is clearly in the interests of women's organisations to emphasise their Muslimness in applying for funding, even if they themselves are fully aware that these issues transcend religious affiliation. In Cardiff, I asked Shahien why the Henna Foundation, of which she was Director, and which offers support to those at risk of forced marriage or 'honour-related violence', was predominantly focused on Muslims. She had acknowledged that these crimes were not exclusive to Muslims. She explained that the organisation had not originally been focused on Muslims but told me that there were a number of reasons why she decided to "have clear terms of reference". The change took place in 2007 which coincides with the rolling out of Prevent.

Superficially this story is consistent with this idea of 'strategic pragmatism' but it is only partly the case since it was not the only reason she gave. Shahien told me that although she respected the work of SBS ("credit where credit's due") she felt that it was important "to get the men on side". Initially her organisation started out as a drop-in centre/one-stop shop which handled case work around families and as such, necessarily dealt with forced marriage and honour related violence. To some extent she had learned from the problems that pioneer organisations like SBS had encountered (as had Fajer in Manchester and Khalida in Brent) by framing these as family issues rather than women's issues particularly. This tactical decision, coupled with the fact that "Sikh men had stopped the Sikh women working with" her and the basic fact of demographics (90% of her clients are Muslim), led to the organisation's explicit focus on supporting Muslim women.

Shahien's experience highlights the impact of events such as 9/11 and 7/7 and the ensuing Prevent agenda on 'inter-community relations', by which I mean relations between different BME groups. Although clearly there is an element of pragmatism in emphasising 'Muslimness' strategically at a particular moment, it also intimates possible responses by non-Muslim BME groups to a hitherto predominantly, although not exclusively, Muslim organisation in this same moment, post 7/7.[17]

The case of An-Nisa and the Henna Foundation show two different paths to establishing Muslim women's organisations. Although the timing is almost twenty years apart, I suggest that these trajectories are also a feature of the diversity and the composition of Brent and Cardiff in these instances. This argument extends further, since these factors are not static and vary over time with economic and demographic changes. So, SBS was established at a particular political, historical moment and endured over time. It was a response to racism and patriarchy and particular conditions, yet clearly its survival is partly due to the local specificities of Southall as well as the dynamism and tenacity of those involved in it; Pragna told me that other Black Sisters organisations set up at the same time had not survived.

Conclusion

This chapter has explored the importance of taking into account local differences in delivering a national initiative. It argues that both the delivery of the role model road show, as well as the way in which Prevent played out locally in different places, was contingent on local circumstances. With regard to both, the chapter has explored differences between and within different geographical locations. It has also considered how the responses to these initiatives as well as the outcomes have varied in different places, both in terms of the recipients as well as other communities.

In relation to the role model project the chapter looked at how the idea of local difference was built into the project in the choice of some less obvious places in which to hold the road shows. There was thus an implicit recognition that there were differences arising in different geographical contexts. Not only were there differences between different places, however, there were differences between the role models attending the road shows. Despite local connections, they were differentiated by social class and cultural capital. These differences between the role models highlighted the multifarious, yet at times nebulous, objectives of the road show. The primary goals were to inspire Muslim girls into exploring a diversity of careers, suggesting that the reason for economic inactivity was a lack of inspiration and knowledge, rather than discrimination or structural inequalities at the point of entry into the labour market (if not the education system itself). As organisers and NMWAG members made clear, some of the reasons for Muslim girls' 'underperformance' might in fact be as a result of failures in mainstream careers services. Moreover, although one of the objectives of the road show was to combat stereotypes of Muslim women which might have challenged discrimination, the scope and scale of the road show was not sufficient to achieve this other than on a very superficial level.

The second half of the chapter discussed how Prevent funding of Muslim women's organisations in different local contexts was experienced. In particular it looked at the impact of diversity in diversity and how stories of migration, settlement and multicultural politics affected how such organisations were received and structured. It suggested that in hyper diverse areas, such as Brent and Southall, there were particular trajectories in the development of BME women's organisations influenced by the different class positions of the organisers, and experiences of migration and engagement with local politics. Furthermore, in relation to Bristol and Cardiff, the chapter discussed how changing patterns of migration had influenced the composition and diversity of Muslim populations and necessitated a strategic pragmatism in relation to securing funding. By contrast, in areas such as Bradford with a relatively homogenous BME/Muslim population, no such pragmatism was required.

A key theme of this book is that policy focused on 'Muslim women' collates together all women who are Muslim, a disparate and multiply-differentiated group and de facto attributes any problematic issues to religious affiliation. As well as perpetuating anti-Muslim racist stereotypes, such policy discourses, focused on religious affiliation alone, also obscure continuities with earlier racisms, as well as other axes of social division in society, such as class and regional inequalities which also affect non-Muslims. In this chapter I have shown the specific ways in which geographical differences in diversity are not taken into account in practice.

The effect of the Prevent agenda, as part of a wider focus on Muslims in contrast to other ethnicised groups, has had particular consequences. In areas with long established minority communities which were predominantly of Muslim origin (for example, Kashmiri Pakistanis as before in Bradford), many of the minority third sector organisations were de facto 'Muslim' ones, even where they were not expressly couched in religious terms. As Adeeba expressed it, she assisted "women who were Muslim," not necessarily "Muslim women". By contrast, organisations in areas with more diverse, transient and newer ethnic minority populations, being Muslim may not have emerged as a way of organising politically until relatively recently, and may undoubtedly have been facilitated by the Prevent agenda itself. Moreover, Muslim populations in these places are more clearly heterogeneous and are experiencing greater flux. The possibilities of inter-community tension were greater as were the incentives to engage in strategic pragmatism.

Notes

1. It was only in December 2009 that Prevent was extended to refer to any kind of extremism including far-right or far-left or animal rights extremists. It had been restricted to 'AQ related threats' (Al Qaida) as opposed to DT (domestic terrorism).
2. Described by the Daily Mail as 'a doe-eyed brunette who would not look out of place fronting an ad campaign for mascara'(Rawi 2010).
3. Chaney (Chaney and Fevre 2001; Chaney 2004) has discussed how devolution and the creation of the Welsh Assembly and its duty to promote equality has impacted positively on the 'meaningful participation' of minority groups in the policy process (Chaney and Fevre 2001: 22).
4. Just as a Muslim woman is a woman – to paraphrase Max Gluckman (cited in Baumann 1996:1).
5. This term gained some currency in 2004 when it was used in a report by the Commission on British Muslims and Islamophobia set up by the Runnymede Trust (Richardson 2004b).
6. Kia's first novel was called 'Life, Love and Assimilation'; she has since written an 'erotic thriller' and occasionally writes in The Guardian.
7. Kia provided an accessible narrative of her own story. As a journalist and published writer she fit the road show requirements of having a non-traditional career. It is also worth remembering that these professions can be difficult to enter, are dominated by people with connections and those willing and in a financial position to work for free doing internships and so on. It is not necessarily a rational decision for parents from deprived backgrounds, of any ethnic or religious background, to encourage their daughters (or sons for that matter) to aspire to such professions.
8. Gillies discusses how middle class parents can draw on their own knowledge, cultural values, social contacts and financial resources, whereas working class parents are more reliant on teachers (2007). See Thapar-Bjorkert and Sanghera (2010), however, in which the authors discuss intracommunal cultural capital among Pakistani Muslims in Bradford.
9. R (Kaur & Shah) v London Borough of Ealing (2008). The Council wanted to stop funding SBS and replace it with an all-women service. It was found guilty of not undertaking a race equality impact assessment as it was required to do under the Race Relations Act (2000). In addition it was found to have misunderstood s.35 of the RRA by suggesting that funding an organisation like SBS would be unlawful; the provisions of the RRA in fact allow for services to be supplied to particular groups only. Lord Justice Moses, the presiding judge said: 'There is no dichotomy between funding specialist services and cohesion; equality is necessary for cohesion to be achieved.' (EWHC 2008).
10. This of course reflects that third sector and voluntary organisations are constantly in competition with one another for resources and patronage. Both longer established

and newer ('invented' or otherwise) organisations would have been competing for the same scarce funds.

[11] Hopkins suggests that the Pakistani population in Scotland is more middle class than elsewhere in the UK and that this is attributable to different patterns of migration (although he does not sufficiently explore the differentiation within the Pakistani population in Scotland). As a result he argues poverty is less salient (31% of BME in Scotland being middle class compared with 16% in UK as a whole) and that Pakistanis tend to live in more middle class neighbourhoods than in the rest of the UK and goes so far as to say that 'related to the issue of class, there was also a sense that differences in the composition of the population influenced the likelihood of periods of urban unrest' (2008: 118).

[12] Husband and Alam (2011:7)

[13] South Asian migration to Bradford (as well a number of other northern mill towns) began in the 1950s and 60s as people came to fill labour shortages in the textile mills in the area. Even then, the textile industry was already in decline and by the 1980s, the industry had almost completely disappeared altogether.

[14] Although see Richmond (1973) for an early study of migration and 'race relations' in Bristol. The city is also renowned for a bus boycott in the early 1960s in response to the local bus company's refusal to employ 'coloured' drivers.

[15] Or in fact that they just did not get on but found it easier to blame 'clan' issues.

[16] Saggar suggests that the structural advantages of the Indian presence among the highly participative sections of the electorate is 'accentuated' by the East African Asian component because of the strong civic culture in postwar societies of Kenya, Uganda and Tanzania as well as the fact that the English language was the lingua franca of public life in several East African societies (2000: 228).

[17] For more on Sikh–Muslim relations in contemporary UK see Sian (2010; 2013) which looks at how historical constructions by Sikhs of Muslims, the Other, have been reshaped in postcolonial Britain and how these have impacted on intercommunity relations. There are also clearly continuities with work on communalism, historical and contemporary, in South Asia and the importance of place, space, proximity and interaction. See also Kundnani (2002b).

FOUR

Giving the silent majority a stronger voice?

> If it's not men within the Muslim community limiting Muslim women then it's people from outside...these attempts to empower us, are actually taking away our space for action (Yasmin)

> what constitutes the position of the subaltern is precisely the impossibility of being heard (Spivak 1996: 289). In other words, the question becomes not so much 'who speaks?' but 'who hears?' (Ahmed 2000: 61)

Introduction

One of the overarching themes of Prevent, and in particular those initiatives directed at women and young people, was to give the 'silent majority a stronger voice'. This was based on the presumption that 'the Muslim community' was best placed to tackle religious extremism. It could be facilitated by the government through its support of the so called silent majority, presumed to be moderate and in a position to determine who was susceptible to violent extremism and, more importantly, to influence would-be-terrorists or report them to the relevant authorities. Women (and young people) were identified as part of that majority. The underlying rationale presupposes that women were previously silent and that government initiatives to empower Muslim women would give them a stronger voice. As Ruth Kelly, Secretary of State for Communities and Local Government stated[1] in light of the:

> inequalities they [Muslim women] face, and the challenges they experience as they seek to take further steps to participate more fully in their communities, and to tackle extremism...we [in government] must do more to ensure that they find their voice more easily.

This chapter examines these assertions in the light of respondents' experiences. It begins by examining whether Muslim women could be described as a silent majority and looks at the extent to which Muslim women's assumed silence arose from 'their own communities' as opposed to from those outside. Among research participants, for example, there were more subtle, nuanced explanations for Muslim women's apparent lack of visibility in the political and policy sphere. The chapter also analyses the wider political landscape during the New Labour era, specifically in relation to women's political participation, which forms the backdrop to the establishment of NMWAG (the National Muslim Women's Advisory Group). Finally, the third section of this chapter examines the experiences of this increased emphasis on Muslim women in political life and how this stated exercise in 'giving the silent majority a stronger voice' worked in practice. Rather than looking at the specific initiatives which were in any case rather small scale, it focuses on the establishment and achievements of NMWAG, analysing the relationship between the members of NMWAG and the women they were supposed to be representing and considering the extent to which NMWAG was successful in providing a stronger voice and to whom. It argues that only certain voices were permitted in particular contexts and that the way this was done was externally prescribed.

The Silent Majority?

In the foreword to *Engaging Muslim Women*, Ruth Kelly wrote, 'Muslim women...have told us that they often feel excluded, sometimes by their own communities and sometimes by those outside it' (DCLG 2006: 5). Many of the respondents agreed that, despite the long (albeit fractious) history of state engagement with the Muslim community, Muslim women were very often absent from this process. They themselves had long been critical of the government for always engaging with the same self-appointed, self-styled 'community leaders', who were invariably men. Social policy discourses imply that this absence reflected the endemic inferior status of women in Muslim communities.[2] Just as Muslim women are 'barred' from mosques, so they are 'barred' from engaging in civic society. On further analysis, however, a more subtle picture emerges which, while recognising some male-dominated groups' objections to women's involvement in public life, draws attention to the state's complicity in, and occasional facilitation of, this process. Research participants offered a variety of reasons for the absence of women which were more complicated than the idea that women were being held back (solely) by community patriarchy.

'..by their own communities'

Some respondents' explanations for the relative absence of Muslim women in public life partially conform to the policy discourse which attributes the position of Muslim women principally to 'patriarchal Muslim men'. Faz Hakim, who had worked at Number 10's Strategy Unit, told me that she "thought there was a genuine feeling that traditionally women had been ignored or left out *by* Muslim men..." (my emphasis). Khalida Khan of the An-Nisa society recalled a dismissive response from "one very prominent Muslim leader" when she presented data to him showing how deprived the Muslim population in Brent was in the late 80s. She told me he:

> just disregarded it all. You know, they just didn't take it seriously; they just...fobbed us off and one religious leader said to us... 'oh yeah, we need sisters to run bazaars and stalls' and basically that's all we were good for... (Khalida)

Khalida added, however, that "there were a few individuals, some Muslim men – our own husbands...who were quite supportive." She also referred to individual men, for example, the Imam at the Central Mosque in Regents' Park at the time, who was "really supportive" in providing food and the venue free of charge when An-Nisa ran training workshops for teachers. Although the An-Nisa Society might not have received universal support, Khalida's account does not suggest that they experienced any direct objections from people necessarily because they were a women's organisation.

Furthermore, rather than any explicit prohibition on women, often it was the type of work that women were involved with which influenced the responses to them. For example, those working in women's organisations offering support to victims of domestic violence had very different experiences. Pragna Patel of Southall Black Sisters (SBS) and Shahien Taj of the Henna Foundation (formerly Saheli) both work in (secular) organisations focused on offering support to BME women experiencing domestic violence. Both reported hostility from men from the wider BME community (although significantly not just from Muslim men as discussed shortly). As a result of their line of work, these women and their organisations have attracted the ire of some BME men, and they, or their families, have been victims of harassment. Shahien, for example, referred to people "coming after her" after she had "grassed on" them to the police or other authorities. She told me how her father's car had been vandalised, in order to harass her saying, "it does happen on occasion, depending on what is going on". She was, however, very stoic about these incidents, telling me:

> So that will happen. Because there will be people in the community who want to take revenge against you even though you've done something good, even though you know Islamically and human rights[wise] it was the right thing to do but when somebody's evil if they wanna come after you, they'll come after you and do you harm (Shahien)

The hostility exemplified in these incidents is, however, directly associated with the type of work she does and such 'revenge' attacks are unfortunately a corollary of the sensitive nature of her work. She did not, however, suggest that any hostility was necessarily because she was a woman or a Muslim per se.

Shahien and Pragna both work in organisations focused specifically on dealing with domestic violence. Other organisations, such as An-Nisa, deal with cases involving domestic violence but did not mention any hostility as a result. Notably, An-Nisa Society is framed very much in religious terms. Its mission, as outlined on its website, 'is to nurture a positive British Muslim identity and develop a dynamic, empowered and healthy Muslim community by promoting societal change and personal growth. This includes pressing for policies, services and initiatives that are sensitive to the Muslim perspective.' It may, therefore, be that (secular) organisations focused principally on domestic violence could be seen as more problematic by certain elements of 'the community' than an avowedly Muslim woman's organisation that deals with a variety of 'family' issues, which might include domestic violence. As well as the obvious hostility one would expect from perpetrators of such violence, it is also possible that the way in which such behaviour ends up being generalised to all Asian or Muslim men leads to a defensiveness which might not otherwise exist. (That is, however, not to condone such behaviour; it is to draw attention to the way that framing matters).

Although there has been some (academic and policy) attention on the effects of multicultural and community cohesion policies on the 'white working class' (Hewitt 2005; Garner et al 2009), there has been little, if any, attention given to the effect of community cohesion policies on other BME communities.[3] In discussions with Muslim and BME women's organisations, however, these themes emerged as salient. Shahien told me how, in addition to experiencing hostility from "people in the [Muslim] community" in Cardiff, she had also experienced hostility from non-Muslim BME men. When asked why the organisation was predominantly focused on Muslims she explained that this had not originally been the case telling me that:

> ....Sikh men stopped the Sikh women working with me. They just did not want this to happen and I wasn't going to go into encouraging another woman from another community, even if she is a friend of mine, 'cos at the end of the day I'll go home, she has to live in that community, she has to go to the Gurdwara you understand? I'm not going to cause her problems and I've always said to them if you wanna come back anytime we're more than happy to...(Shahien)

As a result of that experience, and the fact that 90% of her clients are Muslim (because of the demographics of the area in Cardiff in which her organisation is based), Shahien decided in 2007 to focus explicitly on providing support to Muslim women in order to "have clear terms of reference". This decision highlights the impact of events such as 9/11 and 7/7 and the ensuing Prevent agenda on 'inter-community relations' which the previous chapter examined.

These examples show that Muslim women's organisations have experienced a range of responses from Muslim men, ranging from disinterest to outright hostility and harassment. This is, however, a partial story. The 'Muslim men holding women back' narrative is a convenient common sense way of conceptualising Muslim women's absence in civic society. Hostility has also come from other non-BME men. More than that, however, without underestimating the difficulties faced and overcome by some of the women, such hostility is not the only reason for Muslim women's absence in the political domain. Among respondents there was an acknowledgment that the absence of women was a necessary corollary of how community politics had developed historically. Furthermore, as many respondents argued, the way in which local and central government politics functioned, contributed to Muslim women's invisibility in community politics. The following section discusses this.

...by those outside it

> when they say we don't exist, we do exist actually, the government just doesn't want to see us (Nazneen)

Black feminist critiques of multiculturalism cite the way in which multiculturalist policies have encouraged an informal contract between government and the more conservative leaders of minority communities (Gupta 2003). Wilson (2006) has described how the state's interventions in South Asian women's lives have worked to strengthen South Asian patriarchal relations, arguing that, under pressure from women's groups to provide protection from violence, the state's response has been to try and manage and control, rather than weaken South Asian patriarchy. Khalida's understanding supports this when she explains how local politicians would:

> engage with the mosques, because they want votes; so they'd see the mosque on Friday with loads of people, hundreds of people, thousands of people so ... votes so there's a lot of, you know, like history of mosques with the Labour Party and whatever... (Khalida)

She added that "...it's not only our men that are sexist, it's the government or local authority" and that this was evidenced in their replicating and perpetuating stereotypes about Muslim women. She argued that they saw "the power is with the men" and because of "the stereotyped image that women [...] don't have any say in the Muslim community", Muslim women continued to be ignored.[4] Solomos and Back, for example, cite an interview with a (white) woman from the Labour Party in the early 1990s in which she acknowledges that 'we are doing nothing particularly to change the situation that Muslim women find themselves in' (1995: 99).

Shaista claimed that, prior to her involvement in NMWAG, the Government ignored her contributions despite her extensive research and links with the Muslim community (Gohir 2008) telling me that "when government were engaging with communities [it] tended to be mainly men; the voices of women and youth were missing". This is supported by Faz's comment, "I don't think Government were interested in speaking to Muslim women before, they didn't care, no one asked ever to speak to women". Her explanation suggested that:

> it's just how things work. I think the whole issue of women not being sort of spoken to is a mixture of how it's kind of come on ... it's also because people in politics...they wanted to speak to one person – you represent Muslims, you represent Hindus, you represent Sikhs. For a long time communities were happy with that. And again those tended to be initially people who'd come up through the ranks of the mosque, men anyway.

The absence of Muslim women in the political process meant that interviewees thought that women's interests, needs, concerns (Childs et al 2010) were not considered high priority by male community representatives. Khalida explained that the mosques were not aware of what was happening because of all the:

> politicking going on, there'd be one group and then they'd fight and then they'd split and make another group in another mosque...they were so involved in who wants to be the president or the chair, they weren't seeing that the fire was burning in their own back garden, back home at their families; families were having enormous problems. (Khalida)

Instead, she suggested that the men "just wanted to be councillors". As a result she argues, "because they [councillors] didn't meet the needs of the Muslims, they weren't meeting our needs," that is, the needs of women and the wider community.[5] Women therefore faced dual resistance from the state on the one hand, and male members of their community on the other (Burlet and Reid 1998). As Yasmin stated:

> if it's not men within the Muslim community limiting Muslim women then it's people from outside...these... attempts to empower us, are actually taking away our space for action. (Yasmin)

Furthermore, it is possible that the lack of women's presence is due to the fact that third sector and voluntary organisations are constantly in competition with one another for resources and patronage. As McGhee argues, effective engagement between communities rarely occurs in the context of competition for scarce resources and services (2005). Both longer established and newer organisations would have been competing for scarce funds, suggesting that any objections might not necessarily conform to the 'Muslim men holding back Muslim women' logic alone.

Against a backdrop of scarcity, the experience of Khalida and others may not (only) have stemmed from objections to the idea of women being involved per se. Hostility could potentially be seen as unease at another organisation being established that would compete with existing organisations for funding, both public and charitable. This is of course a much wider issue than just within the Muslim community sector, but must necessarily affect relationships between different BME (women's) groups. As illustrated in the previous chapter, SBS (Southall Black Sisters) had their funding by Ealing Council withdrawn in the interests of community cohesion, whereas local authorities were simultaneously being encouraged to fund specifically Muslim women's groups dealing with the same issues as part of the PVE agenda.

Back et al note how 'studies of Islamic political participation need to be contextualised carefully without recourse to grand generalities about culture and faith' (2009: 2). The last section has demonstrated that the ways in which Muslim women were absented from public life were more subtle, and the reasons proffered, more complex and variegated. Accounts of hostility were often connected to the type of work the organisations did. Those that dealt with domestic violence cases, for example, experienced more direct hostility and this hostility was not restricted to Muslim men. In addition, the workings of local and central government politics may have inadvertently side-lined women. The following section looks at the broader historical landscape of women's political representation in which the EMW initiatives and NMWAG are situated, namely the impact of New Labour.

Finding a Voice

Dustin and Phillips suggest that there was 'a refiguring of public discourse in 1997' (2008: 407) with the election of a Labour government and a doubling in the number of woman parliamentarians.[6] As a result, they argued there were 'more MPs willing to speak out against abuses of women, and a substantial rise in the parliamentary time devoted to matters such as forced marriage and female genital mutilation' (2008: 405). Dustin and Phillips note that these issues appeared on the mainstream political agenda at that particular moment irrespective of the fact that BME women's groups had been lobbying on these issues decades before. It is also symbolic of wider discourses in which feminism is disarticulated, as something that is only necessary in relation to the Other, and specifically Muslim women (Scharff 2011).

Rubina told me that she thought the seeds of NMWAG were sown as early as 1997 when New Labour came to power. Faz suggested this process of increasing the civic participation of women was 'a natural progression', that with time there is change. Early on she had been quite clear in expressing the idea that Muslim women had been excluded by Muslim men. Later though she contextualised this gender imbalance in relation to how ethnic minority community groups had emerged historically in the political sphere, in the context of both local and central government engagement. She admitted that "it's very popular now to attack" male community leaders and say that "'they don't speak for anybody' or that 'they're unrepresentative'". She made clear that we should remember "that they grew up for a reason" which was that:

> there was a time when there was *no* representation for Muslims *at all* and there were some people coming forward and saying, 'hang on, listen to us'. These people turned into community leaders. (Faz)

She added that this situation changed because:

> Maybe because more Muslim women are in the second generation, with better education, they started coming up from the ranks saying 'hang on, listen to us'... again I think it's kind of natural. Yeah, I don't think you can just blame the community...it's pretty much in the round you know.[7] (Faz)

Shaista, by contrast, firmly associated a greater interest in the potential of Muslim women with a 'regime change' both in the Labour party and (consequently) at DCLG (Department for Communities and Local Government), that is, specifically "... when Tony Blair left and Gordon Brown took over in June 2007 and Hazel Blears was appointed as the new DCLG minister". Given that the post had previously been occupied by Ruth Kelly, this suggests it was not necessarily the presence of women parliamentarians *per se* which changed things as suggested by Dustin and Phillips (2008). Perhaps what mattered more was *which* women were in *which* position in government and their relationship to Blair, and later Brown, rather than there simply being a greater female presence across Whitehall. Further, such developments are inflected by local particularities.[8] Vociferous Labour politicians such as Anne Cryer in strategic constituencies with significant Muslim populations, such as Keighley, gained prominence through raising the issues of forced marriage.[9] By contrast, however, politicians such as Harriet Harman and Clare Short who have raised more mainstream feminist concerns (around issues such as 'Page 3' girls) have been derided for doing so.

Raising issues of timing in relation to Muslim women's political participation disrupts the underlying presumptions about their silence. In spite of barriers, whether from 'the community' (overt hostility or indifference) or in the relations of engagement between local government and 'community leaders', it is clear that Muslim women have, in common with many women's groups (minority or otherwise), been organising and working for their communities and 'women's issues' for many years prior to the EMW initiative. Many of the interviewees were high powered OBE-holding women who had established professional or activist careers well before the advent of Prevent and the EMW initiatives. Furthermore, as Back et al (2009) note, we need to think carefully about what social actions constitute participation in the democratic process; mobilization around faith communities can be a form of political participation.

The An-Nisa Society, for example, was "established in May 1985 by a group of young British Muslim women, in response to the needs of Muslim women and their families." When I asked Khalida how they dealt with the lack of support from (some) male colleagues and potential allies, she told me "we had already set it up, we just... no longer looked to the men to help us with everything." She and her peers were, therefore, able to use their own expertise and resources to set up an organisation which is still going strong over twenty five years later. They used their agency and resources in order to provide and develop services which they felt were absent from both mainstream local authority services, as well as those offered by male-dominated mosque based 'community groups'.

In addition, although some respondents' accounts correspond to the idea that women were absent (for whatever reason), it is also interesting to note that many clearly had achieved a level of power and influence prior to the launch of the EMW initiatives. A salient example of this can be seen in the case of a meeting Faz attended in Bradford, as a representative of the New Labour Government, which she used to illustrate that "Muslim women tend to get ignored". She described how:

> There was a time when I was at Downing Street and I was going to meetings ...and it was all men and I had to tell them to go and get some women...I said I'm not going to sit and talk just in front of you, just to men, that's ridiculous, I don't feel comfortable for a start... I want to talk to some

> women, you know... so they went and dragged all their wives in... (Faz)

In this instance, these Muslim men took orders from a Muslim woman working in Downing Street, and seemingly did not object to her request to "go and get some women". She had previously acknowledged that community politics overall were not necessarily representative "in a civic sense" (and as discussed shortly, this issue is not necessarily addressed just by "dragging the wives in"). Nonetheless, this encounter illustrates Faz's power in this particular scenario; she describes how she took control of a situation in which she felt uncomfortable and also the fact that her request was met, seemingly with little resistance.

Many of the women had been very politically active prior to their involvement in NWMAG. Before she was invited to join NMWAG, and in response to being ignored by government (according to her [Gohir 2008]), Shaista set up Muslim Voice UK in April 2005 which was the UK's first Muslim online opinion-polling organisation. She has also been involved with the Muslim Women's Network since 2005 which she describes as "a national network of individual Muslim women and organisations that ensures their voices reach government and provides a platform for sharing knowledge and experiences." Moreover, since her high profile resignation from NMWAG she has continued her work setting up a website 'Big Sister', her answer to NMWAG's 'Our Choices' role models project.

Shaista had been informally involved in government through various networks and suggested that it was in fact Muslim women, such as herself, who highlighted the absence of women to government Ministers, rather than Ministers or civil servants identifying a problem. She argues that "she had been complaining for a while" and as a result of her persistence she, "eventually actually got onto one of these round table meetings".

> in my very first meeting...I raised it very quickly and said, 'where are the voices of women?', you need to empower women, you need to get more voices of women, of Muslim women round the table because I think actually they can be quite, erm, you know, in terms of preventing violent extremism, you know, they could play a role basically (Shaista)

Shaista's use of the term 'empowerment' raises a number of possibilities. First, it could represent an uncritical reiteration of the discourse, or equally it could suggest that she herself was instrumental in the term being adopted. She also uncritically uses the idea of 'voice': that just by 'having more voices around the table', Muslim women would be listened to. In considering issues of silence or invisibility, it is possible that the existence of Muslim women's groups was not recognised simply through a lack of knowledge or awareness. Much of the machinations of community engagement are ad hoc and informal and so Muslim women's apparent silence and invisibility is possibly a consequence of this, rather than an explicit prohibition on women. In addition, perhaps not all of these groups comprised the type of Muslim women the government was interested in seeing. An-Nisa say they were pushing for anti-religious discrimination legislation, based on their experiences of working in Brent, from as early as the late 1980s and claim credit for contributing to finally putting the issue on the government's agenda. In addition, they were vehemently against the Prevent agenda and very vocally contested it. By contrast, organisations focused more specifically on issues like domestic violence and honour related violence often received vocal political support and patronage from the likes of imperial feminists such as Anne Cryer, even if this was not always matched with financial support.

Having questioned the presumption that Muslim women were indeed silent or absent from the political arena, the following analyses the effects and impact of government interventions to redress this alleged silence in the context of Prevent, particularly through the establishment of NMWAG.

(Re)presenting 'the Muslim woman'

> as far as all Muslim women are concerned, we can't say that we represent all of you, it's such a diverse group of people but… you need to feel confident that you are being representative in some shape or form rather than nothing at all (Hadiyeh)

On the 22nd of February 2010 I attended one of NMWAG's quarterly meetings. Not all the members were present, a mixture of apologies and no-shows; the snowy weather had affected national transport links. The meeting began with NMWAG members feeding back to the others on progress on the different initiatives they were involved in (role models, civic participation and theological interpretation). This was followed by a discussion on body scanners which, at that time, were being considered for introduction to all UK airports.[10] There was a range of opinions among the women. There was vehement opposition from those wanting women to have the opportunity to opt for a 'pat down' in private. At the other extreme, there was unequivocal support for body scanners on the basis that women would be happier with a body scan carried out by another woman secreted away who they would never see. In my research diary I noted it was "encouraging to hear the diversity of opinion" among the group. In addition, however, I also reflected on the ad hoc way NMWAG members had consulted 'Muslim women'; one said she had spoken to burqa-wearing family members, as though they were the only (Muslim) women, or indeed people, who might have an opinion on the matter.[11] Others appeared to have utilised slightly more formal channels to consult. This diversity of opinion and the evidence of inconsistent consultative processes highlights the broader question of political representation. This section examines the extent to which NMWAG could be seen to be representative of Muslim women.

The construction of homogenous communities in the multiculturalist policy paradigm has reinforced a particular male- and conservative-dominated ordering of gender relations within social and political spaces (Burlet and Reid 1998; Yuval-Davis 2011). As such, (BME) community leaders have long been criticised for being unelected, unrepresentative, and for not reflecting the diversity of views and contestations in the community. It could also be argued, however, that similar criticisms could be levelled at NMWAG.

To begin with, recruitment to NMWAG was not open and transparent; the original members were personally invited to join. As a result, the group initially consisted of those women who were already known to government through their involvement in particular policy areas and were invited to apply. Shaista thought that she "was one of the people that was invited because I was probably sitting there round the table". Similarly, Shahien told me:

> I was on the Home Office working group...and that came to an end but… I was known to government, and I was still ongoing-ly involved, I'd be asked to go to meetings, consultations, give my views on different things and out of the blue I got this email to say that this is what's happened and we'd like to invite you on the group and that's all I can tell you and that's it. (Shahien)

Further, they were then asked to nominate others in a snowball effect (or, according to DCLG's Muslim Women's Engagement Officer,

NMWAG's membership was guided by the "principle of recruiting people of renown and then getting recommendations from them".) Not only was this process not open, it was skewed in favour of those individuals already known to government officials because they were working on policy areas which were already the target of government attention, such as forced marriage. As well as setting the agenda (in terms of narrowing the issues which were apparently relevant to Muslim women), the routes to engagement were therefore heavily prescribed by government.

The second round of recruitment was ostensibly designed to be more transparent since there was an open application process. According to the DCLG's Muslim Women's Engagement Officer, central government had publicised membership through regional Government Offices and Local Authorities who had much better knowledge of local communities. This was the route through which Kalsoom was recruited. She told me, "I was asked to apply, I think I had an invitation from a local government officer saying that this was something you might find interesting, so I applied and I was told I was selected because of my experience at grassroots." Shaista, already a member of NMWAG by then, told me, however, that she also contacted a number of people and encouraged them to apply. She claimed that of the seven who were recruited to join NMWAG in the second round (out of forty applications in total), four were candidates that she had encouraged to apply. These candidates may also have been invited to apply directly by Government Offices or Local Authorities, but this reflects the narrow pool of suitable candidates. The final decision regarding the women who were recruited was made by officials working in Prevent and DCLG, rather than Ministers.

Political representation is the activity of making citizens' voices, opinions, and perspectives "present" in the public policy making processes. Hanna Pitkin (1972) has described 'to represent' as simply to "make present again."[12] To some extent it is generally accepted that "marginalized groups must rely on surrogate representatives" (Mansbridge, cited in Dovi 2007: 61). Although Dovi makes clear that democratic representation should be understood more broadly as "an activity of political advocates" (2007: 54) and that informal representatives can be democratic, the crucial point is that NMWAG was devised and hand selected by government; it was not a grassroots organically formed group.

One of reasons for the second recruitment was that the Group's initial composition was not seen to be sufficiently descriptively representative (Pitkin 1967) of the ethnic diversity of the UK's

Muslim community.[13] This significance of ethnicised differences was reflected in the recruitment of NMWAG. The launch press release referred to the different "communities, professions and traditions" represented by its members. The emphasis, however, was on ethnic and cultural differences as opposed to differences which might materially affect women's lives. Research participants were clear that ethnic representativeness should be achieved. I was told by the DCLG civil servant ('Women's Engagement Officer') that the original line up of NWMAG had been criticised for its narrow ethnic composition. This was corroborated by one of the NMWAG members as something she had been concerned about:

> there wasn't a single black Muslim woman on the group… there was no Arab representation, the Middle East…I didn't think there was enough Bangladeshi representation so actually I said that this was very Pakistani-dominated; we need more diversity

This issue was considered important enough to warrant a second recruitment exercise to invite another six women to the Group. This superficial concern with ensuring that different ethnicities were represented arises from a broader 'culturalist' framework which centres on ethnicised groups. It relies on essentialist understandings of identity. As Melissa Williams states, "such assertions do violence to empirical facts of diversity as well as to the agency of individuals to define the meaning of their social…traits" (1998: 6). Such an approach perpetuates the idea that it is these women's ethnicity which differentiates them rather than, for example, their differential social positioning as, say third or fourth generation working class Muslim women in economically deprived areas in the north of the UK, or Muslim refugee women living in hyper diverse outer London boroughs. Emphasis on such ethno-national differences thus detracts from deeper structural and material factors impinging on different Muslim women's lives. Factors which they share with other women and Muslims and other men. The way in which Muslim women were engaged with was predicated on their belonging to a particular ethnic group.

It could be argued that the emphasis on ensuring ethnicised representativeness is a response to the fact that NMWAG members were unelected and, therefore, being seen to be representative at even the most superficial level could compensate for the absence of any formalised channels of accountability. The historical policy landscape of multiculturalist lobbying encourages such a view. The emphasis on ensuring that the ethnic diversity of the Muslim community was represented by NMWAG was not because they (Government and NMWAG members themselves) thought it would make a material difference. Arguably, it was because they thought it would grant the Group some nominal representativeness to compensate for their not being elected and, at least initially, not appointed through a fair and open recruitment process.

That said, however, NMWAG members did not feel personally representative of a particular ethnic group. Adeeba, for example, felt particularly strongly about this, telling me that she never "thought that the woman from Morocco was representing the women of Morocco" or that "the woman who was sat there from a Somali background was representing Somali women.." In relation to herself, she was adamant that she had "never claimed to represent any group, do you understand? And I don't think any of us should".

Rather, NMWAG respondents thought instead that they provided substantive representation (Pitkin 1972). That is, whereby representatives' activity consists of actions taken on behalf of, in the interest of, as an agent of, and as a substitute for the represented. Adeeba told me that NMWAG members "should be there because of [their] experience and...knowledge" and that it was important "to make sure this diverse knowledge and experience of different things is on the table..." Hadiyeh reiterated this view, saying that:

> When issues come up, all the members have expertise in all various issues to do with violence, arranged marriage, forced marriage all these things, you know? Even myself with extremism, obviously, I have an expertise there. We all have various expertise in our respective fields which can be drawn on.

Through Adeeba's and Hadiyeh's conceptualisations, those they are supposed to be representing are effectively constructed, constituted, framed and created by the representatives themselves (Saward 2006, cited in Childs et al 2010). Although NMWAG members were clear about who they were *not* speaking on behalf of (that is, not Pakistanis, or women in Bradford or Yorkshire), they were less clear about who they were speaking for. During the course of our interview, Adeeba said she was "there to talk about what [she] felt as a Muslim woman" but she also variously claimed to be "talking about Muslim women as a whole" and, "the Muslim woman" or also just "women who were Muslim".

Closely associated with, if not inseparable from, this idea of representation is that of accountability. According to Mansbridge (2009), there are two models of accountability, the sanctions and the selection model. The sanctions model presumes that there will be differences between what the represented and representatives want. The former will reward the latter for good behaviour through repeat votes. Clearly this is not relevant without a direct constituency that is, there were no electoral routes through which to appoint NMWAG members (although clearly such a view may be applicable in discussions of the 'Black vote' or the 'Muslim vote'). By contrast, the selection model of accountability presumes that representatives have self-motivated and exogenous reasons for carrying out the wishes of the represented. The question for NMWAG members, therefore, becomes one of knowledge of Muslim women's concerns and the paths via which they come to know these.

All the NMWAG members were quite high profile in their respective fields. Nonetheless, they had varying degrees of contact with the potential targets of the EMW initiative. This raises an alternative cleavage of difference between NMWAG members which is more relevant when considering representation and accountability than superficial ethnicised differences. That is the extent to which NMWAG members were connected to the 'grassroots'. This theme came up frequently and created a hierarchy within NMWAG members deemed most entitled to speak for or on behalf of 'Muslim women'. NMWAG members could be distinguished on the basis of their direct involvement in grassroots organisations: first, those such as Adeeba in Bradford and Shahien in Cardiff directly involved in and heading up grassroots organisations (QED Foundation and Henna Foundation respectively); umbrella organisations headed up by Shaista and Kalsoom (Muslim Women's Network and the Bristol Muslim Women's network); and third, successful Muslim women who have some relevant knowledge and experience who can act as articulate advocates (for example, Sabina Lakha who had legal expertise of both English and Sharia legal systems, or Fareena Alam, editor of Q-News). An example of divergent views and emphases between those more directly involved in grassroots and those recruited in a more advisory capacity can be seen in the differing views regarding the inclusion of Amina Wadud in the theological interpretation project (see Chapter 6). The latter thought it was right that she was involved, whereas the former were more concerned about the controversy surrounding her and about how she would be received at the grassroots level.

There is also the possibility that there was a degree of intra-group silencing and that certain voices carried more weight. Sabl has argued, in relation to Martin Luther King's strategy of using Christian spirituality to inform his campaign on non-violence, that:

> moral activists, lacking tangible resources with which to exert pressure, paradoxically are often perceived as having more power to effect change, since they lack the burden of connection to selfish interests (2002: 203).

In the context of NMWAG this tendency works to entrench particular stereotypes; those women with most gravitas within NMWAG were those working and campaigning against forced marriage and honour-related violence thus replicating the idea that the defining characteristic for engaging with Muslim women is via the rescue paradigm.[14] By contrast, those Muslim women working with more prosaic examples of discrimination in employment did not have as high a profile. The relationship between the women NMWAG represent and who they are allegedly speaking on behalf of is complicated and problematic often reflecting class differences between NMWAG members too. For example, Pragna (SBS) distinguished between:

> Middle class women who can shift in and out of whatever identity they choose and when something gets a bit too stifling they move out and shift gear, do something else for a bit and they move back in...(Pragna)

and the alternative, that is "women who really are boxed...[into]... that kind of rigid identification along faith lines". Rebecca, one of the Bristol police officers involved in Prevent, observed that the women she met through police outreach work included "housewives" who just want "their coffee morning". In addition, however, she told me there are "other ladies that go to the group who are really keen to empower women and are keen to get more Muslim women involved in different projects". But she also highlighted a disjuncture here. Reflecting on the Bristol Muslim Women's Network established by Kalsoom, she commented:

> they're more the women who will try and encourage other women in Bristol but...I don't know whether you'll agree with me [addressing her two colleagues] but generally a lot of the women in Bristol are still sort of [pause] not behind,

> but they're not... their voices are not heard as much as the women on the Muslim Network Panel (Rebecca)

Many NMWAG members were concerned at having to justify their position, telling me "it would have been nice if there was an application process". The key considerations are not, however, those of representativeness, representation or accountability. These are overshadowed by considerations of the ability of NMWAG members to effect changes: that is, to wield power and to be empowered as political actors themselves. My research notes on the quarterly NMWAG meeting I attended referred to the palpable desire of NMWAG members to make a difference, but also to be seen to be doing so.

Right on the Periphery

The process of "bringing people who are outside the decision-making process into it" can be seen as a form of empowerment (Rowlands 1995: 102). Phillips (1995) argues that the politics of presence changes the tenor of the debate; issues that would not be there otherwise are thought about. There was undoubtedly some optimism around the idea of NMWAG originally. Rubina told me that the "symbolic value" was immeasurable. Group members appreciated having access to Ministers, civil servants and the corridors of power in Westminster. There was also recognition of the way that membership of a national advisory body and Prevent as a whole had a positive effect on the ability to influence issues at a more local grassroots level. Kalsoom told me that as a result of her membership of NMWAG, she felt that the Bristol Muslim Women's Network in particular "is out there... it's certainly established itself as a voice", adding that:

> I know that people don't like the Prevent agenda but I think it's been fantastic. It came at a time when we really, really needed it. And great steps have been made in Bristol certainly between the women's network sitting down with the Council of Bristol mosques and saying we need to work together; it would never have happened before (Kalsoom)

This enthusiasm, however, was tempered by other respondents' misgivings about what they thought their role in NMWAG was meant to be, and how that worked out in reality. As an advisory body, NMWAG members had anticipated that their role was to advise. The reality was, however, somewhat different. Adeeba told me that she thought NMWAG was always meant to be "an influencing body rather than a delivery body". She told me that it "never worked out like that" and she did not think that "the women around the table expected that either". She was clear that from her "experience of being on influencing bodies, you don't deliver."

This was reiterated by Shaista who explained that she thought, as busy women "successful in their own fields", they would get access to Ministers and could contribute to policy development. She told me that she too was there to influence policy rather than oversee projects and "determine who gets the contracts, to determine if it's meeting all its objectives", as ended up being the case. She thought this was:

> something that the civil servants should be doing. In fact I felt it was cheap labour because we're then being asked to do something for free and I haven't got the time to spare. When there are tons of other projects that they're [civil servants] overseeing, why couldn't they oversee these three? (Shaista)

In addition, this disappointment was compounded by the fact that the initiatives which they were asked to oversee were thought to have been predetermined. Shaista, who eventually resigned from NMWAG, suggested that the workstreams NMWAG was asked to oversee:

> were predetermined… they made us believe we were having a discussion, that they were our projects… [but]… I clearly remember being told, you don't need to discuss role models and civic participation in depth initially, because we're going to do those projects anyway, which kind of left theology … so I felt in a way all three were predetermined – although we ended up saying the third project should be theology – but the whole way it was done it was probably obvious that it was going to be that. (Shaista)

When asked what other work streams NMWAG members would have liked included in their remit, Shaista said that research into the extent of discrimination against Muslim women in employment would have been useful in order to consider ways of tackling such issues. In addition, she and others also raised issues of multiple discrimination, poverty and disparities in healthcare, as well as shortcomings in the provision of ESL (English as a second language) teaching. NMWAG respondents had hoped that their "involvement would have a long term impact on the lives of women", and their empowerment. They did not anticipate that it would be "just a quick tick box, one-off thing that actually has no long term effect". This concern was also shared by Almeena, one of the role models, who told me that:

> these initiatives are all well and good while they've got the funding and it's a year-long thing, but what happens afterwards, you know, what's the point of starting something? (Almeena)

Some respondents told me that the Youth Muslim Advisory Group (YMAG) was given a higher profile than NMWAG. There was also a perception that the group was subject to the whims of whichever politician was in charge. Adeeba told me that changes in DCLG personnel affected morale among the group.

> I think Hazel Blears[15] took it very seriously the fact that she used to turn up at each of the meetings and chair them that's very good so she took it obviously very seriously… what did happen is that there was a change of Secretary of State, and another one comes along and it might not be an important issue for them as it was for the previous one, 'cos they've got their own areas of interest, and I think it was then that it became quite difficult to keep the momentum going because at the end of the day women come around the table, you know they're inspired by the fact that they've got the Secretary of State sat there chairing the meeting who's going to listen to what they tell them (Adeeba)

Not only were the subjects they were asked to oversee limited and seemingly predetermined, there was a sense that dissent would be frowned upon. A recurrent theme in this policy arena has been having 'difficult conversations'. This is founded on the premise that multiculturalism has resulted in cultural relativism and moral blindness in relation to so-called cultural practices, such as forced marriages, honour killings and female circumcision. As a result, one of the positive corollaries of critiquing multiculturalism is the idea that these so-called cultural practices are out in the open and subject to societal scrutiny. No-one I interviewed, however, mentioned this openness as a positive outcome of EMW, other than in terms of there being more funding available for organisations already working in these fields. Instead it was suggested that 'difficult conversations' instigated by NMWAG members or others were not encouraged.

Shaista admitted to becoming, as she put it, quite "renowned" for being very vocal in NMWAG. She explained that there was an e-group which NMWAG members could use to communicate and discuss issues. At the NMWAG meetings, she felt that the timetable was always too tight and that:

> ...We were only discussing the agenda items that the government had put on the agenda; they were not our agenda items. As soon as the meetings were over then... there was no space within the meetings for me or anyone to raise concerns. (Shaista)

She explained that it did not make sense for her to "pick up the phone and ring twenty women", so instead she would raise concerns in an e-group so that everyone could see her views and join in an online debate. She told me, however, that she felt her behaviour was not welcomed and that one of the more senior civil servants working with NMWAG suggested that she contact her to get items on the agenda rather than email NMWAG members en masse directly. Although this could possibly have been justifiable in terms of managing or streamlining communications, Shaista interpreted this behaviour as obstructive, suggesting that it was to prevent debate and to prevent her influencing other NMWAG members. She interpreted the DCLG official's intervention as a "veiled threat" that she should reconsider her position in the group and that it was a polite way of saying, "maybe you should keep quiet or step down". She described how after that incident she was disheartened and contemplated leaving NMWAG. In addition, Shaista suggested that the perks of being on NMWAG prevented other women dissenting more regularly, a theme I return to later.

> I suppose even power gets to women; it does get to women's heads I mean suddenly you've got access to ministers... you're invited to 10 Downing Street not only for the launch but when they've had receptions there, so you get invited there. There were a few trips abroad as well so you get selected on a free trip abroad. Who isn't gonna love that? I went to 10 Downing Street, I went on free trips but I still never forgot why I was there and I think a lot of women didn't want to rock the boat, didn't want to because it looks good on your CV...(Shaista)

For those not directly involved in the Group, there was a perception that it was an empty vehicle which could or would not address substantial material issues. Humera of An-Nisa Society told me that she did not think it was the job of the advisory group to "go and pacify the community". Instead, such bodies needed to be there to be critical of the government, adding:

> But CLG's [DCLG] ...advisers, for some reason, don't believe we have a right to that part of democracy, right? ... I argue with them. We have a right to dissent, we have a right to be critical, and that's what democracy is all about, that's what freedom of speech is all about. But...because we've been critical, we get pushed out so....you know I feel really offended by the whole CLG set-up. But that's the way that they work. As long as you go along, work with them without questioning anything, you're ok. But nobody's allowed to question them. At all. (Humera)

In addition to disappointment with the remit and reach of NWMAG, many interviewees, both inside and outside of NMWAG, intimated that the experience of working in or with central government specifically was itself a marginalising experience. As Ien Ang has suggested, 'othering can take place by acts of inclusion within multicultural discourse' (cited in Ahmed 2000: 97). This was potentially on two levels: first at the level of what was expected of Muslim women and second the exclusionary environment of the Civil Service itself.

Interviewees reflected that the spaces in which they were 'given voice' were narrowly defined. This might be partly explained by the fact that the women were recruited from particular policy areas which were already on the government agenda. One Muslim woman policy consultant, Faz, told me that she avoided Muslim women's groups in government because they were "right on the periphery". She added that the:

> sexy issues are about imams and about, you know, the kind of theological side of things... the *real* counterterrorism side of things and the political side of things... it's almost as though "we'll put women in this group and they just talk about whatever they want to and then we'll talk about real stuff" so I ...avoid them big time. (Faz)

Further marginalisation occurs because the possibilities for engagement are predicated on a certain understanding of what it means to be a Muslim woman, which is to be a victim, to be oppressed. She added:

> Trouble is, as soon as you start saying 'I don't need your help, I want your politics, I want you to treat me the same', they don't care, they don't want to talk to you anymore. They'll say, 'Oh, she doesn't really represent the community'… (Faz)

Muslim women are only intelligible in the political arena if they fit certain norms. Yasmin told me how she always felt that the government did not see her as 'Muslim enough' to be seen as representative of 'a Muslim woman'. Moreover, she felt that Muslim women were only given a voice "as victims or survivors, who were prepared to disclose their personal stories". She explained, "whereas you can talk about the veil, …[but] if you want to discuss any other issues, you know I mean the credit crunch, anything, then you're not allowed a voice because what could you possibly know?"[16] She explained:

> you know, you are limited to these very narrow subjects and I find it really difficult that given the positioning of the Muslim community as a whole, it diminishes the role of women and all the multiple roles that women have in communities generally as gatekeepers, as mothers, as sisters as whatever role you want to have, as active economic participants and citizens, to work with the men and to actually really engage in, not just the Prevent agenda, but in to the wider integration agenda (Yasmin)

She added:

> I actually think it's oppressive the way Muslim women are viewed, and the fact that the government will only speak to erm….certain Muslim women I'm like, I just sit there and go, 'well, who's speaking for me?', 'cause I don't see women who look like me, who sound like me (Yasmin)

This was also reiterated by Faz:

> And part of the reason I get annoyed getting involved in some of these things …is because I've realised that the

> Liberal Left want me to go to them and say: 'I need your help please, can you give me your support and show me what to do. Give me some money. You know, 'help me to overcome this oppression from Muslim men...' and when you trust them like that they love you... and then they're like 'I've got this wonderful friend, she's so amazing, she's speaking out against her own community... doing so much, so brave, you know amazing, amazing!' (Faz)

I also spoke to Nazneen, who framed this in terms of the government not wanting to empower Muslim women like her because they were more interested in empowering, "...women who can't speak English, have hijab on and fit the role model." She thought that in spite of the "rhetoric about Muslim women and empowering Muslim women", civil servants had no intention of empowering "a woman who's educated and who's got a mouth, they don't want you anywhere near... because then you become a threat". She added:

> so you have your own community trying to keep you out, you have a structure in place...which says it promotes diversity, but it really doesn't and it does it piecemeal because there's no support around you so you're going to leave anyway, and they know it, there's a huge business to be made out of diversity and credibility every time I hear [...] or somebody speak about it, it makes me sick (Nazneen)

Building on Fortier's work on the politics of pride, the effect of this way of engaging or interpellating the Muslim woman within this rhetoric is to separate ethnic (and religious) Others into the subjects that must be hailed as figures of the tolerant multiracial Britain, which ultimately reconstitutes the privileges of whiteness (2005). Nazneen described the double bind of being black:

> Whereas in the public sector it's totally not about whether you're good at your job...no way! And I remember when I was there I just gave up I just thought, OK, everyone thinks I got the job here because I'm black, so that's what my staff thought, my peers didn't like me because they thought well, you know a) she got the job because she's black and b) what the hell does she know about employment sort of thing so I was never made to feel welcome (Nazneen)

Dovi (2009) reflects that inclusion is not just about bringing people from marginalized groups into democratic politics; rather democratic representation can require limiting the influence of overrepresented privileged groups. Clearly, issues of social mobility and entrenched privilege are a much broader issue. Neither Yasmin, Faz nor Nazneen were directly involved in NMWAG but had worked in various capacities with central government. Faz, who had worked at quite a senior level in Tony Blair's government, told me how working with (white middle class) senior civil servants could occasionally be an alienating experience if you did not 'bear the signs of "cultural refinement"' (Puwar 2001: 666).

> The biggest thing for me was the Oxbridge thing... they all had this accent which I didn't have and they all spoke in riddles and....lots of Latin, lots of very, very clever jokes, wordplay... and when they talked to you, and you know I'm talking senior civil servants here, I felt very intimidated because they just seemed to be from this different world and...you know I think that's changed...but at that time is was very rarefied you know and they made it clear that you weren't on their level, even though you'd been brought in by the Prime Minister himself, personally appointed... you had to fight for everything you got... you had to fight for information, to be on a distribution list, you had to fight to go to meetings. (Faz)

Nazneen, who had been one of the most senior civil servants under the New Labour government (and incidentally who had been invited to apply for her post) spoke extensively about her experiences of working in both the private and public sector. She told me how she was described by one Ministerial adviser as "scary" because she was an articulate Asian Muslim woman and someone who identified herself as politically Black. She felt that rhetoric "about Bangladeshi women" meant that people made assumptions about her:

> 'oh your husband must stop you', or 'your dad must stop you from doing this' or you know 'men are like this' or 'poor you, poor you,' and actually when you're an articulate Asian women they don't know what to do with you – they really don't know what to do with you. (Nazneen)

Respondents were also subject to experiences arising from patriarchy more generally in the workplace, which affects all women, not just Muslim women. She (problematically) suggested that she thought "white women have been the worst obstacles in my career development", going on to say that, "if you speak to a lot of ethnic minority women they will tell you exactly the same thing; all my black and Asian women friends say the same thing." She suggests this is because white women thought of her as a "threat", "whereas men, particularly older men" had been very supportive to her. Although Nazneen was clear that she did not fit the stereotype of the Bangladeshi woman, she saw no irony in telling me that the white men that had assisted here in her career "were ever so protective, they were really lovely" or that "white men of a certain age...think I'm a little novelty." Nazneen's comments make clear that she does not conform to the widely accepted stereotype of the Muslim woman, yet they also position her as a woman having to bargain with patriarchy (Kandiyoti 1988)[17] and 'sexualised and infantilised at a scale that is over and above white female bodies' (Puwar 2001: 662) – something which she unwittingly appears to collude in. Her experiences with white women are consistent with Scharff's findings which suggest that (white) women's 'self-representation as empowered is intertwined with the othering of Muslim women' (2011: 120)

Occasionally respondents suggested that they too should also be empowered through their appointment to NMWAG. Shaista criticised other NMWAG members for having secured a lot of contract work through NMWAG. Undeniably for some of the women there were perks associated with their position, such as foreign travel and obtaining a high profile (receiving honours and so on). Following her resignation, Shaista claimed that the only two negative emails she received were from NMWAG members who she claimed said she had 'spoilt things' for them. At the same time she herself expressed regret where she had not been successful in securing tenders. She told me that she was disappointed not to have got the contract to run the theological interpretation project and described this as "disempowering".

Conclusion

The rationale for giving the silent majority a stronger voice is based on a number of assertions and common sense assumptions. First, it implies that the reasons for this silence or absence stem from both within 'the community' and outside. Respondents' accounts suggest that any silencing largely came from without and where hostility was explicitly referred to, it was connected to the type of work they were involved in. Second, this rationale for giving women as the silent majority a stronger voice is premised on their having been silent. As this chapter shows many of the women had been active long before the establishment of NMWAG. Third, it is premised on the understanding that government interventions to 'ensure that they [Muslim women] find their voice more easily' (DCLG 2006) achieved that.

As within the multiculturalist policy paradigm, Prevent and the EMW initiatives involve 'group making' and have facilitated processes of reification by 'ethno political entrepreneurs' (Brubaker 2004: 166). Historically men have undoubtedly dominated informal consultations with Muslim communities. NMWAG could, therefore, be seen as an admirable attempt to redress this gender imbalance. It is, however, unclear that the Muslim women involved in NMWAG were any more eligible to represent Muslim communities. The issue of representation is not necessarily rectified "just by dragging the wives in". This is particularly resonant when considering the civic participation initiative which could potentially have been a more far reaching project, but which was not implemented more widely. That is not to deny, however, that many NMWAG members had relevant expertise or knowledge of particular issues, as well as grassroots experience, which qualified them to at least informally advise on issues affecting Muslim women.

In practice, however, NMWAG respondents reflected that, within the Department for Communities and Local Government, they were side lined relative to YMAG which, it was alleged, was given more resources and publicity. Furthermore, there was the feeling that the work streams overseen by NMWAG were predetermined, that dissent was discouraged and that the very experience of working with Whitehall was marginalising. NMWAG respondents felt that they were very well qualified to advise, but that ultimately all they were asked to do was deliver predetermined workstreams. In addition they were not well regarded externally; Humera told me rather disparagingly, "these women are not tackling anything institutional".

What, then, did NMWAG achieve? Quite clearly it had symbolic value. Given, however, that this was a project driven by Whitehall, this symbolic value was directed at increasing mainstream government's legitimacy by tapping into a prevalent discourse about Muslim women. In doing so, it was able to counter accusations that Prevent led to unholy alliances with extremists; women, even ex-Hizb-ut Tahrir members, could never be accused of representing a radical or extremist threat. It is not clear, however, to what extent this crude attempt to increase the policy's de facto legitimacy could ever be successful. Just as the presence of a black President does not mean that the US is post-race; or a woman Prime Minister, that the UK is postfeminist; equally a consultative body of Muslim women advising senior civil servants and Ministers does not mean that women who are Muslim do not continue to be marginalised. The experience of NMWAG reflects Ann Snitow's comment that, '…in a cruel irony that is one mark of women's oppression, when women speak as women they run a special risk of not being heard because the female voice is by our culture's definition, that-voice- you-can-ignore' (cited in Forcey 1994: 170).

The legitimacy of the EMW initiatives, and therefore NMWAG, is undermined by the following: first, that the inception of these initiatives was directly and explicitly connected to the counterterrorism agenda; and second, that Muslim women are not the only underrepresented group that might benefit from being brought into or represented better in political and civic life. Associated with this latter point is the fact that both women and minorities are underrepresented and were these imbalances to be addressed more broadly, then it might follow that more Muslim women may automatically enter the political sphere. In relation to the question of voice, analysing the operation of NMWAG shows that within the category of 'Muslim women' certain voices were louder (or heard more) than others; this was often connected to their particular areas of expertise or that they were uncritical more broadly of the Prevent agenda. Overall, however, for NMWAG members, the very process of being brought into the fold is itself premised on their otherness. As Fortier remarks, 'the embodied multicultural subject achieves unmarked status through the injunction to speak his and her allegiance. One must be *seen* and *heard* to declare her pride in Britishness in order to *achieve* unmarked status. An 'achievement' that is endlessly deferred, as the non-white skin is never fully peeled off, in a continuous process of de/re/racialization' (2005: 573–4).

Although many NMWAG respondents were pleased, at least initially, by government efforts to involve Muslim women, it was as mothers and as guardians of the next generation that they were brought into politics. In this way political engagement with Muslim women perpetuates the image of Muslim women as in need of rescue and empowerment, yet stultifies a more radical liberatory, transformative engagement. The next chapter examines this theme of motherhood.

Notes

[1] In the Foreword to *Engaging Muslim Women* (DCLG 2006: 5)

[2] It also reflects the presumption that Muslim women do not speak English.

[3] Although see Kundnani (2002b) for a discussion of communalism in the context of the UK.

[4] Local situations and circumstances make a profound difference to the way in which local politics functions. The An-Nisa Society is based in Brent and Khalida's account must be understood as specific to the politics in Brent (see Chapter 3).

[5] Eade and Garbin (2002) show the ways in which debates and events occurring beyond the national frontier influence local politics in the context of East London.

[6] This is in contrast to the some of the Left's response to the suffragettes in the early 20th century. Anne Phillips notes that some of the UK's most obdurate opponents of the UK suffragettes were within the ranks of socialist men who thought that the obsession with women's equality was a dangerously middle-class diversion from the more pressing concerns of class (1995). Beatrix Campbell (1984) reflects on the day to day sexism of the Labour movement in the early 1980s.

[7] It may also reflect gendered and staggered patterns of migration.

[8] Burlet and Reid (1998), for example, examine the way that women's political participation in Bradford was prompted by the Bradford riots of 1995

[9] To the extent that it has been said that: 'Anne Cryer has put her life and career on the line to defend Asian women who are forced into marriages' (Alibhai-Brown 2000).

[10] Although since then plans were dropped due to concerns about exposure to radiation.

[11] In addition it is also conceivable that men may have an issue with body scanners or that people would have concerns about children being body-scanned irrespective of religious belief. The fact that this question was asked of Muslim women conforms to the association of Muslim women, dress and modesty.

[12] Strictly speaking, however, it is about incorporating new people to the polity rather than making them present again.

[13] Descriptive representation refers to the extent to which a representative resembles those being represented (that is, look likes, has common interests with or shares certain experiences with the represented). NMWAG members descriptively represent Muslim women since all self-identify as Muslim and share religious affiliation with their constituency, irrespective of whether they practice or are perceived to be Muslim, in terms of dress, for example.

[14] Charlotte Rachael Proudman (The Independent 18 January 2012) wrote about the New Muslim Suffragettes 'increasing number of Muslim women activists are receiving death threats, fatwas and even hate mail...their crime: rescuing fellow Muslim women from violent and life threatening situations'; 'they stand alone in their communities and apart from other prominent Muslim organisations...The NMS provide refuge, advocacy and access to the British legal and welfare system for women whose daily lives consist of beatings, imprisonment, torture and even marital rape, as well as the mental health ramifications that unfold over time...These organisations have emerged post 9/11 as a response to misogynist and extremist views which are contaminating the Muslim community...'

[15] Originally Adeeba referred to Beverley Hughes but I am referring to Hazel Blears as that was who she later confirmed she was referring to.

[16] There is an assumption that minorities should always speak for the communities from which they came. Writing in the Guardian (16 July 2012) Nabila Ramdani criticises Najat Vallaud-Belkacem as someone who had overcome a 'relatively deprived childhood' and prejudice to embark on 'a glittering career' in French politics only to get involved in a pledge to see prostitution disappear whereas, according to Ramdani, she should have been involved in overturning the burqa ban and '…working to try to improve the lot of all women in society, including those in the same underprivileged Muslim communities from which she came.'

[17] As Kandiyoti suggests 'Women's strategies are always played out in the context of identifiable patriarchal bargains that act as implicit scripts that define, limit, and inflect their market and domestic options.' (1988: 285)

FIVE

As a mother and a Muslim: maternalism and neoliberal empowerment

> Muslim women's groups – people have been trying to set those up for a long time. I worked from the kind of view that Muslim women are really important because they're mothers… there's no real other reason for them to be a group of their own (Faz)

> That women mother in a variety of societies is not as significant as the value attached to mothering in these societies (Mohanty 1988: 26)

Introduction

The empowering Muslim women initiative comprised three main work streams. The first focused on 'building faith capacity' in order to ensure that women could provide a counternarrative to extremist ideology and contribute more in the community at a theological level. Second, civic participation was to be improved by encouraging women to become school governors and magistrates in the wider non-Muslim community. The third project was the role models project, whereby Muslim women in non-traditional careers formed part of a road show travelling around England and Wales visiting Muslim school girls and raising aspirations. These three projects envisaged 'empowerment' in a number of ways: empowerment through 'modernising' religious discourse; through encouraging increased civic participation and through raising the aspirations of Muslim girls. Implicit in the three work streams, therefore, are particular understandings of what disempowerment means when speaking about Muslim women, the target of these initiatives. The following two chapters examine how empowerment is articulated through a discussion of two of the EMW (Empowering Muslim Women) initiatives (role models and theological interpretation). These interpretations are then discussed in the context of the way the term empowerment was invoked and understood by the interviewees.[1]

Combined, the following two chapters argue that empowerment is articulated in apparently contradictory ways; it is both individualised and collectivised. On one level, empowerment, particularly as envisaged in the context of the role models road show, is seen as part of an individualistic, aspirational, neoliberal project in which education and employment combine to provide access to consumer citizenship. On another level, however, it is collectivised; an imagined, essentialised Muslim community is pathologised because of its religion. Simultaneously, however, religion emerges as a tool of empowerment.

The title of this chapter originates from a speech given by Hazel Blears about Prevent at LSE (Blears 2009) in which she spoke of the 'the passion and commitment in our communities' by referring to 'one young woman' who told her: 'I am ready to go anywhere, to any audience, at any time, in this country or abroad and say that I believe suicide bombing is wrong – as a mother and a Muslim'. This chapter begins by examining how this discourse of empowerment rests heavily on 'that old trope – that women's citizenship and social status emerge from reproductive relations' (Bhattacharyya 2008: 51). It looks at the importance placed on parenting and mothering specifically as part of neoliberalism's new sexual contract (McRobbie 2009). It also considers the theme of communal mothering and how mothers as a group emerge as specific targets of policy.

The discourse of individual empowerment stresses the importance of mothering and families. It has its roots in New Right ideologies in which the individual is exalted, but with an emphasis on 'traditional' family values. It also reflects the social investment approach of New Labour's third way, orientated towards children and developing social capital to deal with social risks of post-industrial society (Daly 2011). There are explicit commonalities between the discourse on Muslim mothers and understandings of working class mothering. In the neoliberal regime individual mothers and families are the source of both problems and solutions. As Val Gillies argues, however, 'although individualistic values structure contemporary society, they obscure the more relational experiences of the disadvantaged and marginalised. Working class mothers and their children are denied the recognition and resources to construct themselves as worthy subjects' (2007: 92).

Furthermore, in the EMW initiatives mothering itself is gendered; mothers are seen differently in relation to their sons and daughters. With regard to sons, mothers are represented as being in need of empowerment to 'build resilience' against extremism, either through countering extremist views, or being confident enough to report any suspicious behaviour which might indicate radical extremist tendencies to the police or relevant authorities. In relation to daughters, however, it is mothers' support for education which is seen as their primary purpose. This support is seen as pivotal and is an integral part of increasing (the allegedly low) aspirations among Muslim girls. The role models road show is based on two mutually exclusive premises. The first is that Muslim girls underachieve because they (or their parents) under-aspire, do not value education sufficiently, or are fundamentally opposed to it. The second premise is that Muslim parents encourage their daughters in a narrow range of careers. Through exploring the role of mothers in the context of the road show this chapter suggests that this forms part of a wider discourse around parenting, and working class parenting in particular (as identified by Gillies 2007), which is further inflected by race and religion.

The chapter begins by discussing the importance placed on parenting and, in particular, mothering, looking at the way in which it conforms to a simplistic neoliberal logic of aspiration, self-improvement and consumer citizenship. As Dwyer has argued metaphors of home are particularly gendered (2000) and while there is an explicit focus on mothers and daughters in EMW, there are implicit assumptions or directives about: the mothering of sons, and the relationship between fathers and their daughters and sons.

As a mother: individualising empowerment

At an Equality and Human Rights Commission event in Birmingham in March 2009 I met a high profile Muslim activist and during a brief conversation over lunch, I asked her how she saw the link between EMW and terrorism. She was slightly taken aback by what seemed to me to be a fairly obvious question. After some reflection she replied that it was all about parenting. As this section illustrates, however, 'parenting' is in fact a gender neutral way of referring to mothering; fathers are absent in the EMW social policy literature and in the Prevent discourse more widely. A DCLG (Department for Communities and Local Government) report entitled *Engaging with Muslim Women: A Report from the Prime Minister's Event 10 May 2006* refers to engaging with 'Muslim mothers and grandmothers'. In her foreword explaining the impetus for the Prime Minister's event, Ruth Kelly writes of meeting 'forty Muslim mothers and grandmothers' to talk to them about the issues their communities face (DCLG 2006: 5). In addition, there are references to women being at 'the heart of the family' and statements such as the following: 'Muslim women... like all mothers...want the very best for their children and families', and 'We see Muslim women as key to helping with this so we want to hear from you today...how Muslim mothers would like to play an active role' (DCLG 2006: 25). While later policy literature makes fewer explicit references, the themes of mothering, as opposed to parenting, percolate in the practice of policy.

Respondents largely concurred with this emphasis on parenting and mothering. Faz agreed that the impetus for EMW and NMWAG (National Muslim Women's Advisory Group) was founded on the idea that child rearing is women's work:

> ...they want women involved and that's good, and part of it is this whole 'Muslim women have a special role in terms of nurturing the next generation'... and there again I kind of agree, 'cause mothers do play an important role in terms of how they bring their children up... (Faz)

Kalsoom had originally trained as a teacher, but over twenty years her role had developed into a 'community liaison post'. She explained how 'parents, particularly Muslim parents, just didn't have the skills or the tools or the knowledge to be able to appreciate that they were partners with the school and their children's education'. She added that the mothers 'just really lacked the parenting skills' and this led to her becoming a home–school liaison officer, developing parenting courses for mothers. This reflects a broader trend in which parenting has been re-framed as a job requiring particular skills and expertise, which must be taught by formally qualified professionals. This builds on prevalent discourses in wider society about women, femininity and motherhood, and is consistent with a broader discourse in which parenting and child rearing practices have increasingly come to be held accountable for crime, deprivation and inequality. In particular, there has been an overt focus on working class parenting (Gillies 2007) since the late 19th century with the advent of increasing social welfare (Davin 1978).[2]

For Muslim families in the contemporary era, this story is haunted by the ghosts of Britain's imperial past and post war constructions of pathologised 'Othered' families. The bastard offspring of South Asian 'melodrama' and Arab 'despotism', pathological Muslim families are stereotypically characterised (virulently so in the media) by intergenerational conflict between fathers and sons (Lewis 2007) and overprotected daughters constrained by honour, ever at the risk of suicide (Brah and Minhas 1985; Brah 1996; Puwar 2003). There in the background is the submissive, oppressed Muslim mother (Parmar 1982). At worst, an active facilitator, but at the very least, complicit in her silence.

Accordingly, the way mothering is articulated through the Prevent agenda varies between sons and daughters. In relation to their daughters, the emphasis is on the role of mothers in their daughter's education and subsequent employment aspirations. This is apparent in the rationale for the role model road show in which this relationship is explicitly built into the programme. While this is not surprising given that the initiatives are about empowering women, there were no parallel initiatives relating to boys or fathers specifically elsewhere in the Prevent agenda[3]. In relation to boys, the theme of mothering is less overtly discussed. Rather, it is inferred. Since it is only boys that are deemed to be at risk of radicalisation (see Chapter 2), 'empowering women to combat terrorism' refers to women stopping men from being drawn into extremism, or at least having the wherewithal to report them to the relevant authorities if they are unable to.

Mothers and daughters: The role models road show

Although there is an implicit collectivism in targeting 'Muslim women' as a group, the role model road show arises from an individualistic interpretation of empowerment. Broadly speaking, this conceptualisation of 'empowerment' is consistent with broader sociological arguments about individualization (Beck 1992; Giddens 1991). It forms part of a liberal, atomistic privatized form of citizenship (Honig 1999), inseparable from consumerism (Rowlands 1997). Specifically, it is expressed through the meritocratic ideals of (individualised) social mobility in respect of education and employment opportunities. This individualised approach to social mobility sits firmly within the framework of New Labour's (Tony Blair's) mantra of 'education, education, education', which attributes success to individual effort and aspiration in an illusory meritocracy. As such, it averts the need for countering entrenched structural class and regional differences. As Butler and Hamnett argue, 'education is both the means for sorting the population to fit the social positions available in society and the means for individuals to transform their life chances' (2011: 243). Specifically in relation to education, '"hopeful" or innovative approaches based on the widespread belief that raising aspirations... will result in improved educational outcomes for children from low-income households' signifies a policy shift 'away from a sole reliance on an "improvement through teaching" approach towards a broad range of other types of provision…' (Carter-Wall and Whitfield 2012: 3). As discussed later, even if the rationales for the road show were internally consistent, the supporting evidence for such an approach is limited.

In relation to young women in particular, McRobbie suggests that there is a new sexual contract whereby, 'The young woman is offered a notional form of equality concretised in education and employment, and through participation in consumer culture and civil society, in place of what a reinvented feminist politics might have to offer' (2009: 2).[4]

Although McRobbie suggests that 'Black and Asian' women have been recruited into this new sexual contract, arguably Other ethnicised women, such as young Muslim women, occupy a different position in relation to this contract, reflecting the interplay of different axes of power and racialised subjectivities. Within such a discourse this contract is also offered as an opportunity to be modernised.

The stated aim of the road shows was to address the low levels of economic activity among Muslim women. The evaluation report 'Our Choices' (Equal to the Occasion 2010), for example, refers to less than one in three Muslim women in the UK having a job, compared to two in three non-Muslim women. The result of this, according to the evaluation report, is that 'the girls miss out on the diversity of opportunities available and employers miss out on the contribution of an increasingly well-educated section of the population who has much to offer' (2010: 7). Khattab (2009) incorporates religious dimensions into an analysis of the ethnic penalty and finds that skin colour and culture (religion) are to a greater extent (than ethnicity alone) the main mechanisms that operate to reinforce disadvantage among some groups, irrespective of their level of education and qualifications.

The two-fold premise for the road show was, therefore, both a lack of parental aspiration for their daughters as well as over emphasis on a narrow range of careers, and thus conforms to post-feminist neo liberal ideals. The idea of the road show was to present a diverse range of role models from 'non-traditional' careers to encourage higher aspirations to continue on to higher education and also to consider a wider spread of possible careers. In addition to the supposed transformative effects of contact with such role models, parental support was seen as vital. The role of mothers in 'empowering' their daughters was specifically highlighted, reflecting the most basic level at which the idea of mothering operates throughout the EMW initiatives. As a result parenting was explicitly incorporated into the initiative and the workshops. The Equal to the Occasion report states, 'Family support was a critical factor for all of the 12 national role models, so we were very keen that parents should get a chance to meet them, hear their stories and be able to ask questions' (2010: 13).[5]

The role models I interviewed corroborated this. Almeena (BBC Wales journalist and presenter and national role model at the Cardiff road show) told me that her work experience came via her mother. She told me that she had been "totally free" to choose what she wanted to do and that she had got relevant work experience through family contacts. Almeena's parents were clearly in a position to assist her in ways that might not have been possible for all the road show attendees' parents (see Chapter 3). She emphasised that her parents not only accepted what she wanted to do, but provided ongoing "support and encouragement".

A number of respondents had been involved in the Mosaic project, based in Tower Hamlets, which focuses on mentoring Muslim girls *and* their mothers. Almeena told me that her involvement in 'mentoring…the mums' as part of the Mosaic project, made her 'realise just how important parents…but mums in particular, [are] with their daughter's education.' Hadiyeh (member of NMWAG and Three Faiths Forum and former Hizb-ut Tahrir member) was also involved in this mentoring project. She told me how mothers and their daughters attended workshops and discussed a variety of issues relating to aspirations, overcoming barriers to success, and 'how to encourage your children to study'. Then, according to Hadiyeh, the mothers "also went to visit a university and saw how it was, going to the big wide world". This last comment alludes to the isolated seclusion or 'purdah' within which Muslim mothers are presumed to live.

The role of daughters' mothers was explicitly built into some of the role models road shows. Dr Farrah Bhatti (a scientist working on climate change policy at Westminster and national role model at the London road show) was accompanied to the event by her mother. Farrah's mother was involved in a session with the mothers who had attended the Newham road show. (A similar session had also taken place in the Dudley road show.) The London road show was held in Newham on a Saturday morning specifically to allow some of the girls' parents to attend (presupposing that they worked during the week and thus contradicting the view that Muslim women do not work). As well as plenary sessions, there were breakout sessions where the girls were able to interact more directly with role models, away from teachers and their parents. It was during one of these sessions that it was decided that the mothers who had turned up could get together and discuss some of the themes prompted by the event. Around ten mothers attended and the discussion was chaired by the teacher who had organised the event at Little Ilford.

Although initially quite stilted, in time and with a little prompting from Farrah's mother, the discussion flowed. Farrah's mother explained that she had married and had children young, but that she had wanted her daughter to take advantage of the educational opportunities available to her in the UK. Her willingness to be candid about her experiences prompted some of the other mothers to share their thoughts. While it was encouraging to see and hear these women supporting their daughters' educations, the format of this type of event is self-selective. Clearly parents who attended an event such as this were at least, in principle, supportive of their daughters' education, as presumably those less supportive would be less likely to attend. Those that spoke all said they wanted to support their daughters, but pointed out that their fears stemmed from what the 'community' might think. I will explore this idea of 'community' and 'cultural barriers' in greater depth in the second half of the chapter.

Aside from one role model (Zainab), who talked openly about her parents' refusal to support her academic and career endeavours, I saw or heard very little about parents holding their children back. While this might be self-evident, as explained above, it might also reflect an unwillingness to 'wash one's dirty linen in public'; or that girls who genuinely experienced such pressures would not have been present at the road show. Fauzia Ahmad's research on British Muslim women and academic achievement (though based on a small sample) reported that parents viewed 'higher education and careers as an absolute necessity' (2001: 143).[6] Ahmad also noted that mothers with a variety of education levels wished to see their daughters achieve a position of choice and independence in their lifestyles, where they would not be solely dependent upon a future husband and in-laws. This is also supported by the work of Basit (1997b) and Ijaz and Abbas (2010) which showed that South Asian Muslim families valued women in education (and in fact religion was often used as a support, albeit differently across different generations, as is discussed later). Dale et al (2002) suggest that Asian youth value education and have high aspirations relative to their parents' educational and occupational levels and, post-16, relatively higher aspirations than other groups.[7]

According to the aims and objectives set out in the role models evaluation report, not only is women's economic inactivity *per se* problematised, it is the lack of *variety* in their career opportunities and choices which is deemed deficient. To a certain extent this was borne out by feedback on the road shows. Almeena said that many of the girls she had spoken to talked "a lot about parents". For example:

> My parents they want me to become a doctor or a lawyer because that's where the jobs are, that's where the money is (Almeena)

Farrah reiterated this explaining that:

> like many Asian parents, my mum and dad, who are both from Pakistan, would have loved it if I had become a doctor. I was always quite headstrong. I told them I didn't want loads of money and be a doctor, I would rather be a poor scientist because that was what interested me. They were very supportive. They were pleased that I was going to go on to do something in a professional field. (Our Choices booklet)

This is consistent with the road show premise that there is a 'problem' of a narrow range of expectations among parents. Given the time it takes, however, to train to be a doctor it certainly does not indicate a lack of support for educating daughters. The paradox is therefore that Muslim parents are effectively blamed for either not being supportive enough or being *too* supportive in relation to a narrow range of careers and professions.

It could be argued that these parental interventions reflect rational economic choices in response to fears about racism, discrimination, lack of opportunities or a quest for financial and career security. Dale et al, for example, suggest that 'for young Asians, having a specific vocational qualification is likely to provide one means by which labour market barriers can be lowered, either at first entry or on subsequent re-entry following child bearing' (2000: 17). Further, Butler and Hamnett describe an emphasis on a narrow range of prestigious vocational careers as a 'marked example of aspiration' (2011: 116). That is not to deny that some parents might have limited knowledge of available careers, particularly if they are not employed or have had limited careers opportunities themselves. In terms of the road show, however, the explanations for both a lack of support or particular career preferences among parents are seen through issues of parental control or pressure and the lens of intergenerational 'cultural conflict'. While not denying the existence of parental pressure leading to particular subject choices, Dale et al (2000, Working Paper 10) suggested that this pressure sometimes resulted in *continued* study by young people, since minority parents have much higher expectations of education than white English counterparts of similar socio economic positioning. Thapar-Bjorkert and Sanghera (2010) also challenge the discourse that fathers prevent their daughters from pursuing higher education.

If it is not a lack of parental support, then what are the causes of Muslim women's apparent or alleged lack of success in education and the labour market? Almeena told me that a lot of the girls she had spoken to at the road shows did not know what they wanted to do. She explained:

> that's what seemed to come across. A lot of them didn't know, they're year tens [14–15 years old] so they're first year of GCSEs, they're still trying to find out which subjects they're good at and which subjects they aren't, you know? So I guess when they turn 16, they'll probably have more of an idea (Almeena)

This is arguably not a problem per se; many teenagers are not sure of their career choices at such a young age. Further, it could be argued that this might be common across the board for youth of a particular class, whose parents may not be in regular salaried or professional employment. Yet, even if this is characterised as a problem, the family, 'community' or 'culture' cannot be held uniquely responsible. A Joseph Rowntree report of April 2012, *The Role of Aspirations, Attitudes and Behaviour in Closing the Educational Attainment Gap,* stated that the real difficulty was knowing *how* to fulfil their ambitions and that 'rather than raising aspirations in order to raise attainment there is a real need for children and parents to be offered support to learn more about educational and career options so they can make more informed decisions about their future' (Carter-Wall and Whitfield 2012: 4).

Research participants' comments indicated a failure in the ability of mainstream services (both at schools or careers services) to deliver appropriate knowledge and information (whether generally or specifically to minority or marginalised groups). Almeena suggested there was a general lack of knowledge in this regard and commented that "work experience in schools doesn't seem to be too joined up" and as a result, one of the girls she had spoken to who wanted to be a doctor, got work experience in a charity shop. Furthermore, there was an unfortunate "dislocation between what they want and how to actually translate that into reality".

This is consistent with what Fajer from Inspired Sisters, which offers a drop-in centre in Manchester, told me. She was surprised because she thought "all of these young people should be aware of their career choices", adding that "they seem like they don't know anything", and that she had expected them to have received one-to-one sessions with a careers adviser. She thought there were "real problems" with mainstream services and wondered whether they were giving out advice properly. She added that this had knock on material effects on her own organisation, explaining that they spent a lot of time "just dealing with people's enquiries", even though that is not what their funding is for. She complained:

> there are other organisations who are funded to do things and they're not doing them, that pisses me off to be honest because I think they need to do their job properly. Makes it easier for us and then we can do what we're supposed to do so, or just give us the money! (laughs) (Fajer)

This emphasis on parenting skills and culturalist interpretations clearly detracts from wider influences on academic performance which affect many groups, not just Muslims. As Yasmin told me, she did not think it "made any difference whether you're working class white British or from an ethnic minority...if you don't know the systems" you are disadvantaged and need support. The rationale for the role model road show includes no recognition of the role of inequalities in education more generally, which in turn reflect inequalities in wider society, and how these might affect achievement for both girls and boys. State education is increasingly part of the neoliberal agenda. Gillies (2007) argues that a family-centric view, focused on working class mothering, wilfully ignores how these women fit into a hierarchy, in which material inequalities structure society in a variety of different ways. This could be in terms of spatial effects regarding schools, as well as the way in which middle class values predominate. A refusal to acknowledge material or financial capital as significant resources in evening-out life chances is accompanied by an '...evangelical faith in the power of parenting to compensate for social disadvantage' (Gillies 2007: 150).

There is also a contradiction in the fact that this debate about aspirations happens at the same time as an increased emphasis on performance and league tables. The latter highlights the importance of schools in pupils' performance, yet at the same time the veneer of choice again situates the burden of responsibility on parents for securing the best possible school for their children. The reality, however, is that choice is constrained. For example, Little Ilford School in Newham, where the London road show took place, was not one of the more popular schools in the borough with only 2.9 applications per place (Butler and Hamnett 2011: 178). Those from poorer socioeconomic backgrounds, or who live in social housing, cannot exercise the much vaunted 'choice' through mortgage and ensure that they live in the catchment areas of the best state schools. As Tomlinson (2005) has argued, despite the rhetoric of New Labour promoting social justice and equity, '...contradictory policies in education, particularly market policies which encourage parents and students to compete for good schools and educational resources, and allow for the further segregation of social and ethnic groups, do not ensure justice and equity' (2005: 167).[8]

This broader picture of inequality in education impacts on the lives of the Muslim girls (and children) in areas targeted by the role models road show, which are necessarily areas with high concentrations of Muslims and where there is likely to be ethnic or social segregation on spatial lines.

Significantly, in the EMW initiatives there is little recognition that the lives of 'young British Muslim women are inscribed by gender relations and class structures' (Dwyer 2000: 476). For example, there is no consideration of discrimination, whether that is: in the way (Muslim) girls are taught at schools; how they may be stereotyped by their teachers (Basit 1997b); or the type of careers advice that is given to them; or, finally, most importantly perhaps at the point of entry to the labour market. As girls, in any case, they are subject to a gendered education. While no longer solely educated for the purposes of domesticity, access to education alone is not sufficient; content is gendered and there is a bias away from science thus affecting labour market opportunities (Pascall 1996: 130).[9] Equally, as Muslim girls of predominantly South Asian origin, there is the legacy of being regarded as the 'image of passivity' which makes them both 'ideal students' on the one hand, while simultaneously casting them as pupils on whom education is ultimately wasted on the other (Cole 2009: 45). Furthermore they are classed subjects for whom their class positioning will affect their labour market successes. One respondent told me:

> they don't want people from a working class background you know, I had a shit education in South London, you know, a really shit education, so I didn't go to the top universities... (Nazneen)

Assuming a process of rational self-actualisation explicit in aspirational citizenship (Raco 2009), the presence of racism and discrimination would themselves lead to particular outcomes, which might be described as 'non-aspirational' aspirations. Dale et al in their extensive study conclude by saying that it is 'of vital importance that the labour market provides these young women with job opportunities at a level commensurate with their abilities and qualifications' (2000: 28). Youth unemployment and a substantial gender pay gap still exist and, therefore, it is hardly surprising that as higher education becomes increasingly privatised, it makes less economic sense for certain people to go to university. Furthermore, as the 2007 EOC report *Moving on Up: Ethnic Minority Women at Work* showed, Pakistani and Bangladeshi women graduates are around five times more likely to be unemployed than their white counterparts because of discrimination.[10] There is therefore a strong case for undertaking further research into Muslim women's experience of discrimination (and ways of tackling such discrimination).

Indirectly, the road show was also in part about showcasing high profile Muslim women in order to combat stereotypes about Muslim women which might contribute to discrimination. Helen, who managed the road show, explained that the third target audience was the 'general public' and countering stereotypes underlying any discrimination. The DCLG Women's Liaison Officer explained that the project 'started out as being about getting more positive images of Muslim women in the media', in an effort to 'showcase influential Muslim women'. While at a very localised micro level it could be argued that this might have affected employers' perceptions of Muslim women, the scale and emphasis of the project meant that these effects on the 'general public' would necessarily be very limited.

The logic of the road show therefore conforms to a convenient and prevalent discourse which relies on a presumption of parental objection, ignorance or lack of support for their daughters' education. It represents a 'feel-good' response on the part of the organisers that something is being seen to be done. Empowerment is being 'performed'. The road shows were perceived to be the most 'successful' aspect of the EMW initiatives; there were visible outputs such as the road show itself, an accompanying booklet and website, as well as positively filled in feedback forms from the attendees.

What is not clear, however, is the extent to which such events *make a difference*. To what extent can role models compensate for broader more far reaching influences on academic achievement and entry into the labour market? Rather than tackle any structural discrimination which might occur because of class, 'race', ethnicity or religion, simply proffering a role model road show as a solution presumes that any underachievement stems from an unwillingness or inability of girls or young women to engage with education, or enter the labour market. Role models are seen as a 'common sense' solution to this problem, but there is little empirical evidence to support this. It ignores the adverse effects of peer pressure, overt racism, low teacher expectation and stereotyping (D'Souza and Clarke 2005).[11] Current evidence 'offers only limited support for the impact of most interventions aiming to improve outcomes through AABs' (Carter-Wall and Whitfield 2012: 1). Instead such evidence suggests that attainment might be positively affected through: improving the home learning environment; the allocation of funding toward pupils from the poorest backgrounds; and, direct teaching support to children who are falling behind. Goodman and Gregg (cited in Carter-Wall and Whitfield 2012) further add that the links might not be so straightforward; what might appear to be low aspirations might be high aspirations that have been eroded by negative experience. Parental disengagement may in fact arise from disappointment at their inability to provide the necessary support commensurate with their ambitions for their children or secure the effective support of the school.[12]

Mothers and Sons

Having looked at the way in which mothering daughters features explicitly, this section addresses the more implicit way in which the mothering of sons is perceived. As discussed earlier, the corollary of the focus on Muslim women's status within their communities is that Muslim men are simultaneously demonised. They are perceived as uniquely violent and patriarchal; it is women's role as mothers to avert this.

The fact that the 7/7 bombers were 'home-grown' aroused great concern. Much of the ensuing debate was focused at a macro level having prompted much broader discussions about Britishness and integration. Aspects of these themes, however, can also be seen at the micro level in the references to mothering and homemaking. In Chapter 2, Sadiq Khan MP suggested that if women were empowered they could prevent misogyny. By extension, so the logic implied, if they were empowered they could prevent terrorism too. This assumes that only men are singularly at risk of radicalisation. Although Hadiyeh (NMWAG), a former member of Hizb-ut Tahrir, acknowledged that 'there are female suicide bombers' she felt that in Britain and Europe, the trend 'seems to be [that] the men are put up to do the bombing and that is with the consent, support and encouragement of *their* women' (my emphasis). Women were therefore 'just as much a part of that act as the men'. She referred to various reports where it was suggested that:

> ...if it wasn't for their wives or the woman they wouldn't have gone out and done it and women who have that level of anger and that type of psyche of anti-western government and a feeling of wanting to attack – the jihadi mentality – will encourage their men to do that (Hadiyeh)

This is consistent with Bhattacharyya's characterisation of the extremist mother in the discourse of the 'war on terror', in which terrorism 'arises from a perversion of motherly love' (2008: 55). This might also be extended to include 'wifely' or 'uxorial love'.[13]

Ahmed writes how 'a crucial risk posed by migrant cultures is defined as their failure to become British, narrated as their failure to love the culture of the host nation' (2004: 137). Emphasis on home-making could be seen as a gendered variation of the dominant discourse that violent extremism is related to a lack of belonging.[14] Hadiyeh told me that she felt that Muslim women's sense of having made the UK their home was seen as important. In relation to NMWAG and EMW projects, Hadiyeh explained that the projects were about making people "happy" and encouraging people to make the UK their home on the basis that:

> ...if you make your home here, if you participate in your surroundings, your community and government, then you wouldn't want to call for anything else or attack this country, you know, because you see it very much as yours... (Hadiyeh)

Implicit in Hadiyeh's explanation is that women in the British context have sufficient power to either encourage or combat terrorism, even if they are themselves not inspired to commit such terrorist acts themselves. The argument goes that, the more Muslim women feel 'at home', the more they will be galvanised to counter extremist views. In addition it can be argued that the incorporation of women specifically was about getting mothers, wives or sisters to look out for the possibility that their sons, husbands, or brothers may be at risk of radicalisation. It follows that empowered women can contribute to 'community resilience,' either by being able to counter such views, or where that does not work, being emboldened to report anyone who holds such views or engages in suspicious activity to the relevant authorities.[15]

When we discussed whether there was a direct relationship between EMW and Prevent and the role of women, Hadiyeh explained that she thought it was more a long term project "with an unfortunate name". She acknowledged that the "role modelling, arts, capacity building" were not "directly preventing" extremism, they were about "empowering women, personally":

> and hopefully they think that more empowered women... means more confident women, therefore more women are able to influence what's going on in their communities, more women having a say... empowered mothers....can challenge within families, within communities, that's the link, that's the only link, indirect link... (Hadiyeh)

The social policy discourse is based on stereotypes of patriarchal Muslim men, suggesting that women need to be empowered to counteract patriarchy.[16] In contrast to this stereotype, the reality presented by respondents was more complex. More often than not, rather than representing an over bearing presence, it was the *absence* of fathers that was highlighted as a problem. Kalsoom makes a specific reference to absent fathers and this is corroborated by Khalida who explained that, in her area of Brent in north-west London, there were "a lot of absentee fathers in the community". She attributed this to the fact that:

> most Muslim men tend to do unskilled or semi-skilled work and they tend to do work which has very antisocial hours, so like mini-cabbing or working in restaurants or factories or things like that (Khalida)

Absent fathers might apply in any number of scenarios (although clearly in the upper echelons of white society this absence is never regarded as a problem; only women's absence matters, irrespective of class). The reference to absent fathers was accompanied by fear about the impact this had on families more generally, but also the extent to which radicalism or extremism might become more appealing as a result. Although many respondents were positive about the road show, a number thought that role models were in fact more important for boys. Fajer told me that:

> I seriously think that should be done, I think that's really needed, really needed for young men, that so lack role models and have nobody to look up to, most of the time they can't even look up to their parents because they're not maybe properly educated, they're not doing anything, you know... (Fajer)

Khalida told me that Muslim men in Brent had very little to do with their children and therefore as a result:

> there is a disconnect between, often between the children and the fathers; very, very dangerously between fathers and sons which then leads young boys to look for father figures because they don't have that in their family (Khalida)

Humera added:

> ...The problem with boys is, often they have absent fathers for whatever reason, they don't have positive role models and ...er they because it's that male gene of not being too introspective (slight laugh) right? Whereas women tend to be a little bit more introspective. They don't therefore have the skills in order to work it out for themselves, because of all the factors in their lives. I think they become de-skilled. Right? (Humera)

Less sensationally, while government focus is on mothers, both Humera and Yasmin spoke about outreach work they had done with fathers too. Humera told me An-Nisa had been involved with a project with Muslim fathers for the Fatherhood Institute. She described how she:

> ...went as a Muslim woman to these men so I was very conscious of all the different things...[and I]...just listened to what they had to say. I felt the report is a reflection of their feelings, you know, and shows Muslim men in a much more...err... normalising them. A lot of this academic stuff I think pathologises people more than it normalises them (Humera)

Similarly, Yasmin explained how she had been involved in conducting focus groups with young and old Muslim men in Waltham Forest in 1998–99, describing how they were happy to be involved and "were really open about... relationships with women, not just with intimate partners but with their mothers, with their grandmothers...". She remembers it as "really open and...free flowing" and although some attendees "were a bit circumspect", overall she had found it to be "a really interesting event". It might be argued, as is clear in feminist critiques of social policy (Pascall 1997), that the state perpetuates retrograde gender relations in the family. Humera and Yasmin's accounts show that at least some Muslim women activists have possibly been more progressive in that regard.

Many of the respondents told me that they, and other Muslim mothers they knew, lived in fear for their sons too. Humera described it as "a sort of depression" or paranoia among mothers which meant that:

> ...particularly with boys, teenage boys, [they] don't allow them to go anywhere, don't want them to do anything. They either completely lose control because they themselves are in a bad way so therefore they can't handle it. (Humera)

Others raised concerns about sons going away to university and coping as non-drinkers in a very alcohol-centric environment; about anti-Muslim racist insults on the football pitch; about anger at detention under anti-terror legislation, and fear for their safety from racial harassment. As Yasmin explained:

> ... my son had been attacked after the bombing; he doesn't have a beard, he doesn't wear a jilbab or anything, he's just Asian, as he would say (Yasmin)

In relation to the role model road show empowerment is individualised. Despite the liberatory 'feminist' rhetoric of empowerment, the emphasis on mothering which permeates the policy discourse is hardly transformative. Rather it reflects a wider arena of a patriarchal system in which 'men control women as daughters, much as they control their sons, but they also control women as the mothers of men's children...it is women's motherhood that men must control to maintain patriarchy' (Rothman cited in Forcey et al. 1994: 141). Specifically, at the level of education, there is emphasis on individual aspiration and effort at the expense of wider societal factors. The wider social policy framework within which EMW sits is predicated on the idea of Muslims as a pathologised community; an enemy within, which requires civilising (see Chapter 2). As such, many of the debates and discussions are about cultural barriers to empowerment. The following chapter analyses these in greater depth. The next section, however, discusses how the theme of 'cultural' barriers impinges on individual mothers.

Community Barriers and Communal Mothering

During the London role model road show none of the mothers indicated that they themselves individually had any objections to their daughters seeking academic or career success. Many did, however, refer to real and imagined fears about what the 'community' might think and were concerned their daughters might get bad 'reputations'. Negative attitudes were therefore projected on to 'the community'. This suggests the presence of collective barriers or collective disempowerment.

Research participants reflected how perceived community attitudes could work unfavourably against educated girls. Almeena's story shows how, despite her parents' supportive attitudes to her education and career choices, she and her parents were not immune from judgements by 'the community'. Almeena described how her parents had to contend with 'people in the community' questioning their daughter's achievements, given her Cambridge education and job as a TV journalist, and the perceived lack of morality particularly associated with being on TV. This tallied with what Kalsoom had told me, that young women who were getting "themselves an education were finding it really difficult to find marriage partners within their Muslim community" because she said that:

> ..the young men all want to marry who their mum wants them to marry, or they want them to go abroad and it's...you've got highly intelligent women unable to find marriage partners erm because the Muslim community is so judgemental in what they're looking for. (Kalsoom)

This is consistent with the idea that higher education for girls may be frowned upon and that there may be some justification in fearing the views of the 'community'. Fauzia Ahmad (2012) highlights the possible tensions (for British South Asian Muslim women specifically) between the idea that holding a degree for Muslim women confers greater choice in matrimony and the lived realities around difficulties in meeting suitable partners when factors such as increased age or being 'over-qualified' become significant. Ahmad argues that processes of social change are fluid and subject to continual negotiation and renegotiation and are contingent instead upon localised, personalised, religious and transnational interpretations and influences (Ahmad

2012). Anecdotally, Kalsoom suggested that as a result Muslim women were increasingly marrying 'Western' converts to Islam. Importantly, however, the existence of these views has not prevented either Almeena or the girls Kalsoom is referring to getting an education. In fact, Almeena's parents' support for her career and education, despite hostile views from within 'the community', shows the diversity therein.

Many of the respondents' comments reiterated the stereotypes of Muslim women as 'victims of culture' which populate the social policy discourse. This can be seen in the idea that girls specifically are seen as the site of struggle. When I asked why role models were only required for Muslim girls, Almeena told me that, even though boys should not be ignored, given that "boys do tend to underachieve... [and]...girls are far more competitive and motivated in school", she felt that ... "*culturally*, where girls have been and how they're pushed is very different from what it is now". Similarly, although Fajer acknowledged shared experiences between boys and girls and Muslim and non-Muslim girls, she suggested that Muslim girls experience "a little more difficulty":

> ...because their parents have come from different countries and their parents are more scared, and try to protect the girls more than your normal white parents would do, basically, and they're trying to hold onto their culture as well so badly.

The concept of communal mothering is based on the premise that different communities are seen to be at different stages of 'development'. There are historical antecedents of these initiatives in the UK context among different diasporic communities. Susan Tananbaum, for example, has written about the way this idea of communal mothering worked for the Jewish community in London at the start of the 20th century. Although not formally instigated or sanctioned by government, she explains how a 'native born, established, and largely middle class, Jewish community' were involved in 'communal mothering' through voluntary, Jewish sponsored, social service programs in an effort to 'anglicise immigrant girls and their mothers...training them to be good citizens' (cited in Glenn 1994: 312).

This resonates with the discussion in Chapter 3 that different communities make progress or advance in different ways and that potentially there was scope for Bradford's Pakistani community to learn from other Pakistani communities in other cities. This idea was discussed more explicitly by Hadiyeh who explained how:

> people whose parents came back in 70s or 60s or whatever, we've been brought up here and have done very well, taken advantage of going to university, getting a good job....we're pretty much sorted in that area.[17] (Hadiyeh)

As a result, therefore, she argued that second generation Muslims could be used as role models "for those who are quite new to Britain and don't understand the dynamics". In this way different sets of Muslim women are positioned against one another; new immigrants are positioned against longer established groups, even though there may be different factors influencing their differential experiences or degrees of 'empowerment' other than the length of time they have been in the UK. These second generation women were positioned against:

> some of the newer immigrants who have come from Bangladesh and Somalia they...[...].... still live in a very closed circle and have separated themselves off from the rest of society in a way because they've got their shops, they've got their schools, they've got their madrassahs, everything all contained and it's about getting to them. (Hadiyeh)

It could be argued that the shops, schools and madrassahs, which for Hadiyeh indicate a lack of integration, represent better and longer established communities, rather than newer communities. Khalida, for example, thought a lack of infrastructure indicated a reluctance to settle or integrate. What is absent from this interpretation, however, is that these 'original' migrants, who are assumed to be integrated (notwithstanding what that means in practice), managed to become integrated without the presence of such policy initiatives. Their different 'starting positions' on arrival and the impact this has had on 'integration' are not taken into account as having any explanatory value.

Hadiyeh, however, also mentioned "some of the other quite closed communities like Bradford's Pakistani communities" who, in spite of their long-established presence in the UK, she argues, remain closed off, disempowered and in need of such initiatives. Again, possible reasons for why Bradford's Muslim community may still be seen as requiring empowerment, despite its long established presence in the UK, are not explored. The position of Bradford's Pakistanis is 'ethnicised' (Mirza and Meetoo 2007) and any discussion of the socio-historical or geo-political context within which migration and settlement has occurred and which might explain their current status is absent (Bujra and Pearce 2011). Hadiyeh's description is consistent with Adeeba's position, outlined in

Chapter 3, that problems attributed to the 'Muslim community' were essentially about Bradford's Pakistani population which has become an emblematically problematic Muslim community. Notably, where I tried to explore ideas of differences *within* the 'Muslim community' with interviewees, such as those based on socioeconomic class or regional variations (which might at least partially explain different communities' positioning or 'development'), I was overwhelmingly met with bewilderment.[18]

This maternalistic role of longer established migrant communities towards newer arrivals is consistent with the way that EMW initiatives rely on engaging with Muslim women primarily as mothers; as cultural reproducers of the nation, or more aptly, as cultural reproducers of a 'pathologised community within'. This sense of patronage among, for example, the middle class Pakistani women living in the suburbs of Bristol which Kalsoom discussed (see Chapter 3) could be interpreted as internalised dominant racist discourses combined with a fear of being mistakenly associated with these newer Muslims who 'bring the religion into disrepute'. It could potentially be motivated by a sense of group shame or what might be called '*vergüenza ajena*' ('Spanish shame') characterised by feelings of ownership, responsibility and solidarity (Iglesias 1996).[19]

There were frequent references to 'culture' and 'cultural barriers' more generally. Hadiyeh (NMWAG) reflected on the idea that 'culture' acted as a barrier to 'empowerment' which, for her, referred to the achievement of academic qualifications and a career. She said that the mothers had 'high aspirations' for their daughters, "it's not like 'no they're going to have to stay at home and get married'." At the same time, however, Hadiyeh suggested that girls "need the support to go out there and follow their, you know, their education and their dreams in a way that is not going to be a threat to their culture as well".[20] This reflects the potential paradox of communal mothering; that the process of integration could be too successful and lead to a loss of culture (Tananbaum 1994).[21]

Hadiyeh also referred to the tension experienced by those girls and their mothers who have those high aspirations, but at the same time "feel that they are pressured by those who hold *very cultural views*" (my emphasis), reflecting the mothers' feedback at the Newham road show. In that context therefore 'empowerment' for those women means, "to, one, go out there and not feel scared to obtain those [and] two, overcome pressures of communities". She perceives that such women are caught between their own desire not to "go against their culture" and those who "hold very cultural views" and might therefore hold them back. In this way, Hadiyeh intimates that there is an acceptable level of 'culture' which permits empowerment, but also suggests that 'culture' might be threatened by too much 'empowerment'. This logic implies a spectrum, with empowerment and culture at opposite ends, fundamentally opposed to one another, but with the possibility of being balanced at the presumed point at which they coincide. Such characterisations interpret culture as always static, necessarily problematic and something 'done' to women, rather than something they constitute, produce or live through. By contrast, as the following chapter shows, the relationship between empowerment and religion is not seen as similarly problematic; uncontaminated by 'culture', religion does not hinder and potentially even facilitates empowerment. This highlights broader debates about whether religion can be experienced or practised outside a socio-cultural context.

Fajer's analysis is more nuanced on the issue of 'culture'. Although she assumes that a monolithic concept of 'culture' could be a barrier ("You know everybody wants to preserve the culture, they don't want to lose that, so I think they have more barriers to break in that sense"), for her it is not an exclusively 'Muslim' thing and she extends this concern to other BME communities, such as the Chinese community in Manchester:

> ...So that's why I think kids have got this added thing to do now where they have to hold on to their culture, understand what their own identity is and you know make their parents understand what they want to do (Fajer)

Although Fajer's comments are more nuanced than Hadiyeh's, she continues to speak about culture in terms of common sense discourses (as something which needs to be preserved or overcome), despite her own experience. Fajer had come to the UK from Pakistan a decade before (at the time of interview). Although she refers to not wanting to lose her 'culture', it is not clear that her own experience of her 'culture' entailed unsupportive or obstructive parents, which she attributes to BME parents more generally. Speaking about her own experiences of growing up in Pakistan, she explained that she had been involved in helping her mother who was involved in charity work. She told me that she was allowed to do things many other young girls were not. Furthermore, her thoughts about how she was bringing her children up in fact indicate a different interpretation of culture. She herself did not see any conflict between 'preserving culture' and educational aspiration, success and employment (and did not envisage any such conflict for her children either). Despite her contradictory statements she still identified a shared common culture between her own family and that of the families she deals with in Manchester.

Conclusion

This chapter has illustrated that analysis of the role models road show defines empowerment in neoliberal terms. Just as neoliberal development discourses have (mis)appropriated feminist language and emancipatory goals (Cornwall et al 2008)[22], individualistic liberal feminism 'has been absolutely incorporated into political and institutional life' in the UK in lieu of a more transformative politics (McRobbie 2009: 7). This can be seen in the way that the 'agentic self is valorised' (Daly 2011: 17) in the role models road show. As Yuval Davis and Anthias (1989) argue the reproduction of culture within national and ethnic collectives primarily falls upon women, serving to reinforce particular constructions of gender roles and femininity. The focus is therefore on Muslim women as mothers ensuring their daughters' academic success through sufficiently high aspirations. Structural inequalities that Muslim women may experience as a result of their socio economic position or citizenship status, which are exacerbated by regional variations, are not seen as something which needs to be dealt with collectively; such influences are instead subsumed within the discourse of aspirations. Furthermore, inequalities in education and society more widely, and discrimination at the level of careers services and entry into and within the labour market are obscured. This chapter concluded with a discussion of how the 'community' is referred to in abstract terms as a barrier which mothers might face in striving for educational and employment success.

This chapter has also examined how the Muslim woman is engaged with principally as a mother. This engagement rests on the assumption that women will only engage politically as mothers. Yet, as hooks argues, although the home can be a site of resistance, by 'romanticizing motherhood, employing the same terminology that is used by sexists to suggest that women are inherently life affirming nurturers, feminist activists reinforce central tenets of male supremacist ideology' (Cited in Forcey 1994: 363). Although ostensibly at the heart of this project is the will to 'civilise' the Muslim population into embracing secular feminism, what is also curious to note is the way in which the romanticisation of motherhood is in fact consistent with certain aspects of Islamic discourse. As Peteet (1997) illustrates, despite its reputation for the treatment of women, the status of mothers is exalted in Islam.

This theme of Islamic feminism is one which will be developed further in the following chapter.

Notes

[1] I do not discuss the work stream related to civic participation but Chapter 5 discusses the themes of representation and political participation

[2] In fact these ideas are constitutive of the very foundations of the Welfare State. The Beveridge Report includes the following 'in the next thirty years housewives as mothers have vital work to do in ensuring the adequate continuance of the British race and the British ideals in the world' (1942: 53) cited in Pascall (1997: 12)

[3] Although it could be argued that YMAG was implicitly focused on boys since 'youth' tends to refer to males unless specified otherwise.

[4] The trope of the Muslim woman does not fit easily into this argument. This postfeminist analysis is predicated on a particular middle classed whiteness. The asexual, repressed sexuality of Muslim women is in sharp contrast to these postfeminist hegemonies. Muslim feminists are regarded as acceptable because of the virulence of patriarchy in their religion. Muslim women can afford to be defeminised because of their religiosity. McRobbie's critique illustrates the (white) empowered postfeminist woman as characterised by aggressive individualism and hedonistic female phallicism in the field of sexuality. By contrast Muslim women's position as individuals in the neoliberal framework is different. Motherhood is glorified and reflects the culturally essentialised position of woman as always mothers and peacemakers.

[5] As well as inviting parents directly via the letters sent out by the schools, local community organisations were invited to bring parents along to the event. The road shows were open to men as well as women, to enable male relatives to attend if they wished to do so (Equal to the Occasion 2010: 13).

[6] Of course, she only interviewed Muslim women already in HE (higher education) rather than those who had not been able to attend.

[7] The phasing out of EMA (educational maintenance allowance) grants has disproportionately affected BME students and there will be major consequences for Black learners in FE (further education) and their ability to participate in and benefit from higher education (Mamon 2011).

[8] Recently, through the creation of academies, some local authorities have forced the integration of schools with majority white and ethnic minority pupil cohorts in response to fears about self-segregation and insufficient community cohesion, following riots in northern towns in 2001 (Burnley, Blackburn, Leeds and Oldham). This has led to increased racial attacks and a 'white backlash' (Miah 2012).

[9] This could even suggest that parents' instrumentalism in encouraging girls to do a narrow range of subjects is progressive! This also leads to potential discussions about the value of single sex education. On one level it is widely accepted that single sex education is good for girls whereas where this occurs in religious schools the presumption is that this must be disadvantageous. Furthermore, equality in access to the labour market does not lead to equality of outcome in the labour market. Non-paid work gender imbalances affect many women's experiences.

[10] The report also concluded, in relation to Bangladeshi, Pakistani and Black Caribbean women overall (not just graduates) that 'Those who want to work are finding it more difficult to get jobs, progress within them and are more likely to be

segregated into certain types of work, despite leaving school with the same career aspirations as white girls and similar or better qualifications than white boys'.

[11] Even D'Souza and Clarke (2005), the authors of a book dedicated to setting out the biographies of inspirational black and ethnic minority role models reluctantly recognise these external influences.

[12] Having listened to a number of the role models' presentations, the ones which aroused most attention were the more unusual and glamorous careers. While possibly inspirational, they are by no means practical. If your parents do not know someone who works in BBC Wales, a law firm, and so on, it is difficult to know how to get access to those positions.

[13] This can be seen in the case of Bouchra El Hor, the Dutch wife of Yassin Nassari who was convicted of terrorism offences in July 2007. Headlines at the time included 'Wife "urged man to die a martyr"' (BBC News Online) and 'Wife cleared of hiding husband's terror plans' (www.telegraph.co.uk) According to these reports, the prosecuter, Aftab Jafferjee said, 'His wife was not only aware of his intention but positively encouraged it, despite the fact that his actions would almost certainly result in his death in some form of combat and would also result in their son being without a father.'

[14] Devadason (2010) based on a study in north London suggests a sense of belonging is not evenly accessed by different ethnic groups.

[15] This can be linked to John Reid's comments about parents being 'taught' to spy on their children (Batty 2006; Travis 2006) (see Chapter 2).

[16] This is in contrast to the way that African Caribbean families have been portrayed, where an excess of matriarchy is deemed to be problematic.

[17] It is interesting how Hadiyeh uses the term 'we' since she has already told me she is a convert, albeit of South Asian origin, thus highlighting the easy slippage between ethnicity and religion

[18] Brah and Phoenix, citing Sayer (2002) have remarked that 'the manner in which class is discussed in political, popular and academic discourse has radically changed to the point that…some sociologists have found it embarrassing to talk to research participants about class. This tendency is also evident in government circles as when the discourse on child poverty comes to substitute analysis of wider inequalities of class' (2004: 18).

[19] In this context there are comparable historical parallels. Tananbaum noted how middle class established Jewish women volunteers were motivated by 'their concern with anti-Semitism, Judaism's requirement of caring for the less fortunate, feelings of ethnic solidarity, and appreciation of the commonality of experiences among women of different classes' (in Glenn 1994: 315).

[20] In this way, she too iterates early 20th century middle class Jewish concerns about 'cultural preservation' (Tananbaum in Glenn 1994).

[21] Although in the context of turn of the century Jewish East End accounts, Tananbaum refers to Anglicisation rather than integration.

[22] For example, it has been argued (with the development programmes) that such neoliberal approaches reproduce and reinforce conservative notions of womanhood and of women's role in the family.

SIX

A community of communities: privileging religion

> Women are currently being disempowered through the very discourses of empowerment they are being offered as substitutes for feminism (McRobbie 2009:49)

> It doesn't take a rocket scientist to see that some interpretations of religion, all religions, not just Islam, are not necessarily favourable to women (Yasmin)

> You're right, what's the definition of empowerment? Economic empowerment, intellectual empowerment, cultural empowerment, you know what kind of empowerment are we talking about here? (Almeena)

Introduction

This chapter develops the theme of collective forms of (dis) empowerment in the form of cultural barriers in greater depth, focusing on the way in which religion is positioned as both disempowering, but also as potentially empowering. The broader Prevent agenda incorporates Huntington's thesis (1993) of the 'clash of civilisations' and, despite emphatic disavowals to the contrary, the discourse suggests that the roots of violent extremism and terrorism lie in Islam itself. Problematic interpretations of Islam are seen as responsible for Muslims' marginalisation. In relation to women this logic is best exemplified by 'building faith capacity' or the 'theological interpretation' strand of the work of NMWAG (National Muslim Women's Advisory Group).

Cultural differences in religious practice arising from ethnic differences were seen by respondents as a source of contamination of a pure Islam which was compatible with women's empowerment. This framing was persuasive, particularly in understanding problematic so-called 'cultural practices', such as forced marriage which are seen as the result of a culturally determined aberrant version of Islam. In this way, Islam itself is not at fault, rather cultural interpretations of it are to blame. Therefore, as well as being the problem, religion is also posited as the solution. At the government level this can be seen in the quest to fix the 'right type of Islam' through NMWAG's theological interpretation project and this chapter examines how this project was received. It also discusses respondents' views regarding Islam as a potential source of empowerment. The NMWAG-led initiative was supported by some respondents in principle but its impact was not far reaching. This chapter argues that this emphasis on religion as a collective source of (dis)empowerment has negative consequences in terms of privileging religiosity. Further it reflects on the myriad ways in which research participants interpret and utilise the terms religion, race, culture, and ethnicity; ways that are sometimes consistent with the social policy discursive formations and sometimes resistant.

The 'problem with Islam' and cultural contamination

Social policy discourses around the EMW initiatives and associated policy areas rely on Orientalist tropes about Muslim women and religious essentialism in order to make the case for empowering Muslim women. This section examines whether respondents thought there was something specific about being a Muslim and Islam which contributed to Muslim women's disempowerment. Despite recognition of commonalities with other non-Muslim women, many respondents felt that there were specific factors affecting Muslim women. Shaista, stated that:

> all women need empowering and not even just ethnic minority women. You only have to look at the political landscape there's not even...enough white women in politics there's 20% of MP's are women and it should be 50% so *all* women need empowering (Shaista)

She thought, however, that Muslim women need empowering "a bit more than white women". This was due to the straightforward view that Muslim women were first and foremost disadvantaged because Islam, or at least the way it was interpreted and practised, was uniquely patriarchal among religions (Kumar 2012). I was told that Muslim women suffered, "particular disadvantages that are unique to them because of their faith." The following comments from respondents further illustrate this:

> with Muslims [the problem] is a lot of men use Islam and misinterpret Islam...so therefore they [Muslim women] face a lot of internal barriers within the community, things that perhaps other Asian women don't. Like, for example, polygamous marriages. It's not really happening in Sikh and Hindu communities so those need to be challenged, right?

> Sometimes Muslim men try to use ... an Islamic verse in the Quran to justify domestic violence and they're wrongly misinterpreting that verse so there's issues like that...

> if you look at forced marriages even though it's a South Asian thing... you only have to look at the statistics from the Foreign Office to see there's high proportion of Bangladeshis and Pakistanis on there; the Indians make up a small proportion. So what is it about Pakistanis, what is the commonality? It's their faith, isn't it?

When Almeena, a BBC journalist who was one of the national role models, described what disempowerment meant to her, she relied on stereotypes about Asian and Muslim women not being able to access local services because they were not "allowed out of the house" or did not have very good English.[1] She added that, "the Muslim community itself, what help do they provide their own people, you know? It's a very patriarchal society still, very patriarchal." For Almeena this meant that there was a specific case for focusing on girls on the road show because, "there was some kind of notion that denying girls' access to education or further education or not letting them go is somehow religiously justified." This is despite the fact that Muslim boys do worse at school than Muslim girls and in fact is contradicted by girls' academic attainment levels.[2] Such responses conform to the view that Islam is a uniquely patriarchal religion and that Muslim women and girls warrant special attention. This is consistent with the dominant social policy discourse which is imbued with a rescue paradigm in relation to Muslim women.

While recognising the supposedly unifying effects of shared religious affiliation, the issue of diversity within the Muslim community (and potential problems arising from that diversity) was also frequently invoked by respondents. These differences were principally deemed to be 'cultural'; as Almeena said:

> you can't just band Muslims together as if we're one ... homogeneous group because we're not. *Culturally* there's so many different types of Muslim and within Muslims, you know...it's just easier to stereotype and categorise people because that's the way you can put them in that box and it's just not, when you look at it, the complexities are far greater.... [my emphasis]

In academic literature, culture and religion are frequently regarded as interchangeable or, at the very least, intimately linked. Kurtz, for example, argues that 'any given religion is also part of a people's culture' and, even in a secular state, he argues that religion constitutes at least 'a part of the culture' (2007:12). Equally, 'culture and faith are structured by and in turn structure the cultural, institutional and deliberative landscapes through which they are articulated' (Back et al 2009: 2). In relation to this policy sphere, and as research participants' responses suggested, however, the relationship between culture and religion (principally in relation to Islam) is conceptualised rather differently. The problem lies with the fact that, even though Quranic text is regarded as sacred, the unmediated 'word of God' (Jacobson 1998), the 'fundamentally egalitarian nature of Islamic debate lends itself to differences in religious practice and differences in social profile of distinctive congregations of particular mosques' (Back et al 2009: 9). Rather than faith and culture being interchangeable, they are seen as discrete entities. Respondents frequently positioned 'culture' as problematic, reflecting wider discussions about the pitfalls of multiculturalism, whereas by contrast religion emerged as something distinguishable from culture and therefore potentially a source of empowerment. Problematic 'cultural' interpretations are therefore regarded as contaminating an authentic pure version of Islam which is deemed to exist outside of culture.

This can be seen in the way that forced marriage was discussed by respondents. As demonstrated previously, so called 'cultural practices' such as forced marriage and honour related violence have been conflated with violent extremism in the Prevent agenda. Consequently, forced marriage has come to be widely accepted as a uniquely Muslim crime. Humera described, for example, how "there's a generic view that this is endemic in the whole Muslim community", such that in public policy "all it sees when it sees Muslim women is forced marriages, domestic violence or all that". Furthermore these discourses were not generally resisted among respondents. Yasmin suggested there was:

> a contradiction between, I mean they launched the violence against women strategy today erm so on one hand they've done more than I think any previous government in terms of that whole gender advance...erm but you've got the faith agenda running alongside. You know we've got the anti-abortionists in America... (Yasmin)

Even if Islam is deemed principally to blame, forced marriage is not perceived to be prevalent across *all* Muslim communities. What was clear from participants' responses was the idea that particular ethnic communities were associated with particular Muslim 'crimes'. Earlier on in the chapter, for example, Shaista referred only to Pakistani and Bangladeshi Muslims in relation to forced marriage. Humera, for example, referred to "all these Kurdish families where other than Pakistani that's where you hear [about]...these situations". (Although she associated this to their "traumatised past" and her experience is situated in the context of Brent). Notably, however, forced marriage is not perceived to occur widely among other Muslim communities such as Somali, North African or Arab communities, again contradicting Shaista's assertion that forced marriage and honour related violence were uniquely Islamic crimes. By contrast, issues such as FGM are more associated with non-South Asian Muslims.

The outcome of this stance understates the incidence of forced marriage and 'honour related violence' among non-Muslim women. Domestic violence is underreported and particularly so by BME (black and minority ethnic) women (Gill 2004 cited in Anitha 2008). As Anitha (2008) argues in relation to BME women, however, the focus of policy attention is often on the women themselves and their 'culture', rather than any inadequacy in service response. Brittain et al (2005) showed that whereas on average a woman facing domestic violence had to make 11 contacts with agencies before getting the help she needed, in the case of BME women, this figure rose to 17. In addition, even within BME groups, it is clearly not just Muslim women who experience domestic violence; Shahien Taj's organisation in Cardiff, the Henna Foundation, which dealt with domestic violence and forced marriage, served both Sikh and Muslim women,[3] while SBS (Southall Black Sisters), itself an avowedly secular organisation, deals with a wide spectrum of women, both Muslim and non-Muslim.

Building faith capacity and Islamic feminism; turning up religious self confidence

> Before the summer, we will organise a series of roundtables with academics, theologians and community leaders to stimulate debate on this important issue and to gain an understanding of why women are sometimes not allowed access [to mosques]. We will then support and encourage local communities to help break down these barriers" (DCLG 2007: 10)

That religion, or specifically the right type of Islam, can potentially counter violent extremism is a view clearly exemplified in a number of work streams in the Prevent agenda. Within the EMW this imperative is combined with the discourses of maternalism, which position Muslim women as cultural reproducers and as the victims of a uniquely misogynistic religion. Religion here becomes a specific solution for women, and is exemplified in the faith capacity project (theological interpretation). This overtly positions (a) corrupted version(s) of Islam as a collective barrier to Muslim women's success. The theological interpretation project is about ensuring that the right type of Islam is promulgated and assisting reform 'from within'. Islam is therefore framed as at once oppressive and potentially liberatory depending on how it is interpreted.

Among respondents there was an acceptance that Muslims needed to 'get their house in order' and that a perverted or corrupted version of Islam was at fault. When Kalsoom had to explain to her Sikh colleagues in Bristol why Muslims needed additional support she had to argue that:

> people are using religion as an excuse to alienate themselves from the wider community...once we ... put across that... this is not what Islam teaches...then we can go back to, you know, more cohesion work with other communities, but at the moment the Muslim community here have set themselves apart, they're using religion as that excuse and we've got to start all over again if you like (Kalsoom)

Kalsoom's justification, which suggests that there is a particular version of Islam which is more compatible with cohesion, implies that segregation or marginalisation is the result of following a particular isolationist version of Islam.[4] Such interpretations do exist and some people may believe and act on them. Equally, such an argument ignores more structural factors, such as employment patterns or housing policies that might also contribute to some Muslim communities' spatial isolation or segregation (Finney and Simpson 2009).

In relation to women's rights, the rationale for the theological interpretation reflects the Islamic feminist position, in which religion is potentially empowering for women; that Islam can be a source of strength for women and a tool for negotiating against restrictions that might be imposed on them (Macey 1999[5]; Dwyer 1999; Mahmood 2005, Phillips 2007), even if 'such choices [are] made within social, economic and cultural formations' (Dwyer 2000: 484).[6]

Kalsoom was one of the NMWAG members involved in the theological interpretation work stream. When we spoke (April 2010) the project had just been commissioned and the output would be a two day seminar attended by scholars from all across the world. She was optimistic and described how

> ...the aim was to use religion as a tool for social change. We realised that actually a lot of women really did not know the erm rights that women, that Islam gives them...and we really thought, well we'll turn it on its head and use religion, you know, to empower us. (Kalsoom)

The issues that she expected to come up included marriage, for example, whether Muslim women can marry non-Muslim men or 'people of the book' ("you know, there are grey areas and nobody's brave enough to actually say..."). When I asked her whether the eventual aim was to have a definitive view she told me that it was "a scholarly based approach" aiming to be more like the 'Contextualising Islam' report which was more fluid and discursive (El-Affendi 2009). She told me, "it's about being intelligent and discussing it for God's sake, otherwise we're no better than book burners are we?"

Hadiyeh too was clear about the empowering effects of particular interpretations of Islam. Rather ironically, however, it was in the context of discussing her time as a member of the proscribed group Hizb-ut Tahrir prior to joining NMWAG. Sadiq Khan suggested that because radical Islamic extremists are misogynists, empowering Muslim women would go some way to preventing extremism. He explained:

> But it (women's rights) also has serious consequences for preventing extremism, given that the majority of the extremist and radical ideologies that lead young men to turn themselves into human bombs are also deeply misogynist.

> The Taliban and their barbaric laws towards the women are a good example of this misogyny. (Khan 2008)

Although Hadiyeh was aware that some of the strict Wahabbi groups were very segregated and insisted on particular forms of dress for women, she told me that one of 'the big misconception(s)' about organisations such as Hizb-ut Tahrir were that they were misogynist. Instead, she described how "within the women's group [of Hizb-ut Tahrir] there was a feeling of empowerment, that we could get involved in politics". She went on to explain:

> the men had the respect, of allowing us to do our own thing as well, so we weren't at their command; the men did their thing and the women did our thing; there was some … collaboration, various huge events that pretty much we were in charge of our own thing… (Hadiyeh)

This was particularly resonant for Hadiyeh as a convert, who told me that, as a result, she was able to assert that she came "as an independent person" free from any attachment to a particular community. Instead she felt that she was able to link herself to all diverse Muslim communities. She told me, "I'm part of the Moroccan, part of the Somalian, Pakistani, Bangladeshi… [I am] in all of them…" In this way she reiterates the idea of a 'pure Islam', uncontaminated by ethnic and cultural differences. It was during her time at Hizb-ut Tahrir that she learned that she could:

> …[leave] culture behind, it was the culture that was bringing down the Muslims, we needed a revolution, a political idea, so it empowered women to go out there and have the rights that Islam gives to women and we took those on board

Others were more cynical about the theological interpretation initiative. When I described it as potentially something new, Humera interjected:

> It's not new – we've been working at a theological level for ages, yeah? So…er….you're not going to get, what's the point of it, you're not going to get the people you want to influence theologically, are not going to take anything from a government led women's led theological thing. You are not going to get it. Even if they do something which is spot-on they're not going to do it. Those women aren't

> the sort of women who are going to influence those people that need to be influenced, right? (Humera)

She told me that as an organisation An-Nisa had got "to a point after twenty five years of working continuously in the community and tackling, challenging, to the point that we get taken seriously by what we say". She explained how when she dispensed advice in cases of forced marriage:

> you support the woman…and her key question is, 'am I going to make God angry?' … and [they think] the Koran says 'don't say no…to your parents'…so you have to work, step-by-step, through all of those things with them, to let them know if the circumstances are as they say, they have every right *from an Islamic point of view* to leave that situation; you have to stand up against it, right? But what we've found is the more you turn up their self-confidence religiously and they know that God is not going to punish them or that they're not going to go to hell...they actually develop the confidence to resolve the situation themselves…[my emphasis] (Humera)

The contrasting impact of NMWAG and An-Nisa can be seen in their experiences of engaging with potentially controversial characters. Humera said she had been involved in a scholars' tour with Radical Middle Way, involving Halima Krausen (a 60 year old German convert and 'Europe's leading female Muslim scholar'). She explained that:

> because we'd been promoting her, and all this publicity about her, people know the name, people hear about it, see the connection with us and everything, er, we don't get any trouble whatsoever, right?...we went to different places, mixed audiences, and…she was really well-received.

By contrast, Kalsoom described the controversy prompted by the possible involvement of Amina Wadud, who infamously led a mixed congregational prayer, in the theological interpretation seminar. This revealed a tension between the NMWAG members involved in that work and the 'grassroots' which I explored in chapter 4. When we spoke, Kalsoom told me they were still at the stage of deciding who to invite but she explained that "we felt it was imperative to have grassroots people there as well because it's about looking at, it's in context with issues facing Muslim women today." She explained, however, that such grassroots women "perhaps…don't have the theological perspective…[they] just see the controversy" and she was told that "if we have this woman [Amina Wadud] on this board our local imams will just say, if you have her, you can have dogs on this panel basically".

A slower, steadier and more organic approach may seemingly have proved more productive. Humera explained that because people know that "…we're working within the framework of an Islamic community, Muslim communities and they know the issues that we raise are positively for the benefit of the community" that they did not experience controversy.[7] She told me that they had "to take it strategically, theologically at the level where you can influence people positively." What Kalsoom aspired to achieve in terms of credibility at a top down level could be seen as irrelevant to others. Humera told me how she had been discussing the Contextualising Islam project (on which the EMW theological interpretation project was based) with civil servants at DCLG (Department for Communities and Local Government), "the Muslim advisers". She told them how she had been to a seminar which she had found productive and that it had been different from the usual events because "they had a lot of time for conversation, debate and discussion" but then said to them:

> OK you've done this, what next? 'Oh, nothing.' Well, aren't you going to implement it? What's the point of it? 'Oh no, we can't, we just gave the resources, we want the government to take a back seat on it…we can't force implementation'. So what's the point of the women's one then? (Humera)

The Faith and Fashion project which was described in the opening to the introductory chapter is also premised on accepting the possibility of a multiplicity of views within Islam. I had met Sophia through Hadiyeh at the Three Faiths Forum. Sophia was a white British convert who had spent time in Yemen learning Arabic. On her return to the UK she converted to Islam and worked briefly with Majid Nawaz at the Quilliam Foundation. After leaving there she had started working on devising projects to counter problematic representations of Muslims, particularly Muslim women.

The workshops and school visits I attended were focused on discussing concepts of modesty.[8] Over the period of a school term, speakers of different faiths (Judaism and Christianity) had spoken to the girls about modesty in the context of their particular religions.

During their trip to the Victoria and Albert Museum the girls looked at the rooms displaying the history of fashion. Sophia's guided tour also looked at portraits of men and women through the ages. I recall a particular painting of Puritans which Sophia used to explore the idea of modesty; this was to illustrate modesty as an absence of ostentation and showed how it applied equally to men and women. In her conversations with the class I noted how she was very open with the girls about her own (self-confessed) low level of knowledge about Islam. She was also very clear that she was not telling them what they should think, only that they should recognise that there were a variety of views regarding what modesty might constitute. When we discussed the project she had explained to me that she wanted,

> to create a safe space where we could look at why some Muslim women have chosen to interpret some verses of the Koran to support the burka and opening up that space allows opportunities for other choices and other interpretations. (Sophia)

This project illustrated the multiplicity of different interpretations that are possible within Islam and was also done in the context of a cross faith based project and so could be seen to be in the interests of cohesion (albeit only with other Abrahamic religions).

Reducing all problems simply to misinterpretations of Islam, however, results in the increasing privileging of religiosity.[9] The next section looks at the negative consequences of characterising empowerment collectively with reference to religion in relation to a broader debate about multifaithism or 'de-secularisation'. There are a number of problematic outcomes ranging from producing a hierarchy of Muslims based on religious practice; contributing to increasing discrimination, both subtle or more overt; and impacting on the potential for solidarity with other marginalised women.

Becoming Muslim

> I did not come into Parliament to be a Muslim MP. And I have never held myself out as a Muslim spokesperson or community leader. Just as ordinary citizens have multiple identities, so do MPs. I am Labour first and foremost. I am also a Fabian, a father, a husband, a Londoner, and yes, of Asian origin and Muslim faith…But no matter how hard I try not to allow my faith to define me as an MP – no matter

> how many times I ask not to have my religion precede my occupation when I am introduced or described – the fact is that others do define me by my faith. (Sadiq Khan 2008: 1)

This quote from a pamphlet, subtitled 'How to reconnect with British Muslims', shows that Sadiq Khan is clearly aware of the ambivalent position he occupies; he recognises his identity and social positioning are multi-faceted, yet acknowledges the burden of responsibility that comes with being regarded as a representative Muslim MP. Only a few pages later, he criticises the Tory party for having appointed Baroness Warsi (2008), suggesting that this appointment was only made so that the Tory Party could claim to have the most senior Muslim in Parliament. Khan seemingly revels in the fact that Baroness Warsi is unelected and criticises her for trying *not* to be seen as just a Muslim politician. Clearly this position contradicts his own, set out in the quote above, in which he has grudgingly adopted the mantel of British Muslim politician, tasked with pontificating about the compatibility of Britishness and Islam. Moreover, his criticisms of Warsi being unelected also seem hollow in the context of the stated *raison d'être* underlying the EMW initiatives and the establishment of NMWAG (see Chapter 4).

Khan's comments highlight the disjuncture between what one thinks one is and how one is considered by others. This section explores this theme in the context of the research participants' reflections; how their ideas of 'the Muslim woman' compared with their own experiences as Muslim women. It discusses the consequences of being defined by others according to one's faith. It can be seen in the way that respondents (and Muslim women more generally) carry the burden of responsibility for being Muslim (in a similar way to which Sadiq Khan describes his experiences of being a Muslim MP). Furthermore, it can also be seen in crude stereotyping, discrimination and hate crime, all of which enact violence (whether symbolic or real) on them as Muslim women (Mohanty 1988). All reflect the way in which the significance of religion is over determined. Much of this has emerged as a consequence of media representations of Muslim women, but social policy framings, such as that entailed in the theological interpretation initiative, have undoubtedly contributed to this phenomenon.

Discrimination: 'others do define me by my faith'

Shaista acknowledged that in addition to the difficulties caused by Islam for women, they were also "more discriminated against than other BME women's groups," arguing that they had to "face multiple discrimination" as a result of their gender, ethnicity and faith. Furthermore, such discrimination was particularly acute for those who appeared visibly as Muslims, as a result of wearing headscarves or veils. The focus of this section is therefore to explore experiences of discrimination, ranging from stereotyping to discrimination in employment and hate crimes.

Few interviewees made an explicit distinction between the idea of 'the Muslim woman' and the reality of 'Muslim women'. Respondents adopted non-oppositional rather than oppositional subject positions (Brah 1996). Although there was an awareness of the insidious effects of stereotypes, there was little self-awareness regarding their potential complicity in this process; thus they frequently reinforced rather than contested the social meanings (Brah 1996) embodied in discourses about the Muslim woman. By contrast, Adeeba notably distinguished between "women who are Muslim" and "Muslim women". Equally, Humera explicitly discussed the discrepancy between the image of Muslim woman and the reality of the Muslim women she knew. She described how:

> when you're in the family, you don't see what people talk about, because it's normal for you, you see strong women, and you see stupid men (laughs) you see a whole range of different types of people (Humera)

She explained, however, that as she had got older, "news affects you more; you suddenly see *this* is what they're saying". She described how in the early 1980s when "niqab-ed women were first coming from the Middle East", she found it difficult to reconcile but realised:

> the way that people are projected and even women that I knew who dressed like that, I know that they're not what the image says. Behind is something else... (Humera)

Being defined by one's faith also impacts upon women who themselves have not experienced any of the cultural or religious barriers which Muslim women are assumed to have faced. I asked Almeena, the Cardiff role model, whether she had experienced any discrimination. Given we were at the Muslim girls role model road show, implicit in my question was whether being Muslim had affected her career. She told me:

> ...at the BBC, the fact that you're a brown face, you're suddenly put forward for big things...you're able to apply for diversity things that nobody else can apply for and you kind of think, My God...but you just take whatever opportunities you can...they're so keen on, you know, rebalancing everything and being seen not to be 'hideously white' as Greg Dyke called it. (Almeena)

Almeena's response illustrates the slippages between ideas of 'race' and religion which are deeply entangled in discussions on anti-Muslim racism. From referring to her "brown face" it is clear that she at least is speaking of her 'race', rather than her religion, when talking about not having experienced discrimination. Despite such positive experiences, she also described how she had been bestowed with the burden of representation (Mercer 1994) of being Muslim through no conscious desire or efforts of her own. After saying that she "had nothing but er...positive experiences," in the BBC, that is, she did not feel she had been discriminated against, she also described how there:

> was a point when I just sort of thought, every time there's a Muslim story or some kind of Asian story, or honour killing story, everyone would turn to me as if I was some kind of expert and I'm like, 'What?'...So, you know, you kind of get over that, you kind of understand that, and then you explain, 'actually I don't know much about that', or you know (Almeena)

This tendency for her ethnic and religious background to shape what she was given to do as a journalist echoes the phenomena, described in Chapter 4, in which the spaces in which Muslim women can speak (or can be heard) is often narrowly defined and delimited externally. Her general feeling that she had not been discriminated against sits in stark contrast to her own conviction that she was a suitable Muslim role model. This was despite not having personally experienced any of the barriers which allegedly hold back Muslim girls on which the entire role models road show was premised (see Chapter 5). This shows a willingness to conform to a positive stereotype of the model minority (namely, to be a role model)[10] whereas when the associations are negative (such as with forced marriage and honour related violence), no such incentive exists. Despite this, and even though she did not wear the veil, she was very aware that appearing visibly Muslim was a disadvantage.

The young hijabi girls at the role model road shows were concerned at how their veil wearing would impact on their future prospects. On one occasion, at the Q and A session of the Cardiff road show, one of the school girls asked Almeena whether she thought there would ever be a newsreader on the BBC who wore the headscarf. Almeena explained to me:

> Yeah, that's a really interesting question. I can't see it happening on mainstream news I mean there was, you know a huge debacle when Fiona Bruce wore her cross, it was recently, and people complained, saying that our news readers should be completely without…you know, so it's… Can you imagine someone with a hijab?...And also, you're on TV, it's about presentation, it's about people being able to see you, you know, I'm not justifying it but I can see… I don't know if ever on mainstream telly there'll be a lady. I hope so. How fantastic would that be? But whether it'll happen I don't know…I hope so, but do I think it will happen? I don't think so…

It is interesting that she places reactions to a cross, a symbol of the main religion of the UK, as equivalent to responses to a headscarf which is symbolic of a minoritised (Gunaratnam 2003)[11] religion which is perceived to be uniquely problematic. She described how she was "stumped" by the question, but tried to be positive and realistic at the same time, again showing the gulf between her and the targets of some of the initiatives.

Humera also told me how "Muslim women, of course will be affected by the generic Islamophobia suffered by the Muslim community as a whole", but added that they were especially vulnerable because "they will get affected by the perceptions of the general public on them because they are the most visible if they are dressed in a particular way." She told me that she observed everyday encounters in supermarkets suggesting that checkout assistants "will be less helpful to these kind of [hijab wearing] women". She added that:

> I've seen drivers when they see a group of Muslims wearing jilbabs I see drivers, er …not slow down, but go faster… so Muslim women are really, really vulnerable if they are visibly Muslim or perceived to be Muslim, right? Because even non-Muslims who look like Muslims, you could even get Jewish women who sometimes wear scarves and do

> whatever. Errr they are targets not because of who they are but because they they're perceived to be Muslims.[12] (Humera)

The Bristol police officers I spoke to told me that Muslim women experienced harassment and hate crime because of their dress. They described how their involvement with the women in Bristol's Muslim communities was partly driven in response to hostility directed at Muslims in Bristol after the 7/7 bombings. They realised there was quite a lot of hate crime being reported. While the police were quite good at responding in terms of engaging with the mosques, they thought that women were being "side-lined" in terms of underreporting hate crime, particularly those wearing headscarves. As a result the police told me they had felt that "there was a need for someone to specifically engage with women in the community".

Throughout my field work I noticed a palpable sense of 'veil-fatigue' permeating many of the discussions. This could be seen, for example, in Adeeba's weary response to my question about what empowerment meant specifically in relation to Muslim women or girls. At that point I had not even mentioned the issue of clothing but the first thing she said to me in response was:

> I'm going to say something here [pause] I think the groups need to stop making a view about niqabs, scarves and covering and all that stuff...I think it needs to be closed and I think the Muslim women have to talk about things that are of wider importance....I'm not saying the hijab isn't important, I'm not saying that the niqab isn't important, but it's about, how do you develop yourself and how do you create a scenario for that particular group which is seen to be broad, it's not stereotyped as being a group that's just linked to the hijab. It certainly is at the moment...(Adeeba)

Adeeba's heartfelt exhortation is commendable in its attempt to move beyond the veil as a defining trope through which Muslim women are viewed and which is a crucial source of discrimination for those that wear it. The association between Muslim women and the veil continues to be perpetuated by politicians, as shown by the Jack Straw episode, and more broadly in the media, irrespective of how many Muslim women and others in the policy sphere may want to move beyond that. The veil is imbued with symbolic power, acting as a very visible marker of difference and regarded as a symbol of gender oppression and self-segregation.

When asked what was specifically Muslim about the issues faced by the women she worked with in Bradford, Adeeba seemed quite perplexed. After a long pause I rephrased the question asking whether we needed the label 'Muslim' if the things that really mattered were education, employment and poverty; what was the value in talking about a Muslim community? After a further extended pause, she replied quite pensively:

> It didn't happen when I was a child, it didn't happen in my teens, it didn't even happen in my twenties and I'm talking about this as a person here who was brought up in a very... traditional Muslim Pakistani family but also, er, was very linked to the white community through their education, through work. But unfortunately I don't think it set out, it set itself out to be labelled as this Muslim community. (Adeeba)

Yasmin felt that these stereotypes were "disempowering". She told me that when she spoke to "older people, [her] mum's generation but also... middle aged women with adult children" they felt that:

> one, that they're excluded from the dialogue and two, all they ever get is criticism, this is Muslim people, that they are criticised on every level, if they're not terrorists, then they're slaughtering animals in an unacceptable way or they're murdering their children... (Yasmin)

She explained that the consequences of this were that the people she was talking about felt there was "no space for them to be actors or take action in a positive way". Nor were they able to explore "finding a new path" that allowed them "to embrace a British identity and a religious identity"; in fact the climate of fear and hostility reinforced the idea of the incompatibility of the two.

Moreover the presumption of religiosity potentially excludes as many as it includes. Islamic identities may be the only opportunity some individuals have for gaining greater freedom, but equally, it may simultaneously limit opportunities for others (Dwyer 2000). For example, it over-determines which women are recruited to particular initiatives or nominate themselves to become involved. I asked Sarah from the Bristol police force how the women that she worked with were recruited to the community events organised by the police. She told me that the women all volunteered to be involved, but that very often they were invited at public meetings "advertised...through the All Mosques Together initiative which is a group of mosques and the representatives that meet".[13] As Yasmin pointed out, however, when community engagement is principally through the mosque, many other people who might describe themselves as Muslims could be excluded. She told me, "a lot of Muslims do not go to the mosque [and] there's... just no acknowledgment that there's anything outside of it."

In addition, the idea of a 'pure religion' contaminated by 'culture' may lead to a hierarchy of Muslimness between different ethnic groups, intersected by 'race' and global positioning. Kalsoom implied that South Asian Muslims started wearing the hijab because that was more akin to the Middle East/Arab version of Islam and therefore 'purer'. Yasmin had also used the term "cultural Muslims" to describe people like her who had grown up as Muslims but are not necessarily (fully) practising (Ruthven 1997). Yasmin had told me that she knew:

> an awful lot of people who fit within that ...you say that you're of Muslim heritage and from a Muslim background you're almost afraid to say that you practise it because maybe you're not practising on a daily basis but erm you haven't got those links through the mosque and through faith leaders and to the wider community (Yasmin)

Yasmin's use of the term 'cultural Muslim' was in the context of not being seen as Muslim *enough* and therefore not representative of 'the Muslim community', and reflects how the wider trend of privileging religion means certain Muslim women become invisible.

From the above it is clear that one unifying characteristic of Muslim women's experience is, at best, being stereotyped or, at worst, being discriminated against or becoming victims of hate crime. What then might empowerment mean? Adeeba explained:

> Can I just say, in terms of the empowering of the Muslim women, I think it's really important... that the agencies, institutions and employers....change their perceptions... because you know we want them to be also thinking about how they see this particular community; that if a Muslim woman does apply for a job, you know the stereotype that I have of her has gone out of the window and they look at that CV on the basis that it's a good CV. (Adeeba)

A siege mentality?

Writing in Bradford in the aftermath of the Rushdie affair, Haleh Afshar observed that 'At times of hardship, particularly when the Muslim community has perceived itself a beleaguered minority, women have had to submit to much greater degrees of restrictions than at times of success and prosperity' (1994:130). Yasmin's account suggests parallel developments in the post 7/7 era. She told me that a siege mentality has emerged in some of the more marginalised communities she has been dealing with over the years. She described how in the 80s, when she was working on what she described as "very taboo issues" within 'the Muslim family', "you had to tread carefully because it was so new" because "the community weren't at the stage where they were ready to talk about things". Over time, however, by the late 90s she felt things had changed, she talked about focus group discussions she'd been involved in, talking to men across different generations and described that they had been very open about their relationships with mothers, daughters and wives and that although there were some people who were "a bit circumspect" on the whole "it was really open and...free flowing". She suggested, however, that "post 9/11 but certainly post 7/7 in the work that I've done...there's been a reluctance to come forward" particularly among women who may be experiencing domestic violence:

> because Muslim people do not want to engage with the police and not because they've got anything to hide but there's this fear of... if we go and talk to them about something that has been happening at home will they start asking me questions about how many times he goes to the mosque, and does he have a beard and all sorts of things? ... not being believed, not being taken seriously but what ..just a few of what the repercussions might be you know, that it's pretty frightening. (Yasmin)

This is not necessarily inconsistent with comments from the police, mentioned earlier, about an increasing willingness to report hate crime. What it could suggest, however, is that, while police engagement might encourage reporting certain crimes, such as hate crime, a community which perceives itself to be under siege may not be so keen to report domestic crimes due to the perennial fear of 'washing its dirty linen in public'. This can, Yasmin suggested, be seen in relation to the impact of a higher profile being given to forced marriage in the public policy arena.

During the New Labour era forced marriage became a cause celebre, becoming the rallying cry of imperial feminists such as Anne Cryer MP. The high profile given to forced marriage in the New Labour era was unsurprisingly welcomed by many BME women's organisations. Yasmin had been a senior advisor to the Metropolitan Police on Forced Marriage. She agreed that the issue had come to greater prominence when the Labour government came to power, even though, as she explained, "work was going on and the work was being done quietly and the work was being done by communities". Accordingly, previously "...the communities were seen as, particularly the women's sector as...the ones with a solution to the problem". Despite government involvement and funding being welcome, it is also clear, however, that the *way* in which this involvement was implemented meant that such 'top down' interventions were not wholly unproblematic.

Not only do such top down interventions perpetuate the idea that Muslim women are victims purely of cultural relativism (Yasmin spoke of "the sensationalisation of it all, the othering"), they also ignore the more nuanced and multi-directional ways in which some BME organisations had been engaging with these issues. When I had asked Pragna how SBS avoided colluding in racist stereotypes about pathological Asian families, she was very clear that SBS was also committed to fighting racism; their approach took into account the intersectional aspects of BME women's lives. By contrast, in relation to forced marriage, Yasmin was critical of the fact that the way it was portrayed changed once the issue got on the broader political agenda. She explained that previously such work "was couched within, the violence against women agenda...clearly set in that context but also racism which nobody wants to talk about now." She told me it was seen as part of a continuum of violence (Kelly 1987). She added, "No one wants to talk about racism or Islamophobia". As Meetoo and Mirza suggest, 'young ethnicised women have become highly visible... problematically contained and constructed in the public consciousness within a discourse of fear and risk posed by the presence of the Muslim alien "other"' (2007:6).

Moreover, this external involvement, if not done sensitively, has potentially been counterproductive. Not only have such interventions been closely associated with immigration control (Anitha 2008), this experience and response of communities already 'under siege' is to make feminism 'other', to make it 'western' rather than look for continuities and solidarity. For example, Dustin and Phillips (2008) have criticised the symbolic use of legislation in lieu of costlier interventions, such as educational initiatives or support work, while at the same time lending them to cultural stereotyping. Yasmin suggested this may have affected how people sought help, to the extent that it may have even "driven the issue underground". This was in part due to the association of some of the forced marriage groups with Prevent. She said she knew of people "in pretty damned awful situations" who "will maybe go to a woman's group, or will go through a religious group, but they're damned if they'll go to the police".

When I had spoken to Humera at An-Nisa about the issue she told me that part of this reluctance to involve the police was that "there is a difference between really the sort of criminal activity of forced marriages and between parents who are in fear of their girls, in particular… going off track". She told me that "what we always argue is: a crime is a crime and therefore it needs to be dealt with". On the other hand, she suggested, "with those families who are actually afraid, you have to tackle them differently". She was adamant that "what they do is categorically wrong", but thought that "the root of what they are doing is fear" which needs to be dealt with. They need to be asked "why are you afraid that she's making a different choice?"

Whither Solidarity?

> Separate electorates, along with reservations and weightages, gave birth to a sense of Muslims being a religio-political entity in the colonial image – of being unified, cohesive and segregated from the Hindus. They were homogenised like 'castes' and 'tribes' and suitably accommodated with political schemes and bureaucratic designs. Self-styled leaders were emboldened to represent an 'objectively' defined community and contend with others for patronage...in this way separate electorates created space for reinforcing religious identities, a process which was, both in concept and articulation, profoundly divisive. (Hasan 1997)

The quote refers to the experience in British India and the lessons here are salutary. The previous section discussed how the tendency to privilege religiosity works to make certain Muslim women more or less visible depending on whether they are seen to count as Muslim. Equally, this trend of privileging religion over 'culture' has had adverse effects on relationships within South Asian communities by working to reduce historically 'cultural' commonalities and obscure potential solidarities[14]. The legacy of a shared South Asian religiously syncretic culture is elided by emphasis on strictly demarcated religious affiliation, particularly where acknowledging this shared history might position South Asian Muslims as inferior to Muslims from the Middle East[15]. In this section I want to examine the consequences of privileging religion on solidarity.

Popular, political and academic discourse associates the splintering between different South Asian communities and the ascendancy of religion as the determining signifier to the Rushdie affair (Malik 2009). During our discussion about the politicisation of religious demands in the context of the post-Rushdie policy landscape, Pragna acknowledged that religion had featured in earlier anti-racist struggles. She distinguished such instances, however, as "cultural religious" (such as the demand for halal meat in schools) as opposed to "pure religious values' terms" (for example, blasphemy laws).[16] Pragna's narrative referenced a halcyon era of black feminists' unity against racism and patriarchy reflected in a diverse range of Black Sister groups across the country. Then the Rushdie affair happened which was accompanied by:

> a serious agenda which was that you know 'as Muslims we want to be recognised, we want our religion to be privileged in the same way that Christianity is privileged'... and that manifested in demands for example to extend the blasphemy law ... more religious schools was the other big demand and of course we've seen that that's kind of now just gathered momentum to the point that we are at, at the moment so the politicisation of religion was not there before...(Pragna)

Pragna's understanding would fit Macey's position that such moves constituted a *demand for special treatment* on the basis of religion (2010: 39). There was clearly a demand among some Muslims for a greater politicisation of religion. Indeed, both Humera and Khalida told me that they had been lobbying for legislation against religious discrimination from the late 1980s onward. They also told me that this had stemmed from their perception that the apparent successes of the anti-racist movement in the 1980s concealed the under-representation of Muslims in civic society from scrutiny (in Brent at least). As such their demands did not necessarily constitute 'special attention', rather they were an attempt to secure equality. That there were calls to widen the scope of the blasphemy law to incorporate Islam is undeniable. This is, however, only a partial view. What also needs to be considered is that asking for Islam to be recognised by existing blasphemy legislation was not necessarily asking for 'special treatment'. It can only be regarded as such if one accepts that only believers in the Church of England are eligible for protection from religious offence. Furthermore, such a request did not preclude other religious groups from demanding the same.[17] Equally, the demand for separate schools also needs to be considered in this context. As Haw (1994) has argued the demand for separate Muslim schools was by no means unanimous and often reflected shortcomings in mainstream schools' responses to religious and cultural demands. This has obvious parallels with the supplementary school movement among black parents, as well as precedents in the form of Roman Catholic and Jewish schools.

Not only do we need to consider the presence of such demands, we also need to look at whether these requests for 'special treatment' were met by those in power and if so, to consider the motivations for this. These developments therefore need to be considered in the context of the wider post-Cold war political landscape. The Rushdie affair did not escalate purely because of book burnings in Bradford, it occurred because of the wider geopolitical environment in which the controversy erupted. By contrast, the 2004 furore over the play *Behzti* which depicted a rape that took place in a gurdwara did not escalate in the same way in the absence of wider global or supra national links, despite public disorder and death threats to the author emanating from the UK (Branigan 2004). At a micro level the growth in Muslim schools was facilitated by the Education Reform Act (1988) which encouraged schools to opt out of local authority control as well as the emerging faith agenda. Equally, the growth in academies and free schools has also facilitated this process (Kulz and Rashid 2014).

It is, therefore, undeniable that there have been profound effects on opportunities for solidarity with other marginalised groups. The historic syncretism of South Asian religions and more recently, experiences of British Asian-ness have in the past formed the foundations of a shared solidarity (Ali et al 2008). While research participants were ostensibly supportive of the idea that Muslim women needed empowering as Muslim women, some were aware of the potential for antagonisms with BME women which might be associated with this. Pragna told me about some protests SBS had been involved in against the EDL in Harrow. As well as telling me she had been disappointed that there had not been more visible support from Muslims, given it was at a mosque, she told me that:

> whereas in the past you would have seen Asians coming out and saying, 'well this is an attack on Asians, you know, it's a

> mosque, but it's an attack on Asians', here it's kind of 'well it's Muslims, they deserve it, they're the trouble makers, they're the terrorists and we Hindus – aren't we wonderful, we're law abiding Hindus', and it's precisely why the BNP think they can get away with this focus on Muslims because they've[18] split that kind of solidarity potential (Pragna)

Equally, Yasmin told me how over the course of her lifetime the situation had gone from one in which "there was this sense of commonality, solidarity, of you know, we're Asians together" but that now it is:

> 'we're not Muslims, we're Sikhs', 'we're not Muslims, we're Hindus, we don't do things like that' and... I think it's a shame that people don't feel that they can stand together and have to distance themselves...it's like 'we [the Sikhs] have these problems but we're not as bad as they [the Muslims] are...' and it's scapegoating almost which ..... I think is really sad...now creating more boxes to pigeonhole people in, narrowing down the agendas to the point where you lose the focus and you lose the continuity... (Yasmin)

This regret was accompanied by pragmatism (see Chapter 4). After saying that it was not wrong to get funding as Muslim women, Shaista admitted that it should not have been "at the cost of BME women". She said she could see "why they are upset" but that ultimately it was "the government's fault". She concluded:

> I mean if someone's saying, 'We're going to empower you', you're not going to say 'OK, don't empower me because BME women are gonna be upset' you're gonna grab that opportunity right? So I think...they've created a lot of animosity between the groups and that's wrong...(Shaista)

Shaista's justification for 'special treatment' for Muslim women, therefore, is tempered by the recognition that other BME women need empowering too, but that the realpolitik of Prevent funding for Muslim women means that political ideals and potential solidarities can be easily compromised or squandered altogether. She does not, however, take into account that her initial agreement to be involved in NMWAG could be seen as colluding in this historic tactic of 'divide and rule'. A more timely alternative strategy of resistance might have consisted of presenting a united front which resulted in no Muslim women's organisation taking funding unless its association with the Prevent agenda was retracted or unless other marginalised women were involved.[19] By contrast, the An-Nisa society had originally been involved in the pathfinders projects (forerunners to EMW) but then chose to withdraw from the scheme out of principle, as they set out in their evidence to the Prevent Enquiry.

Equally, there needs to be awareness among secular feminists of the fact that Muslim women do experience racism *as* Muslims. Although Pragna was clear that anti-Muslim racism existed as a separate strand within racism generally, she also suggested that it was often just directed at any one "who's Asian-looking" and that it was "not just Muslims". She told me that sometimes she thought "it gets relabelled as anti-Muslim racism when actually it's just pure and simple racism". The example she used to illustrate this point, however, did not support this:

> and a lot of the women like this woman she also talked about how she went into one shop and the security guards surrounded her and she had a rucksack and they must have mistaken her and so clearly it's not even about whether you are Muslim or not, you are just going to face racism...

Does the racism directed at non-Muslims who are mistakenly assumed to be Muslim not constitute anti-Muslim racism? The implication is often that the problem is in the fact of making a mistake. This has obvious parallels with the 'don't freak, I'm a Sikh' response of Sikhs in the US who were targeted in the post 9/11 climate (Sian 2010; Puar and Rai 2002).

Conclusion

This chapter has built on the idea of (dis)empowerment which was analysed in the previous chapter. It has developed the themes of 'cultural' and 'community' barriers, discussing how 'culture' and religion are positioned as a collective source of oppression for Muslim women which needs to be tamed and modernised. While potentially more hopeful since it takes into account more than just individualised disadvantages, it is problematic because it privileges religion to the exclusion of any other factors. Furthermore, it is not always clear at whose behest this privileging occurs.

The theological interpretation work stream of the EMW initiatives encapsulates this idea of collective (dis)empowerment. It potentially disrupts the idea of a homogenous Islam practised equally and unquestioningly by adherents across the board. Such efforts disrupt the notion that Islam is absolutely patriarchal since they acknowledge that alternative interpretations exist, in particular those promoted by Islamic feminists. Respondents partially accepted that the need for empowerment was almost exclusively the result of religious identity, although they emphasised the importance of cultural differences. These differences, however, are privileged at the expense of other cleavages of difference such as socio-economic class.

Given that religion *is* used to justify patriarchal and separatist behaviour, considered alone, this work stream is difficult to dismiss entirely. The flaw with its rationale, however, is that although religion can be used to justify patriarchal violence by its perpetrators (and this is well documented in WAF 1992), patriarchal violence still occurs in its absence and can be justified by alternative means. For example, there are legal precedents regarding more lenient sentences for men convicted of killing their female partners for socially unacceptable behaviour, so called 'nagging and shagging' defences (Siddiqui 2005). Furthermore, even though laws exist against violence against women, they do not guarantee that either problematic views or actions disappear in wider society. There are ongoing contemporary debates within mainstream society about 'rape culture' and the effects of increasing sexualisation in the media.[20]

It is not clear what the theological interpretation initiative has achieved. On one level the government's reticence about implementing its findings was understandable since it is true that doing so would be difficult in terms of logistics and it would have been criticised for being heavy-handed. Irrespective of the desirability of doing so, there were no channels for disseminating the outputs of this project more widely, since there is no equivalent institutional structure akin to the Vatican or Synod through which such a process might take place. Moreover differences in priorities between those involved in the project from a 'top down' level and those involved at the grassroots illustrate the difficulties with the project. The question, therefore, becomes: what work does this initiative do if it cannot achieve its purported aims?

The tendency to privilege religiosity reflects the tautology at the heart of a project focused on Muslim women *as* Muslim women. It supports the view that Muslim women only care about whether they can wear the veil and getting access to mosques. Clearly such campaigns have been instigated by Muslim women themselves in particular localities and under particular circumstances, but the involvement of the state not only undermines these 'grassroots' projects, as Katherine Brown

(2011) has argued, it also ignores the question of whether all Muslim women even want access to mosques. State involvement, rather than merely accommodating religious difference, makes political capital out of those differences as well as potentially reinforcing the structuring effects of religion in Muslim women's lives.

Notes

1. As Ahmed (2008) notes there is often an emphasis on this from the point of view of segregation rather than as something that might enhance women's lives.
2. Experiences of women and girls in countries such as Afghanistan under the Taliban are frequently extrapolated to all Muslim women and girls across the world.
3. One of the highest profile activists in this area is Jasvinder Sanghera who is of Sikh heritage.
4. This mirrors work which organisations such as An-Nisa Society and Radical Middle Way have undertaken 'to develop relevant Islamic approaches to contemporary challenges to facilitate change' *Faith, Khidmah and Citizenship* (2012) Birmingham.
5. Macey (1999) reveals that there is a difference between male and female attitudes towards Islam. Some men are using it to justify violence against women, while women of all ages and backgrounds are using it as a source of strength and to negotiate the cultural and religious requirements which men try to impose upon them.
6. This can be seen in relation to the use of sharia courts where women seek Islamic divorce certificates (Bano 2012)
7. This has parallels with the way I discuss how issues around domestic violence were less likely to be met with hostility if they were put in the context of family rather than women's rights (Chapter 4).
8. The other aspect of the project was that the girls built up fashion portfolios which were judged and 20 girls were given the opportunity to attend a course at the London School of Fashion).
9. This can also be seen in the research arena. I attended an early career researcher workshop at LSE in 2009. One attendee was at the early stages of devising her research which was looking at the relationship between [Somali] mothers and daughters. When asked about access, she explained that her gatekeeper was based at the local mosque which was attended by some of the local [Somali] population. She seemed surprised when I asked her whether she thought all Somali women went to the mosque and whether she was going to take into account that her sample was more likely to be practising Muslims as a result.
10. Peterson (1966) cited in Suzuki (2002)
11. I use Gunaratnam's term here to refer to the *process* of becoming a minority
12. This has clear parallels with attacks in US on turban wearing Sikhs in the aftermath of 9/11 and more recently in the gurdwara shootings in Wisconsin (Williams 2012).
13. This might also ensure ethnic diversity since, as Kalsoom told me, the mosques are frequently organised around ethnic differences.
14. Not that these syncretic 'traditions' were not without their critics. In India arguably the British operated policies of divide and rule which were accompanied by various religious revivalist (Deobandi and Brahmanical, BJP/RSS) trends as part of the nationalist movements.

[15] In the Bangladesh civil war of 1971 one of the alleged issues was that West Pakistanis felt superior to the Bengalis in East Pakistan because they were Aryan, descendants of Mughals whereas Bengalis were seen as Hindu peasant converts (van Schendel 2009)

[16] This possibly says more about what secular people are prepared to accommodate. It may also be seen as the difference between cultural needs and cultural wants as distinguished by Jayasuriya (cited in Yuval-Davis 2011)

[17] For example, Sikhs who, despite being a religious group, were considered as an ethnic/racial group for the purposes of the Race Relations Act [Mandal vs Dowell Lee] but were not similarly accused of having sought special treatment.

[18] Unfortunately it was not clear from the transcript whether "they" referred to the government or to Muslims themselves or both.

[19] Rather than saying so after a high profile resignation once NMWAG was set to be dismantled.

[20] This can be seen in online campaigns against Facebook for not censoring sexist pages founded on 'rape' humour. It can also be seen in the debates around Julian Assange's extradition from Sweden on rape charges and the kinds of comments this has led to. For example, comments about 'real rape' by George Galloway.

SEVEN

The Muslim woman: victims of oppression or agents of change?

> The idealising of the victim is useful for a time; if virtue is the greatest of goods, and if subjection makes people virtuous, it is kind to refuse them power, since it would destroy their virtue. If it is difficult for a rich man to enter the kingdom of heaven, it is a noble act on his part to keep his wealth and so imperil his eternal bliss for the benefit of his poor brethren. It was a fine self-sacrifice on the part of men to relieve women of the dirty work of politics.
> Bertrand Russell (1950: 73)

Introduction

A survey article regarding the impact of the Arab Spring laments its failure to deliver on its potential in terms of women's progress (Booth et al 2011). The article conforms to the tendency to homogenise all Arab women's experiences (Abu-Lughod 2013) and builds on the fixation with the uniquely patriarchal nature of Islam and Arab countries. It conflates the divergent experiences of women across countries as (internally) diverse as Libya, Yemen and Tunisia. The authors suggest that 'Arab women are barely one small step forwards on the road to greater equality with their menfolk', a statement which reveals more about the journalists' own preconceptions than the complex realities of different women's experiences in each of the countries involved. The same article, for example, makes various references to female university graduates and women from highly educated elites, suggesting that some women at least had not done too badly under the old totalitarian regimes. In terms of women's role in the 'Arab Spring', the article is littered with references to their relationships with 'their menfolk' as 'mothers, sisters and widows', inferring that this represents their motivation for involvement in the movement. Moreover their involvement is primarily framed with reference to food deliveries and the provision of blankets.

The discursive framework established in this article replicates many of the themes raised in this book in relation to how the idea of 'the Muslim woman' in the UK is produced. I have shown that the experiences of Muslim women are homogenised and also seen solely in relation to patriarchal relations with 'their menfolk', rather than the multiplicity of their social positionings in terms of class, region and citizenship status, amongst other things. Equally, their political involvement is seen as part of 'modernising' discourse even if, paradoxically, it is framed within narrow perceptions regarding the role of women as maternal and nurturing. In contrast to the EMW (Empowering Muslim Women) initiatives, however, at least women's mobilisations in the context of the Arab Spring are spontaneous, emerging from the grass roots rather than imposed from above as in the case of the EMW initiatives.

This chapter is divided into three sections: the first addresses the key findings of the research on which this book is based; the second situates these findings within wider debates regarding multifaithism and the consequences for solidarity with other BME (black and minority ethnic) and marginalised groups; and the third section offers some thoughts on the limitations of the study and suggests avenues for possible further research.

Unsettling policy paradigms

This book has examined the rationale and practice of the EMW initiatives, which formed part of New Labour's Prevent strategy from 2008, when they were launched, until 2010 when NMWAG was disbanded. The objective of the research on which this book is based was to provide a historically located intersectional analysis of initiatives to 'empower Muslim women' as part of the UK government's Preventing Violent Extremism (PVE) agenda. Social policy contributes to constructing the social problem which is the target of its intervention (Ladner 1987; Harding 1987). While the initiatives were undoubtedly on a relatively small scale (less than £70m), they offered the opportunity to consider a variety of different sociological issues and political concerns. Informed principally by black and post-colonial feminists such as Mohanty (1988) and Narayan (1997) who interrogated developmental discourses around the 'third world woman', this research has analysed the way in which the EMW initiatives fit into this framework; specifically, how the Muslim woman is produced in policy and public discourses.[1]

In examining the relationship between Muslim women's 'empowerment' and preventing violent extremism I approached the subject from a number of perspectives. To begin with I situated the initiatives within a broader policy context in relation to, at the national level, multiculturalism and debates on Britishness and community cohesion, and at the global level, the 'War on Terror'. Second, the logic of these initiatives is premised on the basis that Muslim women need empowering, thus presupposing their disempowerment. I analysed how 'empowerment' in the context of these initiatives was characterised and by extension, therefore, 'disempowerment'. Third, I examined how the EMW initiatives functioned in practice.

In Chapter 1, I set out the five key strands of Prevent (set out in the Prevent Strategy (HM Government 2008: 6). I revisit these objectives having now considered the wider policy discourse in order to suggest how we are to understand them. I argue that '*Challenging* the violent extremist ideology and supporting mainstream voices' assumes that terrorism (and misogyny) is principally the outcome of incorrect interpretations of Islam. There is a presumption that mainstream voices, implicitly from 'within the Muslim community', have the power to effect change. It strongly rests on the idea that there is a 'them' and 'us' and that mainstream voices require external support. *We,* that is, the government will help *them* to 'get their house in order', partly through supporting a reformation of Islam or a re-codification of Islam which is consistent with British values, including liberal feminism.

The second objective of the Prevent agenda 'Disrupting those who promote violent extremism and supporting the institutions where they are active' does not relate directly to the scope of EMW; it is more in the work of Mosques and Imams National Advisory Body (MINAB) in reforming madrassahs, for example. Since Muslim women are presumed to be peacemakers and at no risk of radicalisation, however, they too may be recruited into assisting in this endeavour of disrupting those who promote violent extremism. Taken together with the objective of 'Supporting individuals who are being targeted and recruited to the cause of violent extremism', these are (barely disguised) euphemisms for encouraging surveillance. The objective of 'Increasing the resilience of communities to violent extremism' suggests that the Prevent agenda is akin to an immunisation programme. Once the backward and barbaric practices are treated and the community modernised, partially through the 'empowerment' of women, then it will be resilient from the disease of radicalism. Finally, 'Addressing the grievances that ideologues are exploiting' suggests that dealing with inequalities and discrimination is only important in so far as it removes a potential grievance to be exploited; it falls short of addressing inequalities and discrimination as a route to securing social justice. It builds on the idea that radicalism is a feature of incorrect interpretations of Islam. It does not necessarily imply that discrimination and inequality are equally risk factors, only that they can be exploited. Nor does it suggest that those who commit such acts are disadvantaged themselves, only that they are politically motivated by and are able to exploit the presence of these inequalities.

A key theme in this book has been the way in which Muslim women are seen solely in relation to their religious affiliation. This is based on Orientalist stereotypes of the uniquely misogynist Muslim man, inflected with contemporary representations of problematic Islamic masculinity in the post 9/11 world. The primacy given to this cleavage of difference reinforces the idea of a narrowly bounded internally homogeneous Muslim community. Other axes of inequality arising from region, class and citizenship status are elided. The research did not set out either to prove or disprove the common sense assumptions underlying the EMW initiatives. Rather its objective was to unsettle them and move beyond the simplistic binaries which dominate discussions on this field.

This books represents a critical intervention by offering an alternative stand point to much of the existing literature in this field (described in Chapter 1). Rather than conform to the social deviancy paradigm within which much research on Muslims is located, it disrupts it by turning the focus of attention on the production of dominant discourses around Muslim women within the field of social policy. Equally the focus on policy rather than media draws attention to the institutional structures within which the idea of 'the Muslim woman' is produced and circulated. It therefore also unsettles the often problematic relationship between policy and research.

This book has illustrated the process of 'discursive reiteration' (Narayan 2000: 82) by looking at the way in which these discourses are engaged with, co-opted, contested and resisted by those working within this policy arena. Such reiterations operate 'to help construct the senses of gender identity and cultural identity that shape the self-understandings and subjectivities of different groups of people who inhabit these discursive contexts' (Narayan 2000: 82). It has analysed the EMW initiatives from an intersectional perspective attending to the historical juncture at which the initiatives took place.

I have not claimed that 'the Muslim woman', as characterised in the EMW initiative, came into being purely as a result of this initiative. The discursive formation of the Muslim woman outlined in this book builds on previous and parallel constructions, both throughout history and contemporaneously across the globe. Since conducting the research the political and policy landscape has changed. Many of the themes discussed remain salient, however, since these are not new dilemmas; they are expressed differently in different places and at different times. Nor does the trope disappear with the demise of the initiative. As such the analysis remains pertinent for informing the analysis of future iterations. I will explore its relevance to more recent events in the epilogue.

Revisiting the War on terror

> Counterterrorism is a form of racial, civilizational knowledge, but now also an academic discipline that is quite explicitly tied to the exercise of state power (Puar and Rai 2002: 122)

Through examination of the wider social policy discourses within which EMW was situated I analysed how, at a particular historical moment, with all its concomitant geopolitical contingencies, the discursive frame exemplified in Huntington's thesis of the 'clash of civilisations' (1993) permeated the policy language related to Prevent in the UK. This broader framing depoliticises the roots of Islamist terrorism and reinforces the idea that a belief in Islam is of itself sufficient to risk radicalisation. Any discussion of the role of foreign policy was absent from discussion of the Prevent agenda. This reflects the way such issues have been elided in the debate more generally. As Butler writes with regard to the US, it is impossible to consider the causes of terrorism as this is considered to be tantamount to justifying it (2004). Instead the focus in the Prevent agenda is on an assumed process of radicalisation and women's role in countering this.

Furthermore, within the discourse of Prevent and the associated discussions about multiculturalism and community cohesion, the issue of women was seen as a principal fault line along which this civilisational clash was being played out; it was the *true* clash of civilisations. I described how Muslim women were seen only in relation to patriarchal relations within their communities. They were seen as victims of cultural relativism and symbolic of the self-segregation of which 'the Muslim community' stands accused. The only direct links between Muslim women's empowerment and preventing terrorism can be seen in initiatives to equip Muslim women to uncover and report potential terrorist or radical behaviour from within their families - whether that be as mothers, wives or sisters. The idea of rescue which imbues discussions of the status of Muslim women makes 'the Muslim woman' automatically a victim. The possibility of women themselves being radicalised is not entertained in the discourse. Such characterisations necessarily foster the demonisation of Muslim men, since it is principally from them that Muslim women need to be rescued.

In the context of the UK, the 'oppression of women' and 'violent extremism' are metonymies. The discourse which positions Muslim women as victims of oppression contributes to a broader anti-Muslim rhetoric which, combined with the emphasis on 'soft power' and 'shared values' and 'the battle for hearts and minds', has real effects in terms of allowing for the dramatic and asymmetric curtailment of civil liberties. As Kundnani writes, 'never before has such a vast and rapidly expanding accumulation of state power confronted young Asians, Africans and African-Caribbeans, Muslim and non-Muslim, immigrant and British born' (2007: 167). The following is worth quoting at length.

> Under anti-terrorist powers, they face mass stop and search without reasonable grounds for suspicion, the virtual return of the 'sus' tactics…new powers of arrest that dramatically extend the time held in police custody prior to any charges being brought. They face threats of raids in the early hours, often on the flimsiest of suspicions of involvement in terrorism or 'immigration offences'. They face virtual house arrest without the right to defend themselves in a court. They face mass surveillance at places of worship, at train stations and at airports. They face the risk of armed police deploying shoot-to-kill tactics. They face prosecution for expressing unacceptable opinions, for protesting, for supporting foreign charities, for being members of political organisations deemed unacceptable to the government. Finally, they face the ultimate sanction of having their citizenship itself stripped away at the behest of the state. (Kundnani 2007: 167–8)

The discussion of women in the broader policy framework in the UK therefore echoes the way in which the idea of the oppressed Muslim woman in the Afghan context was instrumentalised to justify the invasion of Afghanistan. Within the context of EMW specifically, however, women are simultaneously positioned as potential agents of change. They, along with young people, were deemed to constitute a silent majority who needed to be supported to be given a stronger voice to combat terrorism.

Muslim women as agents of change

> …may Allah give you an opportunity to use your voice (Nazneen)

What is clear in the EMW discourse is that Muslim women are being engaged with solely as Muslim women, whereas clearly such women have multidimensional identities (on both subjective and structural levels). The proposed routes to empowerment envisaged in EMW were both individualised and collectivised. The two are deeply implicated in one another. At a simple level both involved blaming the victim. First, conceptualising disempowerment as a 'lack of aspiration' is attributed to 'bad parenting', specifically mothering, and a failure to inculcate good neoliberal values. Second, religion itself is identified as a source of disempowerment.

Women's individual empowerment does not conform to feminist definitions of empowerment, other than the most faux-liberal ones. Rather they are couched in maternalism and promulgating good neoliberal values to secure individualised aspiration; consumption is indirectly promoted, but the emphasis is more on 'modernising' recalcitrant Muslims to be good citizens. The idea of empowering 'Muslim women' presents Muslim women's lives as removed from class, ethnicity, region, age, sexuality and race. These other axes of identity do not emerge in the policy discussion and are subsumed within the presumption that Muslim women's disempowerment is rooted principally in religious affiliation or identity. By contrast, collective but 'secular' forms of oppression (or causes of marginalisation) which might arise from different class positions are redefined as individual challenges which need to be overcome. Important structural inequalities which are not based on religion and which impact on (some) Muslim women's lives are assiduously ignored.

The empowerment of Muslim women acts, therefore, as both a proxy and a conduit for integrating what is assumed to be an internally homogeneous, yet inassimilable community. Rather than acknowledge the complex inter relationship between societal and community attitudes, the agency of individuals and quirks in circumstance that combine to produce particular outcomes, certain 'cultures' are deemed to be pathological or deficient instead, as suggested by Huntington. A clear expression of this is in the way that Muslim women, symbols of the dangerous consequences of 'too much multiculturalism', are positioned collectively as constrained by 'cultural barriers' which they must overcome.

Both ways of articulating empowerment rest (implicitly) on particular notions of subjectivity. The individualised discourse presumes the autonomous aspirational neoliberal subject, whereas the collectivised discourse evokes an image not of individuals but of people as members of a group, the 'other' of neoliberal subjectivities. This reflects different understandings of culture and how they produce different forms of subjectivities (Brown 2006). In this way Muslim women are seen as either neoliberal agents, which disregards structural constraints on their lives, or as members of a group in which they themselves *are* culture and therefore determined by culture. This articulation of empowerment is pathologising, homogenising, and, by disregarding internal differentiation, is itself disempowering since it does not grant full subject status to particular individuals, denying their agency instead.[2]

EMW efforts to represent Muslim women need to be considered against a broader discussion regarding women's political participation and democracy more generally. It is clear that women are as a group marginalised, more generally in political institutions such as Parliament, local government or local councils. While there was potentially symbolic value in an organisation such as NMWAG its presence did not ultimately alter the wider structural political relations in society. In fact Allen and Guru described the group as 'an intensive care patient struggling to survive' concluding that it was 'more akin to 'political fad' than an organisation with the capacity to achieve any real meaningful political empowerment (2012: 8.3).

Multiculturalism to Multifaithism

As a whole, the EMW reflects the paradox described by Yuval-Davis in which there is simultaneously an assimilationist focus on Islam 'in order to try and make our Muslims the 'good ones'' and faith is regarded as 'the only legitimised difference within the nation' (2009: 134). The EMW initiatives discursively privilege religious affiliation. In doing so, the initiatives are arguably an expression of the transition from multiculturalism to multifaithism. I now want to reflect on how the findings in the book relate to the emerging debates on multifaithism which I set out in Chapter 1.

The social policy framework analysed in this book shows an increasing emphasis on religion. These developments could partially be a response to demands from Muslims themselves. They are, however, also the product of a particular historical juncture, not only in the context of the post 9/11, post 7/7 landscape, but also in terms of neoliberal policies of 'rolling back of the state', whereby the faith agenda works to fill in the gaps left by neoliberalism in third sector resources (Patel 2008; Yuval-Davis 2011). Associated with this, however, is the increasing reliance on 'culturalist' explanations for social problems thus effectively blaming the victim (for being Muslim) and reducing the scope for solidarity with marginalised groups (whether BME or white). This needs to be analysed in relation to the wider economic and political environment, for example, the impact of national and global recessions on inequality and further marginalising already marginalised constituencies.

To an extent research participants' responses conform to Yuval-Davis's characterisation of faith being the only legitimised difference within the nation. Some respondents uncritically accepted the homogenisation of Islam as oppressive to women, while others readily took comfort in its potential for salvation. In both scenarios religious difference was privileged. This could be seen in some respondents' wishes for specifically Muslim organisations vis a vis other religious groups, or because of the failures of multiculturalist policies in addressing intra cultural disparities. Within the category Muslim, respondents differentiated between who counted as a Muslim. While there was little explicit mention of sectarian differences, respondents distinguished between themselves and others in terms of perceived religiosity (as did I in my interactions with research participants). Yasmin referred to the concept of a 'cultural' Muslim and the possibility of not being considered 'Muslim enough'. Given the wider discursive framing of good v bad Muslims (Mamdani 2005a) there is the implicit possibility of being *too* Muslim, or having too much culture (as an obstacle to empowerment) as suggested by Hadiyeh in Chapter 5.

The research also showed, however, that respondents continued to identify complexities or cleavages of difference between Muslim women in terms of ethnicity, whether ethno-national or ethno-religious (discussed below). Respondents differentiated between ethnic communities within 'the Muslim community' and explicit connections were made between the cultural differences arising from these ethnic and ethno-national differences which caused variations in religious practice, for example, in the way in which people dressed. Kalsoom told me how the arrival of Arab students in Bristol had affected the way Bangladeshi and Pakistani girls veiled. As the discussion in Chapter 6 about 'cultural practices' showed, some 'practices' or crimes (such as forced marriage or FGM) were more strongly associated with particular groups. In addition, as Chapter 4 showed, there was an emphasis on ensuring the ethnic representativeness of NMWAG. Notably respondents did not themselves subscribe to the view that they were ethnically representative of particular groups, with the exception of Hadiyeh. She negatively asserted her ability to represent different Muslims since, as a convert, she was *not* restricted to a particular ethno-religious community, implying, therefore, that others were. According to the respondents the problems of Islam were attributed to its 'cultural contamination'. A 'pure' Islam could only emerge therefore by transcending ethnicised differences to reveal a new Islamic feminist utopia.

During the research, through discussions with interviewees, there were variations between those adopting an overarching definition of Muslim, and those speaking about a particular ethnic group in a city or region of the UK with very specific experiences of migration and settlement and disadvantage. On occasion there were slippages between the two. The argument is not necessarily that we should differentiate more keenly by different ethnic group or different sect, but rather that we should be problem focused and then consider difference within that. I argue that we should disentangle the various problems encountered by 'Muslims' and other groups of people to deal with those problems. So, problems arising from citizenship status and socioeconomic status should be addressed principally through those lenses, rather than ethnic or religious group identity.

The failure of mainstream services to meet the demands of Muslim women was a theme among respondents. This was often related specifically to faith based services, as could be seen in comments from Humera and Khalida regarding their rationale for establishing An-Nisa. Their argument was that even once multiculturalist policies were adopted in Brent, not all BME groups experienced these benefits equally, with Muslims in particular being 'left behind'. Such requests could represent an apparent shift to multifaithism on the basis of Omoniyi and Fishman's definition in that it constitutes 'institutional recognition of multiple faiths by the state and the granting of equal rights and protection to devotees by law' (2010: 315). Multiculturalism was, however, never resolutely secular. Different ethnic minority groups' demands were not purely 'cultural'; they frequently had religious underpinnings, for example dietary requirements, prayer rooms, uniforms being more religiously sensitive (permission to wear turbans for Sikh men and headscarves and trousers for women) and paid leave from work for religious holidays. Much, if not all of the liberal plural accommodation of minorities in the legal context even prior to the Rushdie affair (which was widely regarded as the watershed moment for 'religious demands' being made more explicitly) has been around religious accommodation (halal/kosher slaughter of animals, religious wedding ceremonies, wearing of turbans). It was the law that characterised, that *named* these issues as being about race and ethnicity.[3, 4] Having said that, not all the shortcomings in mainstream services raised by respondents had a religious character, as I will explore later.

In a similar vein, there seems to be some element of amnesia regarding the significance of religious identity prior to the Rushdie affair. Pragna's comments regarding Indian and Pakistani workers' associations being secular ignore that the very foundations of the difference between Pakistan and India was a religious divide. Pragna also told me she thought memories of communal violence in South Asians' countries of origin meant that in the post-war era people preferred not to privilege their religious identity. Equally, however, it could be argued that memories of Partition and communal violence have remained salient issues. Sian (2013), for example, explores how historical discourses of forced conversions to Islam among British Sikhs continue to circulate in the contemporary UK.

Accommodating faith is therefore nothing new even though *how* it has been accommodated institutionally might have varied. It is nonetheless true that issues are now couched more explicitly in terms of religious identity. There is more overt political mobilisation and organisation around religion and this process has been facilitated by government. We need to think carefully, however, about the origins of that more overt religious discourse and recognise that part of this mobilisation around religious identity is also directly attributable to social policy measures and discourses, influenced by broader geopolitical issues and concerns. Since 1997, when New Labour came to power, the government has engaged more publicly with faith groups and communitarian ideals. Within this, religious communities have been identified as a particular source of social capital, especially in deprived areas where other forms of social infrastructure may be absent.

Even if religious based demands are regarded as a continuation of multicultural demands, one of the clearest developments accompanying a greater emphasis on faith is the rise of anti-Muslim rhetoric and racism, which I explored in Chapter 6. As many of the research participants recognised, the issue of discrimination against Muslim women *as* Muslim women was a pertinent one, particularly for those who wore veils.[5] In the context of this I revisit and reframe Okin's question.

Is Multifaithism bad for women?

To address this question we need to distinguish between the theory and practice of multifaithism. The theory of it refers to incorporating religion into the existing multicultural paradigm, offering equality and recognition to religion not just freedom and tolerance (Modood 2010). In principle, as I have suggested, to some extent this is a continuation of what multiculturalism involved. The practice of it can be criticised, however, since it often results in formalising gender discrimination and cultural relativism (Patel and Bard 2010). Yasmin recognised that there was a contradiction between the way in which the EMW policy initiatives ran alongside a faith agenda, given that some interpretations of (all of the world's) religions are not necessarily favourable to women.

Given the potential for women (across various religious faiths) to be adversely affected by the entrenchment of religion (Patel 2008; Jeffreys 2011), the immediate logical response is to advocate a retrenchment. The dilemma emerges, however, from the fact that religion is clearly important to some women. As I discussed in Chapter 6, respondents recognised the value of Islamic feminism and using alternative religious interpretations in their work against forced marriage, for example. Given that there are clearly women who are Muslim for whom religion is an integral part of their values or an important source of comfort, overtly secular spaces as advocated could be seen as exclusionary (Mahmood 2005).

I observed how, in the context of New Labour's faith agenda, middle class women could "shift in and out of whatever identity they choose" (Pragna). Equally it was also clear that there were other women who were "boxed... [into]...that kind of rigid identification along faith lines" (Pragna). One solution to this is of course to advocate a retrenchment away from multifaithism as a necessary and sufficient solution. It is also possible, however, that the solution to this dilemma lies more in addressing the factors which facilitate the ability to 'shift in and out of' different identities. These could be the result of a variety of factors such as racism and patriarchal relations in wider society. Equally, as Pragna herself notes, the issue of class too is of great importance and I discuss this further below.

Conversely, there are those who conflate the marginalisation of some Muslims to all Muslims, without paying due attention to the diversity caused by other modalities of power. The experience of anti-Muslim racism is constituted through both 'race' and class. There are extensive socioeconomic variations within the Muslim community. These inequalities contribute to some Muslim women's marginalisation in terms of poverty, access to health services, access to learning languages, or unemployment. Conflating the experience of all marginalised Muslims who may be marginalised for reasons other than their religious affiliation alone is therefore equally problematic if understandable. As Nancy Fraser argues, today's struggles for recognition assume the guise of identity politics in response to 'demeaning cultural representations of subordinated groups' (2000: 119). Muslim women are certainly often the subject of such demeaning cultural representations. As Fraser argues, however, such struggles for recognition 'abstract misrecognition from its institutional matrix and sever its links with political economy' which 'lead to enforce separatism, conformism and intolerance'. She states that such 'struggles for recognition simultaneously displace struggles for economic justice and promote repressive forms of communitarianism' (Fraser 2000: 120).

This dichotomy of 'multifaithism is bad for women' on the one hand and 'all Muslims are equally marginalised solely because they are Muslim' on the other is reductive. Both approaches over-determine the role of religion, privileging it to the exclusion of other salient factors. This research has demonstrated the importance of drawing greater attention to these other modalities of power.

Intersectional contestations[6]

This book attempted to deconstruct the idea of 'the Muslim woman'. More significantly, its objective was to draw attention to the axes and modalities of power which get ignored in the context of the dominant discursive framework in which religious affiliation is privileged. Crucially, differences arising from class or socioeconomic background (in access to cultural, economic and social capital) were not explicitly identified. They were, however, ever present. Such factors, for example, differentiated between different role models. As well as ethnic differences in the composition of NMWAG, there were also class differences between members which reflected the grassroots/high profile expert split in the composition of the group. In Chapter 5 I showed how some of the shortcomings attributed to 'Muslim mothering' were in fact attributable to wider societal and socioeconomic factors, for example, in the provision of careers services and the inability of schools to provide adequate careers advice or work experience to students. This was therefore often indicative of a wider problem in schools attended by working-class pupils whose parents' access to social, economic and cultural capital is limited. Pupils from marginalised backgrounds share these conditions irrespective of their faith.

Chapter 3 provided an explicit focus on the impact of local variations in both how the role models project worked in practice, and the impact on intercommunity relations. Adeeba's comments regarding the difference between Bradford's Pakistanis and Bangladeshis and London's Bangladeshis reflects the different economic realities of these two cities. Kalsoom mentioned the relationship between Somali and Pakistani women in Bristol. It would be too simplistic to reduce these simply to ethno-national differences. I analysed the way in which local particularities, incorporating local politics and stories of migration which have affected the composition of populations played a crucial part in these dynamics. Although Kalsoom did refer to class when she shared the problematic views of some middle class Pakistani women in Bristol towards Somali women, she did not mention difference arising from their citizenship status or their specific reasons for migration. The fact that even NMWAG respondents recognised that the Group was dominated by Pakistani-heritage women reflects at least an awareness of a larger Muslim population with whom they may have had little in common.

Race and Religion

'Race' too emerges in the data as a salient factor and there is often slippage showing the way in which race and religion are mutually constituted. Shaista referred to there being no black representation on NMWAG, for example. Equally, Almeena's responses to my question of whether she had ever experienced discrimination reflected the easy slippage between race and religion. She referred to her 'brown face' never having been a problem for her at the BBC, but also said that she simultaneously carried the burden of representation as a Muslim since colleagues expected her to be an 'expert' on forced marriage and 'honour' violence. It also shows that religious identity is constituted through race since it is difficult to conceive of a white Muslim having the same experiences. In addition, it reflects her being 'ethnically' South Asian since it is equally unlikely that a black Muslim would have been associated with 'forced marriage'. Almeena's experience also shows that while she merely carried the burden of (religious) representation, she was fully cognisant of the impact that looking Muslim through wearing the veil could have on others. This is particularly so given that Blair implied that the wearing of the veil was an indication of extremism. The slippage between race and religion was also mentioned by Pragna who suggested that what was often interpreted as anti-Muslim racism was in fact 'ordinary' racism towards South Asians.

Religious affiliation cannot be ignored. The presence and influence of anti-Muslim rhetoric is undeniable. It results in specifically anti-Muslim discrimination and hate crimes and forms the basis of contemporary mobilisation of the far-right (into which non-Muslims have been recruited irrespective of their 'race'). At the same time, however, we must also resist the lure of religious essentialism that this fosters and recognise the role of the state and its motivations for colluding in this process. The diversity of the Muslim population and the underlying material non-culturalist reasons for that diversity need to be given greater attention, whether that be regional inequalities or byzantine immigration laws. Equally, racism and patriarchal relations in wider society also need to be attended to. As Fraser advocates, 'what is needed...is an alternative politics of recognition, *a non-identitarian* politics that can remedy misrecognition without encouraging displacement and reification' (author's emphasis) (2000: 120).

Recommendations and scope for future research

This book offers a critique of social policy initiatives undertaken at a particular historical moment. It is therefore difficult to make specific policy recommendations. The broader lessons which I hope emerge are that it is important to consider the way that particular groups of people are produced as objects of social policy and the repercussions of doing this. While not necessarily inspired by an explicit decision to stigmatise Muslims, it is also not neutral; it reflects wider ideological and political concerns with potentially long term effects. What are 'problems' to us 'are built into the flesh and blood of the young' (Spender 1969 cited in Arendt 1970: 17).

The limitations of this research reflect the skewed nature of this arena. Just as it could be argued that NMWAG was dominated by particular women, so my research too reflected these constructions embedded within the institutional environment itself. NMWAG's own lack of representativeness and the top-down impetus behind its formation mean that the research only 'gives voice' to those involved in the scheme at that level. This research reflects the side-lining of non-South Asian Muslims within the Muslim cohort of engagement; it also reflects the association of Muslim women with forced marriage and what they wear. Nonetheless, the research has unsettled the dominant discourses within the literature and its critical approach offers scope for future research.

In Khattab's quantitative analysis of 2001 census data he suggests that it is 'important to move beyond a simplistic notion of a Muslim/non-Muslim' and he refers to '… the vastly divergent starting points for different groups' (2012: 570). He describes how ethnic and religious cultural differences characterise aspects of this story and are reflected in the relative integration. He notes, however, that the 'Muslim Black African group experiences greater penalties than Pakistanis on a consistent basis' and therefore that we 'need to move beyond the historical focus on South Asians ….[to one].. that is aimed at a more holistic interpretation and analysis of the Muslim experience in Britain per se' (Khattab: 571). While on many levels I agree with this approach, it does not go far enough. Such an approach falls short because it is still within the confines of talking about 'the Muslim experience', whereas it is important that future research adopts a more intersectional analysis which in particular takes into account socioeconomic differences. Locally situated intersectional research in lieu of an exclusive focus on religious affiliation will be more productive, not only for correctly framing problems, but also for opening up the possibilities for solidarity with others. As Ali states: 'A political will to challenge categories which make up racial hierarchies is the only way to begin to tackle ordinary racism which arises from the instigation of "difference"' (2006: 483).

Finally, in solidarity with respondents who raised the issue, many suggested better research was needed on discrimination against Muslim women as Muslims. As Bulmer and Solomos argue '...it is important that research addresses the impact of racism in real-life situations. Racial harassment, direct/indirect discrimination, racist violence and victimisation are not fictions or figurations that admit of the free play of signification' (2004: 10). Thus research with an 'experiential and analytic anchor in the lives of marginalized communities of women provides the most inclusive paradigm for thinking about social justice' (Mohanty 2003: 231).

Conclusion

> Deconstruction does not say anything against the usefulness of mobilizing unities. All it says is that because it is useful it ought not to be monumentalized as the way things really are. (Spivak 1991: 65)

This research and its approach were designed to provide an analysis of a particular policy initiative at a particular historical juncture. Following the 2010 elections and the coming to power of a coalition,

Prevent as a major policy declined in significance and its profile all but disappeared from the policy landscape. It has, however, re-emerged recently following the murder of the soldier Lee Rigby at Woolwich and in response to young British Muslims going to fight for ISIS who it is thought will pose a terrorist threat to the UK upon their return. (I reflect on these developments in the epilogue.) Policy focused on 'Muslim women' collated together all women who are Muslim, a disparate and multiply-differentiated group and de facto attributed any problematic issues to religious affiliation. As well as perpetuating anti-Muslim rhetoric, such policy discourses, focused on religious affiliation alone, also obscure continuities with earlier racisms as well as other axes of social division in society, such as class and regional inequalities which also affect non-Muslims.

The book has illustrated how the EMW initiative utilised, fomented and produced common-sense Orientalised stereotypes of Muslim women. Such understandings were analysed in the context of a broader policy landscape dealing with counterterrorism, immigration, forced marriage and 'honour killings'. Taken together, the various initiatives were essentialising, reducing Muslim women's circumstances purely to their membership of a religious group. I analysed the way in which social policy discourse around community cohesion and Britishness constructs the Muslim woman in a particular way. I also drew attention to the way in which feminism is invoked and instrumentalised in these discourses, for example, in the use of feminist rhetoric of 'empowerment' and 'giving voice'. Such neo-Orientalist discourses inflect the way in which policy works in practice. Muslim women are engaged with solely as Muslim women at the expense of considering the more complex and differentiated realities of their lives. To be clear, this book does not deny the presence of marginalised women who are Muslim, nor is it a manifesto espousing the liberatory emancipatory potential of Islam, since despite the possibilities offered by Islamic feminism, it acknowledges that some Muslim men can and do persist in sustaining patriarchal relations through recourse to religion.

The extent of diversity among Muslim women has been a recurrent theme throughout the book. What is clear, however, is that different differences are validated differently. Through analysis of qualitative interview material and observation I highlighted the way policy practitioners working in this policy arena (who I interviewed), themselves predominantly Muslim women, conformed, responded to or resisted these characterisations. In the context of the broader policy framework defined by multiculturalism, community cohesion and multifaithism, the discursive repertoires available to characterise this diversity is restricted; ethnic and religious diversity are readily invoked to the exclusion of any explicit discussion of other equally (or more) salient axes of difference, such as class, region and citizenship status.

There have been ongoing reports regarding the issues faced by BME women in general in relation to employment. Both figures and anecdotal evidence show that BME women are suffering discrimination. Moreover, if the trend towards austerity continues (and according to November's 2012 Budget statement such policies are to continue until at least 2018), it will be BME women who suffer because they are over represented in both the public and voluntary sectors which are the targets of the most swingeing cuts. Notably, organisations which offer help to those experiencing domestic violence are also suffering cuts. Against this background of austerity those most marginalised in society are becoming further marginalised. As such I conclude with Nancy Fraser's exhortation:

> This is a moment in which feminists should think big. Having watched the neoliberal onslaught instrumentalize our best ideas, we have an opening now in which to reclaim them. In seizing this moment, we might just bend the arc of the impending transformation in the direction of justice – and not only with respect to gender. (2009: 117)

Notes

1. In contrast, however, I am addressing this by looking at women 'over here' rather than 'over there'.
2. With thanks to Christina Scharff for our discussion on this.
3. See Mandla v Dowell Lee [1983] This case defined the terms 'ethnicity' and 'ethnic group' in UK law, with the latter referring to those with 'a long shared history of which the group is conscious as distinguishing it from other groups, and the memory of which it keeps alive…[and]…a cultural tradition of its own, including family and social customs and manners, often but not necessarily associated with religious observance. Other features were stated to be relevant but not essential. These included a common geographical origin, language, or literature, and "being a minority or being an oppressed or a dominant group within a larger community' (Jefferson 1983: 78).
4. Growing up in London during the 70s and 80s I participated in the GLC's multicultural accommodations for example. Concessions to religious dietary requirements meant that at primary school I wore a small sign around my neck (during my lunch hour) which said 'No Pork' while my friend from a Hindu background wore one saying 'No Beef'!
5. In May 2012 an organisation was launched to record instances of anti-Muslim attacks called Tell Mama UK. http://tellmamauk.org/; they reported that 58% of incidents are targeted at women (Allen et al 2013: 1).
6. Yuval-Davis (2011).

EPILOGUE

Some reflections on Prevent

By the time this book goes to print, five years will have passed since the original research concluded. This is not perhaps unusual in academia and the temporality of my subject was something I was always conscious of. As I made clear throughout the book, the purpose of the research was to capture the discursive formations of 'the Muslim woman' emerging through UK public policy discourse at a particular historical moment. This research was therefore historically and geographically located; it was never conceived of as the definitive analysis of the way the idea of the Muslim woman is constructed in policy discourses in the UK. Rather, the analysis, grounded in postcolonial, intersectional feminist approaches, offered a way to understand and critique the discursive formation of gendered anti-Muslim racist rhetoric during New Labour's final term in office and in its responses to the 7/7 London bombings through the Preventing Violent Extremism agenda. In fact, as I finalised the draft of my PhD in early 2013 it appeared that Prevent had, despite a review in 2011, fallen off the policy agenda.

Yet, as increasing numbers of young British Muslims travel to Syria and Iraq, many to join ISIS, the counter terrorism agenda has again emerged as a key political issue which David Cameron described as 'the struggle of our generation' (Dearden 2015). In February 2015 the Counter Terrorism and Security Bill received Royal Assent. The provisions of this Act have placed a statutory duty on a very wide range of public sector institutions, including Local Authorities, to monitor Muslims for signs of radicalisation. This means, for example, that local authority teachers are now required to officially monitor and report signs of radicalisation and extremism amongst pupils (Rao-Middleton 2015) and council officials and university staff are being similarly enlisted in an 'increasingly expansive, pre-emptive, centralised, top-down and punitive approach' (O'Toole 2015). In July 2015 Cameron made a speech setting out a five year plan which was followed by the publication of a new Counter Extremism Strategy in October 2015 (HM Government 2015).

This renewed interest in Prevent comes at a time when the political landscape across Europe is dominated by the issue of migration, in particular the refugee crisis arising from civil wars in Syria and Iraq. It is against this backdrop that we see the rise of anti-Muslim political movements such as Pegida in Germany in response to the so called Islamification of Europe.[1] There have also been very public pronouncements by elected leaders in Hungary and Poland regarding Muslim immigrants which the UN Human Rights Commission has labelled 'xenophobic and anti-Muslim' and in the US the Republican presidential candidate, Donald Trump, has called for a ban on Muslims (Miles 2015; Pilkington 2015). There has also been an increasing level of anti-Muslim racist attacks in the UK, across Europe, and in the US. And it is those women who appear as visibly Muslim who are most at risk of these attacks (Press Association 2015).

The targets of the Prevent agenda have arguably changed and its primary focus is now on young people leaving the UK to join ISIS rather than committing acts of terrorism on UK soil. At heart, however, the Prevent agenda continues to be founded on the 'radicalisation thesis', the idea that there is a 'conveyor belt' of radicalisation on which socially conservative, fundamentalist or 'extreme' views amongst Muslims are considered to be the precursors to 'violent extremism' and a willingness to perpetrate acts of terrorism. This is despite the fact that there is no clear evidence of a *causal* relationship between religious fundamentalism and perpetrating acts of terrorism (Kundnani 2014); there is scant evidence even of any correlation. In relation to counter extremism there appears to be little of the evidence-based policy making which characterises a variety of other policy arenas in government.

Extremism continues to be couched in 'culturalist' terms and adherence to the 'wrong type of Islam' is regarded as the principal explanation for radicalisation. Consequently, yet again, despite the government's vociferous denunciation of 'Islamophobia' and frequent assertions that far-right extremism is also being targeted by the Prevent agenda, the focus remains on Muslims who continue to be regarded as collectively responsible for terrorism; and if Muslims are not directly engaged in perpetrating acts of terrorism, they are at the very least accused of 'quietly condoning' such acts, as David Cameron suggested in June 2015 (Morris 2015).[2] There have, however, been some important developments in the way Muslim women are represented in the policy discourse which signify an important departure from the Prevent agenda under New Labour.

Representing Muslim women

In the General Election of 2015 the local Labour Party in Bradford West fielded a local woman, Naz Shah, as their candidate. Her victory brought the total number of Muslim women MPs in the British Parliament to eight. Whilst the number of Muslim women elected as MPs is encouraging, the issue of 'representation' remains key, both in terms of how they are portrayed and the terms with which they are engaged. For example, media coverage of Naz Shah's campaign was dominated by her status as a 'forced marriage survivor' (or the 'daughter of a murderer' in the case of The Telegraph) whereas only cursory attention was paid to what she stood for politically. As a result, the incumbent Respect Party MP George Galloway's defamatory counter-campaign focused on undermining her credibility through questioning whether in fact her marriage had been forced. Through this emphasis on her past experiences she was reduced to what are regarded as the 'cultural practices' of her 'community'. As such it fits with one respondent's assertion (in Chapter 4) that Muslim women were only given a voice 'as victims or survivors, who were prepared to disclose their personal stories'.

Nor does being represented in politics necessarily equate to having political power as the vicissitudes of Baroness Warsi's career testifies. Warsi was briefly the most senior Muslim in government. Her background is no less atypical than Naz Shah's in terms of mainstream politicians. Lauded for being one of the most senior Tory politicians, albeit unelected, her career has been beset with controversy. Starting with the expenses scandal and a high profile divorce, she subsequently attracted the ire of her fellow Conservative party members for speaking out on controversial issues. In 2011 she spoke publicly about anti-Muslim bigotry passing the 'dinner table test', alluding to its casual acceptability. Cameron and other prominent Tories distanced themselves from her and Norman Tebbit wryly commented that 'a period of silence from the Baroness might not come amiss'. It was, however, her party's position on Palestine which led in August 2014 to her eventual resignation as a senior Minister in the Foreign Office and which Chancellor George Osborne described as a 'disappointing and a frankly unnecessary decision'.

These instances exemplify the way that Muslim women are used in politics to achieve particular ends but are ultimately expendable (or silenced when they voice unpalatable opinions). As I discussed in Chapter 4, the terms of engagement continue to be set by predominantly white male classed agents who are quick to capitalise on having women or minorities to prove their egalitarian credentials.

Representing 'the Muslim woman'

What has changed most profoundly since the research was conducted, however, is the explicit recognition that Muslim women and girls can be drawn into terrorism or terrorist organisations and this has altered the representation of Muslim women and girls in UK policy discourse.

In early 2015 reports of three 15-year-old British Muslim girls from the east end of London who had gone to join ISIS in Syria dominated the national and international news. These girls form part of an increasing number of British Muslims travelling to join ISIS. The original Prevent strategy and the EMW (Empowering Muslim Women) initiatives were not premised on the idea that girls and women were at risk of being drawn into terrorism; the threat was seen to emanate principally from young men. Instead, the role of women was seen as auxiliary and it was only as mothers, sisters and wives that women and girls were engaged with in the EMW initiatives, as people who might 'prevent' male family members from becoming involved in terrorism. The incidence of Muslim school girls traveling to Syria sits in stark contrast to the way in which Muslim girls were presented in the EMW initiatives. The role models road show was premised on the idea that Muslim girls needed to raise their aspirations in order to achieve both academically and in the labour market. By extension this would mean that they were 'empowered' and in a position to combat terrorism. The three girls in East London were, however, straight-A students and their alleged contact in Syria was a privately educated Muslim girl from Scotland. If nothing else, it shows that academic potential or achievement is not necessarily a safeguard against susceptibility to radicalisation or terrorism. They exemplify the way in which Muslim girls are increasingly being characterised as both 'dangerous' and 'in danger' and are being 'simultaneously constructed as both highly "visible" raced subjects and yet also "invisible" gendered subjects' (Mirza 2015: 40).

The ghosts of Prevent agendas past continue to haunt the latest iteration of the Prevent strategy. Whilst the phenomenon of Muslim girls' 'radicalisation' is clearly something new, policy interpretations and responses remain very gendered. Cameron makes specific references to the different ways in which Muslim youth are at risk of ISIS. He warns that, 'If you are a girl, they will enslave and abuse you' whereas 'if you are a boy, they will brainwash you, strap bombs to your body and blow you up' (Dearden 2015).[3] As with the Prevent agenda under New Labour, the current approach relies on problematically conflating concerns about radicalisation and terrorism with those about FGM, forced marriage, honour related violence and sharia courts. In his July 2015 speech, Cameron provides more information about the number of cases of FGM and honour based violence than he does about the number of young people that have been 'radicalised'. In fact there are no references to the numbers involved in the latter in either his speech or the Counter Extremism Strategy published in October 2015.

Throughout this book I have pointed to the importance of intersectionality and taking into account the wider environment which 'the Muslim woman' inhabits. The austerity measures introduced by the Coalition government following the financial crisis have had a profound impact on the British economy and society; inequality is increasing and already marginalised groups in society are becoming ever more marginalised, with women and ethnic minorities being hit particularly hard (O'Hara 2014). Muslim women will necessarily be amongst those women and ethnic minorities affected by austerity. Arguably these cuts directly undermine some of the policy measures announced as part of the Conservatives' counter terrorism strategy. Whilst violence against Muslim women is regularly invoked and instrumentalised in order to show the 'backwardness' of Muslim communities, this is not matched with a corresponding commitment to funding organisations which deal with these issues.[4] Likewise when Cameron discusses integration in his July 2015 speech he talks about parts of the UK 'where language remains a real barrier' and that 'specific action' is required to 'ensure people learn English'. This is, however, at the same time as deep cuts are being made in the provision of English as a Second Language services (Williams 2015).

Preventing Prevent?

While this book is not directly about the *causes* of 'radicalisation' (in as much as the phenomenon of 'radicalisation' exists in the simplistic manner in which it is frequently represented), having researched the role of women in the Prevent agenda between 2008 and 2010 I would nonetheless like to offer some explicit reflections on the current Counter Extremism agenda.

The Prevent agenda is based on a number of common-sense justifications for which there is little evidence. That is of course not to say that the phenomenon of young people joining ISIS does not need addressing. But in recognising this, there should be greater perspective regarding both the numbers of people who may be susceptible, as well as a clearer focus on the risk that they may or may not pose on their return to the UK. More broadly, in terms of identifying young people who may want to go to Syria to join ISIS, the possible causes need to be established more clearly. There are a range of factors which act as pull or push factors. Determining these and acknowledging which ones can in fact be addressed is a step closer to a better, more targeted policy. Here there is a case for detailed research which tries to capture the complexity and heterogeneity of the issues involved rather than collapse together a diverse range of experiences and circumstances in the interests of political expediency. Alternative interpretations of their behaviour may well facilitate different policy responses. Such an evaluation would be able to assess whether the Prevent agenda is the best way of addressing this and whether the more strategic, tactical use of intelligence services would be more judicious.

It is worth bearing in mind that the recent phenomenon of British Muslims going to fight for ISIS has developed *in spite* of the existence of Prevent, suggesting that it is based on broader socio- and geo-political changes. To acknowledge this and to consider the wider political context as part of a policy response does not amount to 'justification' or legitimisation. But discounting such factors in this way leads to a rather crude expression of the 'either with us or against us' logic exemplified by both George Bush and ISIS recruiters. By perpetuating this logic, the Prevent agenda and its uncritical supporters encourage and entrench this type of binary thinking which posits unequivocal support of the government and its 'war on terror' on the one hand and ISIS on the other. Seeking to take into account the wider (socio-) political context is merely an admission of the complexities involved.

One plausible basis for policy making is the recognition of the need to provide a counter narrative to ISIS recruitment propaganda. In order for such a narrative to effectively compete with the Islamic utopia proffered in ISIS propaganda, however, it needs to be credible. The current focus on teaching Fundamental British Values in school is problematic. Attempts to particularise such values to Britishness could in fact be alienating. Furthermore, the various asymmetries and contradictions of the way in which concepts such as 'freedom of expression' and 'universal human rights' are invoked reduces the credibility of potentially powerful counternarratives. For example, as Europe was rocked by the terrorist attacks in Paris and Copenhagen in 2015, the issue of freedom of speech once again took centre stage as another fault line between the West and the rest, between them and us. Freedom of expression is framed as a Western ideal threatened by ISIS. Yet there are a myriad ways in which UK's counterterrorism policies themselves curb freedom of expression.

Shortly before the Counter Terrorism and Security Act became law a concession was made in response to protests by universities that some of the provisions of the legislation conflicted with academic freedom. The former director of public prosecutions, Lord Macdonald, said the Home Office concession was an important acknowledgement by the government that the new powers could conflict with their freedom of expression duties and might mitigate its impact. He also warned that 'the current official 'working definition' of non-violent extremism, which talks of opposition to fundamental British values, would be hopeless when it came to be applied' (Travis 2015).

Whilst this represents a victory of sorts, it comes in the context of the widespread silencing of alternative perspectives on radicalisation and the question of what draws young British Muslims to perpetrate acts of terrorism, both here in the UK and abroad. Such voices are seen as apologists for terrorism or as condoning such activities. The debate regarding radicalisation therefore remains stilted and effectively censored and there is a reluctance to consider even the remote possibility that any of the young people who have been drawn to ISIS could be politically motivated and that this is a form, however dangerous or misguided, of political agency or youthful rebellion.

There has been a considerable amount of lurid and sensationalist speculation as to the reasons for young girls in particular joining ISIS. The reasons proffered have ranged from: the use of attractive jihadis to lure girls; Nutella and kittens according to CNN; and the perennial appeal of the 'bad boy' (Itkowitz 2015; Alibhai-Brown 2015).[5] What such explanations share, however, is the failure to take into account any agency on the part of the girls, which once again builds on the way in which Muslim women and girls are superficially drawn as only ever being victims or survivors.[6]

Many commentators have been perplexed that girls brought up in the 'West', with all the alleged freedoms that this affords them, would choose to live in a state where they would only ever be seen in an auxiliary role as brides, wives and mothers. These girls' experiences of growing up in the UK, however, will have been affected by the fact that they are Muslim and in many cases visibly so. The negative experiences of girls and women wearing the veil has been well documented (Allen et al 2013) in terms of discrimination and racial violence, but less is known about the longer term impact of these experiences on aspirations and life chances. They are not able to participate in 'the new sexual contract' (McRobbie 2009) which I discussed in Chapter 5. As otherwise intelligent and academically successful girls, perhaps they know that, despite their 'A' grades, there will be a shortfall between what such academic credentials might entitle them to and what their ethnicity and religious identity is more than likely to deny them. It would of course be too simplistic and deterministic to suggest that such marginalisation on its own is sufficient to drive someone to engage in terrorist activities or seek to join ISIS. It may be one of a number of contributory factors none of which are sufficient on their own to be decisive. Beyond this debate, however, more important is surely the fact that any such marginalisation arising from anti-Muslim racism and discrimination is an issue of concern *in itself* in terms of social justice and wasted opportunities.

And while integration is frequently talked about in relation to whether minority communities make enough of an effort to integrate, there is very little public discussion about the environment into which they are being asked to do so. When Muslim girls are being 'criminalised and demonised as the new female folk devils' (Mirza 2015: 42) both in the media and in social policy discourses and when Muslim women who wear the veil are being seen as targets for racial abuse and violence, then the 'lack of integration' must be framed to take into account this hostile environment.

This book argues that not only are the measures implemented as part of Prevent likely to be ineffective, there are also adverse consequences to the underlying narrative in the form of legitimating anti-Muslim rhetoric and anti-Muslim racism. This can be seen in the suspicion with which young Muslims who are politically active are treated in schools (Khan 2015). But more broadly, the association of Prevent with every other social problem or criminal activity which involves Muslims contributes to and legitimates anti-Muslim rhetoric. A policy agenda as nebulous as Prevent, which legitimates anti-Muslim rhetoric and thus makes potentially vulnerable people feel more excluded, is not conducive to addressing the issue.

The aim of the research on which this book is based was to look at the discursive production of 'the Muslim woman' at a particular historical conjuncture. Despite changes in the policy landscape I maintain that the analytical approach remains pertinent beyond the scope of the historical and geopolitical specificities of the Prevent agenda. I am, however, more pessimistic than I was when I initially completed the research.

As the Prevent agenda has become ever more insidious and problematic, and its remit broader and increasingly tenacious, it continues to discursively produce and legitimate anti-Muslim racism partially through recourse to instrumentalising feminism. There is clear evidence of this, not only as part of the growth of far right movements but also in society more generally. In a piece published in 2011 I wrote that:

> The consequences of framing social problems with reference to religion alone and perpetuating dehumanizing stereotypes of the 'oppressed Muslim woman' will have negative effects on the very women that such initiatives purport to assist. This may be through increasing incidents of racial violence, as evidenced in Europe with incidents of 'burka rage' or through increasing discrimination in employment. (Rashid 2011)

If Muslim women were the focus of anti-Muslim racist attacks before, when their primary representation was as victims within their communities oppressed by the uniquely patriarchal nature of Islam, the current situation with (visibly) Muslim women and girls joining ISIS will unfortunately make Muslim women more of a target than ever before.

Notes

1. Attempts are currently being made to establish a branch of Pegida in the UK.
2. David Cameron was speaking at a security conference in Slovakia. The timing of his comments, just as the Muslim holy month of Ramadan was about to begin, was seen as particularly insensitive.
3. Speech in Birmingham 20 July 2015, full transcript available (Dearden 2015)
4. This can be seen in the high profile campaigns against closure by organisations such as Apna Haq (Dugan 2015).
5. Yasmin Alibhai-Brown suggests that "messianic fervour, millenarianism and magnetism can whip up female hormones alarmingly."
6. More measured analysis can be found in the work of Katherine Brown (Brown 2014).

Bibliography

Abbas, T, ed, 2005, *Muslim Britain, communities under pressure*, London, Zed Books

Abu Odeh, L, 1993, Post-colonial feminism and the veil: thinking the difference, *Feminist review*, 43, 26-37

Abu-Lughod, L, 2002, Do Muslim women really need saving? Anthropological reflections on cultural relativism and its others, *American Anthropologist*, 104, 3, 783–90

Abu-Lughod, L, 2013, Do Muslim women need saving?, Cambridge, Massachusetts, Harvard University Press

Afshar, H, 1994, Muslim women in West Yorkshire, in H Afshar and M Maynard, eds, *The dynamics of race and gender: some feminist interventions*, London, Taylor & Francis

Afshar, H, ed, 1997, *Women and empowerment: illustrations from the Third World*, New York, St Martins Press

Afshar, H, Aitken, R, Franks, M, 2005, Feminisms, Islamophobia and identities, *Political Studies*, 53, 262–83

Afshar, H, 2012, The politics of fear: what does it mean to those who are otherized and feared? *Ethnic and Racial Studies*, 36, 1, 9–27

Ahmad, F, 2001, Modern traditions? British Muslim women and academic achievement, *Gender and Education*, 13, 2, 137–52

Ahmad, F, 2003, Still 'in progress'? Methodological dilemmas, tensions and contradictions in theorizing South Asian Muslim women, in N Puwar and P Raghuram, eds, *South Asian women in the diaspora*, New York, Berg

Ahmad, F, 2012, Graduating towards marriage? Attitudes towards marriage and relationships among university-educated British Muslim women, *Culture and Religion, An Interdisciplinary Journal*, 13, 2, 193-210

Ahmed, L, 1992, *Women and gender in Islam: historical roots of a modern debate*, New Haven, Yale University Press

Ahmed, S, 2000, *Strange encounters: embodied others in post-coloniality*, Oxford, Routledge

Ahmed, S, 2004a, Declarations of whiteness: the non-performativity of antiracism, *Borderlands Journal*, 3, 2

Ahmed, S, 2004b, *The cultural politics of emotion*, Edinburgh, Edinburgh University Press

Ahmed, N, 2008, Language, gender and citizenship: obstacles in the path to learning English for Bangladeshi women in London's East End, *Sociological Research Online*, 13, 5, 12

Al-Ali, N, 2014 From Germany to Iraq via WAF: a political journey in Dhaliwal, S, Yuval-Davis, N, *Women against fundamentalism: Stories of dissent and solidarity*, London, Lawrence and Wishart, 182-195

Alexander, CE, 1996, *The art of being black: the creation of black British youth identities*, Oxford and New York, Clarendon Press

Alexander, CE, 2000, *The Asian gang: ethnicity, identity, masculinity*, Oxford, Berg

Ali, N, Kalra, VS, Sayyid, S, 2008, *A postcolonial people: South Asians in Britain*, New York City, Columbia University Press

Ali, SR, Mahmood, A, Moel, J, Hudson, C, Leathers, L, 2008, A qualitative investigation of Muslim and Christian women's views of religion and feminism in their lives, *Cultural Diversity and Ethnic Minority Psychology*, 14, 1, 38

Ali, S, 2006, Racializing research: managing power and politics? *Ethnic and Racial Studies*, 29, 3, 471–86

Alibhai-Brown, Y, 2000, It may be undemocratic, but we need positive discrimination, *The Independent*, 26 September 2000 http://www.independent.co.uk/voices/commentators/yasmin-alibhai-brown/it-may-be-undemocratic-but-we-need-positive-discrimination-701420.html

Alibhai-Brown, Y, 2015, The jihadi girls are just part of a long line attracted to mad, bad men, *The Independent,* 22 February 2015 http://www.independent.co.uk/voices/comment/the-jihadi-girls-are-just-part-of-a-long-line-attracted-to-mad-bad-men-10062909.html

Allen, C, Guru, S, Between political fad and political empowerment: a critical evaluation of the National Muslim Womens Advisory Group, NMWAG, and governmental processes of engaging Muslim women, *University of Birmingham Sociological Research Online*, 17, 3, 17, www.socresonline.org.uk/17/3/17.html

Allen, C, Isakjee, A, Ögtem Young, Ö, 2013, *'Maybe we are hated': the experience and impact of anti-Muslim hate on British Muslim women*, Birmingham, University of Birmingham

Alvesson, M, Skoldberg, K, 2009, *Reflexive methodology: new vistas for qualitative research*, London, Sage

Ameli, SR, Merali, A, 2006, *Hijab, meaning, identity, otherization and politics: British Muslim women*, London, IHRC

Amin, A, 2002, Ethnicity and the multicultural city: living with diversity, *Environment and Planning*, 34, 6, 959–80

Andersen, J and Siim B, eds, 2004, *The politics of inclusion and empowerment: gender, class and citizenship*, Basingstoke, Palgrave Macmillan

Anderson, B, 2006, *Imagined communities: reflections on the origin and spread of nationalism*, London and New York, Verso

Anitha, S, 2008, Neither safety nor justice: the UK government response to domestic violence against immigrant women, *Journal of Social Welfare and Family Law*, 30, 3, 189–202

Ansari, H, 2004, *The infidel within: the history of Muslims in Britain, 1800 to the present*, London, C Hurst & Co

Anthias, F, Yuval-Davis, N, 1992, *Racialized boundaries: race, nation, gender, colour and class and the anti-racist struggle*, London and New York, Routledge

Archer, L, 2003, *Race, masculinity and schooling, Muslim boys and education*, Maidenhead, McGraw-Hill and Open University Press

Arendt, H, 1970, *On violence*, New York, Houghton Mifflin Harcourt Publishing Company

Armstrong, S, 2002, *Veiled threat: the hidden power of the women of Afghanistan*, New York, Four Walls Eight Windows

Ashe, J, Campbell, R, Childs, S, Evans, E, 2010, Stand by your man: womens political recruitment at the 2010 UK General Election, *British Politics*, 5, 4, 455–80

Associated Press, 2007, Britain stops using 'War on Terror' phrase, *NBC News* 16 April 2007 http://www.nbcnews.com/id/18133506/#.Vt7-NEKLSM9

Back, L, Keith, M, Khan, A, Shukra, K, Solomos, J, 2009, Islam and the new political landscape: faith communities, political participation and social change, *Theory, Culture, Society*, 26, 4, 1–23

Bano, S, 2012, *An exploratory study of Shariah councils in England with respect to family law*, Reading, University of Reading, http://wap.rdg.ac.uk/web/FILES/law/An_exploratory_study_of_Shariah_councils_in_England_with_respect_to_family_law_.pdf

Basit, TN, 1997a, *Eastern values, Western milieu: Identities and aspirations of adolescent British Muslim girls*, Aldershot, Ashgate

Basit, TN, 1997b, I want more freedom, but not too much: British Muslim girls and the dynamism of family values, *Gender and Education*, 9, 4, 425–39

Batliwala, S, 1994, The meaning of women's empowerment: new concepts from action in G Sen, A Germain, LC Chen, eds *Population policies reconsidered: health, empowerment, and rights* Boston, Massachusetts, Harvard University, Harvard Center for Population and Development Studies

- See more at: http://www.popline.org/node/288048#sthash.HC8iwSjJ.dpuf

Batty, D, 2006, Reid barracked during speech to Muslim parents, *The Guardian*, 20 September 2006 http://www.theguardian.com/world/2006/sep/20/terrorism.immigrationpolicy

Baumann, G, 1996, *Contesting culture: discourses of identity in multi-ethnic London, Vol 100*, Cambridge, Cambridge University Press

Bawer, B, 2006, *While Europe slept*, New York, Double Day

BBC, 2007, Marriage visa age to rise to 21, *BBC News,* 28 March 2007 http://news.bbc.co.uk/1/hi/uk_politics/6501451.stm

BBC, 2009, MP defends Muslim wedding walkout, *BBC News,* 14 August 2009 http://news.bbc.co.uk/1/hi/england/london/8201461.stm

BBC, 2010a, Belgium veil ban debate in doubt amid political crisis, *BBC News*, 22 April 2010 http://news.bbc.co.uk/1/hi/world/europe/8636605.stm

BBC, 2010b, French parliament debates Islamic veil ban, *BBC News,* 6 July 2010 http://www.bbc.co.uk/news/10517707

Beck, U, 1992, *Risk society: towards a new modernity*, London, Sage

Bhatt, C, 2004, Contemporary geopolitics and 'alterity' research, in M Bulmer and J Solomos, eds, *Researching race and racism*, London, Routledge

Bhattacharyya, G, 2008, *Dangerous brown men: exploiting sex, violence and feminism in the war on terror*, London, Zed Books

Beckett, C, Macey, M, 2001, Race, gender and sexuality: the oppression of multiculturalism, *Womens Studies International Forum*, 24, 3, 309–19

Begum, H, 2008, Geographies of inclusion/exclusion: British Muslim women in the East End of London, *Sociological Research Online*, 13, 5, 10, www.socresonline.org.uk/13/5/10.html.

Blair, T, 2006, Our Nation's Future–multiculturalism and integration. Speech at 10 Downing Street 8 December, Available at: http://tna.europarchive.org/20070305112605/http:/www.pm.gov.uk/output/Page10563.asp (accessed 6 March 2016)

Blair, T, 2007a, What I've learned: Tony Blair reflects on the lessons of his decade as Britain's Prime Minister, *The Economist*31 May 2007

Blair, T, 2007b A battle for global values, *Foreign Affairs* 86, 1,79 https://www.foreignaffairs.com/articles/2007-01-01/battle-global-values

Blears, H, 2009, Many voices: understanding the debate about preventing violent extremism. Lecture at the London School of Economics, 25 February http://www.lse.ac.uk/assets/richmedia/channels/publicLecturesAndEvents/transcripts/20090225_HazelBlears_tr.pdf

Bloch, A, 2000, Refugee settlement in Britain: the impact of policy on participation, *Journal of Ethnic and Migration Studies*, 26, 1, 75–88

Blunkett, D, 2009 Don't let the families of immigrants flock here in a free-for-all, *The Sun* 28 July 2009

Booth, R, Chrisafis, A, Finn, T, Marsh, K, Sherwood, H, Rice, X, 2011, Women have emerged as key players in the Arab spring, *The Guardian,* 22 April 2011 http://www.theguardian.com/world/2011/apr/22/women-arab-spring

Brah, A, 1992, Women of South Asian origin in Britain: issues and concerns, in P Braham, A Rattansi and R Skellinton, eds, *Racism and anti-racism: inequalities, opportunities and policies*, London, Sage

Brah, A, 1996, *Cartographies of diaspora*, London, Routledge

Brah, A, 1999, The scent of memory: strangers, our own, and others, *Feminist Review*, 61, 1, 4–26

Brah, A, Minhas, R, 1985, Structural racism or cultural conflict: Asian girls in British schools, in G Weiner, ed, *Just a Bunch of Girls*, Milton Keynes, Open University Press

Brah, A, Phoenix, A, 2004, Ain't I a woman? Revisiting intersectionality, *Journal of International Womens Studies*, 5, 3, 75-86

Branigan, T, 2004, Tale of rape at the temple sparks riot at theatre, *The Guardian,* 20 December 2004, http://www.theguardian.com/uk/2004/dec/20/arts.religion

Briggs, R, Birdwell, J, 2009, Radicalisation among Muslims in the UK, *MICROCON Policy Working Paper* 7, Brighton, MICROCON

Brittain, E, Dustin, H, Pearce, C, Rake, K, Siyunyi-Silwe, M, Sullivan, F, 2005, *Black and minority ethnic women in the UK*, London, Fawcett Society

Brown, G, 2004, The golden thread that runs through our history, *The Guardian* 8 July 2004 http://www.theguardian.com/politics/2004/jul/08/britishidentity.economy

Brown, G, 2006a, *Moving Britain forward, Selected speeches, 1997–2006*, London, Bloomsbury UK

Brown, G, 2009, It IS great to be British: Gordon Brown reminds us Brits why we should be so proud of coming from these great isles, *The Daily Mail*, 4 April 2009 http://www.dailymail.co.uk/debate/article-1176983/It-IS-great-British-Gordon-Brown-reminds-Brits-proud-coming-great-isles.html

Brown, K, 2006b, Realising Muslim women's rights: the role of Islamic identity among British Muslim women, *Womens Studies International Forum*, 29, 417–430

Brown, K, 2008, The promise and perils of women's participation in UK mosques: the impact of securitisation agendas on identity, gender and community, *British Journal of Politics & International Relations*, 10, 3, 472–91

Brown, K, 2013, Gender and counter-radicalization: women and emerging counter-terror measures, in ML Satterthwaite and JC Huckerby, eds, *Gender, National Security, and Counter-Terrorism: Human Rights Perspectives*, New York, Routledge

Brown, K, 2014, Analysis: Why are Western women joining Islamic State? *BBC News*, 6 October 2014 http://www.bbc.co.uk/news/uk-29507410

Brubaker, R, 2002, Ethnicity without groups, *Archives européennes de sociologie*, 43, 2, 163–89

Bujra, JM, Pearce, J, 2011, *Saturday night and Sunday morning: the 2001 Bradford riot and beyond*, Skipton, Vertical Editions

Bullock, K, 2002, *Rethinking Muslim women and the veil*, London, ITT

Bulmer, M, Solomos, J, 2004, *Researching race and racism*, London, Routledge

Burchill, J, 2010, Poor Lauren Booth: she would do anything to get in with the tough kids *The Independent* 26 October 2010 http://www.independent.co.uk/voices/columnists/julie-burchill/julie-burchill-poor-lauren-booth-ndash-she-would-do-anything-to-get-in-with-the-tough-kids-2117219.html

Burke, J, 2006, Britain stops talk of 'war on terror', *The Observer* 10 December 2006 http://www.theguardian.com/politics/2006/dec/10/uk.terrorism

Burlet, S, Reid, H, 1998, A gendered uprising: political representation and minority ethnic communities, *Ethnic and Racial Studies*, 21, 2, 270–87

Butler, J, 1998, Subjects of sex/gender/desire, in A Phillips, ed, *Feminism and Politics*, New York, Oxford University Press

Butler, J, 2004, *Precarious life: the powers of mourning and violence*, London, Verso

Butler, T, Hamnett, C, Mir, S, 2011, *Ethnicity, Class and Aspiration: understanding London's New East End*, Bristol, Policy Press

Cable, V, 2010, A Minefield of Myths called Immigration, The *Daily Mail*, 19 April 2010 http://www.dailymail.co.uk/debate/article-1227829/VINCE-CABLE-A-minefield-myths-called-immigration.html

Cameron, D, 2001, *Working with spoken discourse*, London, Sage

Campbell, B, 1984, *Wigan Pier revisited*, London, Virago

Cantle, T, 2001, *Community cohesion: a report of the independent review team*, London, Home Office, HMSO

Carby, H, 1982, White women listen! Black feminism and the boundaries of sisterhood, in *The Empire Strikes Back*, ed, Centre for Contemporary Cultural Studies, London, Hutchinson

Carter-Wall, C, Whitfield, G, 2012, *The role of aspirations, attitudes and behaviours in closing the educational attainment gap*, York, Joseph Rowntree Foundation

Chandler, D, 2002, *From Kosovo to Kabul: human rights and international intervention*, London, Pluto Press

Chaney, P, 2004, The post-devolution equality agenda: the case of the Welsh Assembly's statutory duty to promote equality of opportunity, *Policy & Politics*, 32, 1, 63–77

Chaney, P, Fevre, R, 2001, Inclusive governance and 'minority' groups: the role of the third sector in Wales, *Voluntas, International Journal of Voluntary and Nonprofit Organizations*, 12, 2, 131–56

Childs, P, Williams, P, 1997, *An introduction to post-colonial theory*, Harlow, Pearson Education Limited

Childs, S, Webb, P, Marthaler, S, 2010, Constituting and substantively representing women: applying new approaches to a UK case study, *Politics and Gender*, 6, 199–223

Choudhury, T, 2007, *The role of Muslim identity politics in radicalisation: a study in progress,* London, Department for Communities and Local Government

Clayton, J, 2009, Thinking spatially: towards an everyday understanding of interethnic relations, *Social and Cultural Geography*, 10, 4, 481–98

Cole, M, 2009, Brutal and stinking and difficult to handle: the historical and contemporary manifestations of racialization, institutional racism, and schooling in Britain, *Race, Ethnicity and Education*, 7, 1, 35–56

Cornwall, A, Gideon, J, Wilson, K, 2008, Introduction: reclaiming feminism, gender and neoliberalism, *IDS Bulletin*, 39, 6, 1-9

D'Souza, S, Clarke, P, 2005, *Made in Britain: inspirational role models from British black and minority ethnic communities*, Harlow, Pearson Education Limited

Dale, A., Shaheen, N., Kalra, V. and Fieldhouse, E., 2000. Routes Into Education and Employment for Young Pakistani and Bangladeshi Women in the UK. Working Paper no 10, Manchester, University of Manchester: ESRC Future of Work Programme

Dale, A, Shaheen, N, Kalra, V, Fieldhouse, E, 2002, Routes into education and employment for young Pakistani and Bangladeshi women in the UK, *Ethnic and Racial Studies*, 25, 6, 942–68

Daly, M, 2011, What adult worker model? A critical look at recent social policy reform in Europe from a gender and family perspective, *Social Politics, International Studies in Gender, State and Society*, 18, 1, 1–23

Darwish, N, 2006, *Now they call me Infidel: why I renounced Jihad for America, Israel, and the war on terror*, Sentinel

Davin, A, 1978, Imperialism and motherhood, *History Workshop*, 5, 9–65

Department for Communities and Local Government (DCLG), 2006, *Engaging with Muslim women: a report from the PMs event on 10 May 2006*, London, DCLG, http://webarchive.nationalarchives.gov.uk/20070506142013/http://www.womenandequalityunit.gov.uk/publications/muslimwomenfeedrep.pdf

DCLG, 2007, *Preventing violent extremism: winning hearts and minds*, London, DCLG

DCLG, 2008a, Gordon Brown launches the Muslim Women's Advisory Group, *DCLG Press Release* 31 January 2008 http://webarchive.nationalarchives.gov.uk/20120919132719/http://www.communities.gov.uk/news/corporate/680335

DCLG, 2008b, *Empowering Muslim women: case studies,* London, DCLG

DCLG, 2009, *Building community resilience: Prevent case studies,* London, DCLG

Dearden, L, 2015, David Cameron extremism speech: Read the transcript in full, *The Independent,* 20 July 2015 http://www.independent.co.uk/news/uk/politics/david-cameron-extremism-speech-read-the-transcript-in-full-10401948.html

Devadason, R, 2010, Cosmopolitanism, geographical imaginaries and belonging in North London, *Urban Studies*, 47, 14, 2945–63

Dhaliwal, S, Patel, P, 2006, Multiculturalism in secondary schools: managing conflicting demands, *Report on A Pilot Project*, London, Working Lives Research Institute, London Metropolitan University, http://www.southallblacksisters.org.uk/reports/multiculturalism-in-secondary-schools-report/

Dhaliwal, S, Yuval-Davis, N, 2014, *Women against fundamentalism: Stories of dissent and solidarity, London*, Lawrence and Wishart

Dixon, P, 2009, Hearts and minds? British counter-insurgency from Malaya to Iraq, *The Journal of Strategic Studies*, 32, 3, 353–81

Donohoue Clyne, I, 2002, Muslim women: some Western fictions, in H Jawad and T Benn , eds, *Muslim women in the United Kingdom and beyond: experiences and images*, Leiden, Brill

Dovi, S, 2007, *The Good Representative*, Oxford, Blackwell Publishing

Dugan, E, 2015, Forced marriage: Asian victims being put at risk by closures of services set up to protect them, *The Independent,* 21 July 2015 http://www.independent.co.uk/news/uk/home-news/forced-marriage-asian-victims-being-put-at-risk-by-closures-of-services-set-up-to-protect-them-10405731.html

Dustin, M, Phillips A, 2004, UK initiatives on forced marriage, regulation, dialogue and exit, *Political Studies*, 52, 3, 531-51

Dustin, M, Phillips, A, 2008, Whose agenda is it? Abuses of women and abuses of culture in Britain, *Ethnicities*, 8, 3, 405–24
Dwyer, C, 1999a, Contradictions of community: questions of identity for young British Muslim women, *Environment and Planning*, 31, 53–68
Dwyer, C, 1999b, Veiled meanings: young British Muslim women and the negotiation of differences [1], *Gender, Place & Culture*, 6, 1 , 5–26
Dwyer, C, 2000, Negotiating diasporic identities: young British South Asian Muslim women, *Womens Studies International Forum*, 23, 4, 475–86
Eade, J, Garbin, D, 2002, Changing narratives of violence, struggle and resistance: Bangladeshis and the competition for resources in the global city, *Oxford Development Studies*, 30, 2, 137–49
Edley, N, Wetherell, M, 2001, Jekyll and Hyde: men's constructions of feminism and feminists, *Feminism & Psychology*, 11, 4, 439–57
El-Affendi, AA, 2009, *Contextualising Islam in Britain: exploratory perspectives*, Cambridge, Centre of Islamic Studies https://www.exeter.ac.uk/media/universityofexeter/webteam/shared/pdfs/misc/Contextualising_Islam_in_Britain.pdf
El Saadawi, N, 2007, *The hidden face of Eve: women in the Arab world*, London, Zed Books
Enloe, C, 1990, Women and children: making feminist sense of the Persian Gulf war, *Village Voice*, 25 September
EOC (Equal Opportunities Commission), 2007, *Moving on up? The way forward: report of the EOC's investigation into Bangladeshi, Pakistani and Black Caribbean women and work*, Manchester, Equal Opportunities Commission
Equal to the Occasion (ETTO), 2010 *"Our choices" New careers for Muslim women Evaluation of role models roadshow, 2009-10,* Equal to the Occasion
Esterberg, KG, 2002, *Qualitative methods in social research*, Boston, McGraw Hill
Ette, M, 2007, Empowerment, in G Blakely and V Bryson , eds, *The impact of feminism on political concepts and debates,* Manchester, Manchester University Press, 146-161
EWHC (England and Wales High Court), 2008, Kaur and Shah v London Borough of Ealing Judgement 28 July 2008, Neutral Citation Number: [2008] EWHC 2062 (Admin), case number CO/3880/2008 http://www.southallblacksisters.org.uk/savesbs.htm
Fairclough, N, 2001, The discourse of New Labour: critical discourse analysis, in M Wetherell, S Taylor and SJ Yates, eds, *Discourse as Data, A Guide for Analysis*, London: Sage, 229-266

Fallaci, O, 2002, *The rage and the pride*, New York, Rizzoli
Fanon, F, 1968, *The wretched of the Earth*, New York, Grove Press
Fernandez, S, 2009, The crusade over the bodies of women, *Patterns of Prejudice*, 43, 3–4, 269–86
Finney, N, Simpson, L, 2009, *Sleepwalking to segregation? Challenging myths about race and migration*, Bristol, Policy Press
Flint, J, Robinson, D, 2008, *Community cohesion in crisis: new dimensions of diversity*, Bristol, Policy Press
Forcey, LR, 1994, Feminist perspectives on mothering and peace, in EN Glenn, G Chang and LR Forcey, eds, *Mothering, ideology, experience and agency*, London and New York, Routledge
Fortier, A, 2005, Pride, politics and multiculturalist citizenship, *Ethnic and racial studies*, 28, 3, 559–78
Fortier A, 2010, Proximity by design? Affective citizenship and the management of unease, *Citizenship Studies*, 14, 1, 17–30
Franzen, A, Hangartner, D, 2006, Market outcomes: the non-monetary benefits of social capital, *European Sociological Review*, 22, 4, 353-368
Fraser, N, 1989, *Unruly practices, power discourse and gender in contemporary social theory*, Cambridge, Polity Press
Fraser, N, 2000, Rethinking recognition, *New Left Review*, 3, 107– 20
Fraser, N, 2009, Feminism, capitalism and the cunning of history, *New Left Review*, 56, 2, 97–117
Frisch, M, 1986, *Herr Biedermann und die Brandstifter*, London, Methuen & Co. Ltd
Furbey, R, Dinham, A, Farnell, R., Finneron, D, Wilkinson, G, 2006, *Faith as social capital, connecting or dividing?* Bristol, Policy Press
Garner, S, Cowles, J, Lung, B, Stott, M, 2009, *Sources of resentment, and perceptions of ethnic minorities among poor white people in England*, London, Communities and Local Government
Giddens, A, 1991, *Modernity and self-identity: self and society in the late modern age*, Stanford, CA, Stanford University Press
Gill, R, Koffman, O, 2013, The revolution will be led by a 12–year–old girl: girl power and global biopolitics, *Feminist Review*, 105, 83–102
Gillies, V, 2007, *Marginalised mothers: exploring working-class experiences of parenting*, Abingdon and New York, Routledge
Gilroy, P, 2000, *Ain't no black in the Union Jack*, Oxford, Routledge
Gilroy, P, 2004, *After empire*, London, Routledge
Gilroy, P, 2005, Melancholia or conviviality: the politics of belonging in Britain, *Soundings*, 29, 1, 35-46

Githens-Mazer, J, 2010, 'Radicalisation via YouTube'? It's not so simple, *The Guardian*, 4 November 2010 http://www.theguardian.com/commentisfree/2010/nov/04/youtube-radicalisation-roshonara-choudhry

Glenn, EN, 1994, Social constructions of mothering: a thematic overview, in EN Glenn, G Chang and L Rennie Forcey, eds, *Mothering, ideology, experience, and agency*, London, Routledge

Gohir, S, 2008, Muslim women's voice will be heard in debate, *Birmingham Post*, 26 March http://www.birminghampost.co.uk/news/local-news/muslim-womens-voice-heard-debate-3963021

Granovetter, MS, 1973, The strength of weak ties, *American Journal of Sociology*, 78, 6, 1360-1380

Grewal, I, 2003, Transnational America: race, gender and citizenship after 9/11, *Social Identities*, 9, 4, 535-561

Griffin, P, 2007, Neoliberalism and the World Bank: economic discourse and the (re)production of gendered identity(ies) in policy, *Futures in Education*, 5, 2, 226-238

Gupta, R, ed, 2003, *From homebreakers to jailbreakers*, London, Zed Books

Gupta, R, 2009, We don't need Hegel: the burka is a cloth soaked in blood, *The Guardian*, 8 July 2009

Hacking, I, 1999, *The social construction of what*, Cambridge, Harvard University Press

Hajdukowski-Ahmed, M, Khanlou, N, Moussa, H, 2008, *Not born a refugee woman: contesting identities, rethinking practices*, New York, Berghahn

Hall, S, 1992 "The West and the Rest: Discourse and power." *The Indigenous Experience: Global Perspectives* (1992): 165-173.

Hall, S, 1997, *Representation, cultural representation and signifying practices*, London, Sage Publications Limited

Hall S, Du Gay, P, eds, 1996, *Questions of cultural identity*, London, Sage Publications Limited

Hansard, 2005, HL Deb Vol 676 Col 1418-1454, 15 December 2005 http://www.publications.parliament.uk/pa/ld200506/ldhansrd/vo051215/text/51215-16.htm

Harding, S, 1987, Introduction: is there a feminist method? in S Harding, ed, *Feminism and Methodology*, Indiana, Indiana University Press, 1-14

Hari, J, 2008, Dare we stand up for Muslim women? The Independent 28 October 2008

Hartsock, NCM, 1983, The feminist standpoint: developing the ground for a specifically feminist historical materialism in S Harding, ed, *Feminism and Methodology*, Indiana, Indiana University Press, 158-180

Hasan, M, 1997, *Legacy of a divided nation: India's Muslims since independence*, London, Hurst

Haw, KF, 1994, Muslim girls' schools – a conflict of interests? *Gender and Education*, 6, 1, 63–76

Haw, K, Shah, S, Hanifa, M, 1998, *Educating Muslim girls: shifting discourses*, Buckingham, Open University Press

Hewitt, R, 2005, *White backlash and the politics of multiculturalism*, Cambridge, Cambridge University Press

Hirsi Ali, A, 2006, *The caged virgin: a Muslim woman's cry for reason*, London, The Free Press

Hirsi Ali, A, 2007, *Infidel*, London, The Free Press

Hirsi Ali, A, 2010, *Nomad: From Islam to America,* New York, FreePress

HM Government , 2008, *The Prevent Strategy: a guide for local partners in England*, London, HM Government

HM Government , 2015, *Counter-Extremism Strategy,* London, HM Government

Honig, B, 1999, My culture made me do it, in SM Okin, M Howard, J Cohen, M Nussbaum, eds, *Is multiculturalism bad for women? Susan Moller Okin with respondents*, Princeton, Princeton University Press

Hopkins, P, 2008, Politics, race and nation: the difference that Scotland makes, in C Dwyer and C Bressey, eds, *New geographies of race and racism*, Ashgate, Aldershot, 113-24

Howarth, D, Stavrakakis, Y, 2000, Introducing discourse theory and political analysis, in D Howarth, J Aletta Norval and Y Stavrakakis, eds, *Discourse theory and political analysis, identities, hegemonies, and social change*, Manchester, Manchester University Press, 1-23

Hughes, J , 2005, Analyzing women's experiences: race, social difference, and violence against women, in GJ Sefa Dei and GS Johal, eds, *Critical issues in antiracist research methodologies*, New York, P Lang

Huntington, SP, 1993, The clash of civilizations, *Foreign Affairs*, 72, 22-49

Husband, C, Alam, Y, 2011, *Social cohesion and counter-terrorism: a policy contradiction*, Bristol, Policy Press

Hussain, S, 2008, *Muslims on the map: a national survey of social trends in Britain*, London, I B Tauris & Co

Iglesias, I, 1996, Vergüenza Ajena, in H Rom Harré and W Gerrod Parrot, eds, *The emotions: social, cultural and biological dimensions*, London, Sage, 122-31

Ijaz, A, Abbas, T, 2010, The impact of generational change on the attitudes of working class South Asian Muslim parents on the education of their daughters, *Gender and Education*, 22, 3, 313–26

Inglehart, R, Norris, P, 2003, The true clash of civilizations, *Foreign Policy*, 135, 62–70

Itkowitz, C, 2015, CNN: Islamic State uses Nutella and kittens to entice female recruits, *The Washington Post,* 18 February 2015 https://www.washingtonpost.com/blogs/in-the-loop/wp/2015/02/18/cnn-islamic-state-uses-nutella-and-kittens-to-entice-female-recruits/

Jacobson, J, 1998, *Islam in transition: religion and identity among British Pakistani youth*, London, Routledge

Jayawardena, K, 1995, *The white woman's other burden*, London, Routledge

Jefferson, M, 1983 Turban or not Turban- That is the Question (Mandla v Dowell), *Liverpool Law Review*, 5, 1, 75-90

Joly, D, 1995, *Britannia's crescent: making a place for Muslims in British society*, Aldershot, Avebury

Jones, H, 2013, *Negotiating cohesion, inequality and change,* Bristol, Policy Press

Kabeer, N, 1999, Resources, agency, achievements: reflection on the measurement of womens empowerment, *Development and Change*, 30, 435–64

Kandiyoti, D, 1988, Bargaining with patriarchy, *Gender and Society*, 2, 3, 274–90

Kearns, A, Forrest, R, 2000, Social cohesion and multilevel urban governance, *Urban Studies*, 37, 5–6, 995–1017

Kellner, D, 2012, The dark side of the spectacle: terror in Norway and the UK riots, *Cultural Politics*, 8, 1, 1–43

Kelly, L, 1987, The continuum of sexual violence, in J Hanmer and M Maynard , eds, *Women, violence and social control*, Basingstoke, Macmillan

Khan, S, 2006, Muslims! in N Ali, N Kalra and VS Sayid, eds, *A postcolonial people, South Asians in Britain*, London, C Hurst & Co

Khan, MG, 2010, No innocents: Muslims in the Prevent strategy, in S Sayyid and A Vakil , eds, *Thinking through Islamophobia: global perspectives*, New York, Columbia University Press, 85-92

Khan, S, 2009, Speech at the Inspire conference Muslim Women: Pioneering Change in 21st Century Britain (The London Muslim Centre, January 2009) only available online at https://www.youtube.com/watch?v=n3oFdhE0oPQ

Khan, S, 2015, Please can I tell you about a child who is Muslim? Media Diversified, 26 May, http://mediadiversified.org/2015/05/26/please-can-i-tell-you-about-a-child-who-is-muslim/

Khan, S, Katwala, S, Jameson, H, 2008, Fairness not favours: how to reconnect with British Muslims, *Fabian Society*, 624

Khattab, N, 2009, Ethno-religious background as a determinant of education and occupational attainment in Britain, *Sociology*, 42, 2, 304–22

Khattab, N, 2012, Winners and losers: the impact of education, ethnicity and gender on Muslims in the British Labour market, *Work Employment & Society*, 26, 4, 556–73

Kulz, C, Rashid, N, 2014, Education and the prevent agenda: mythmaking and the limits of freedom, *Discover Society,* issue 11

Kumar, D, 2012, *Islamophobia and the Politics of Empire*, Chicago, Haymarket Books

Kundnani, A, 2002a, The death of multiculturalism, *Race & Class*, 43, 4, 67–72

Kundnani, A, 2002b, An unholy alliance? Racism, religion and communalism, *Race & class*, 44, 2, 71–80

Kundnani, A, 2007, *The end of tolerance: racism in 21st century Britain*, London, Pluto Press

Kundnani, A, 2009, *Spooked: how not to prevent violent extremism*, London, Institute of Race Relations

Kundnani, A, 2014, *The Muslims are coming: islamophobia, exremism and the domestic war on terror*, London, Verso

Kurtz, LR, 2007, *Gods in the global village: the world's religions in sociological perspective*, California, Pine Forge Press

Kymlicka, W, 1995, *The rights of minority cultures*, Oxford, Oxford University Press

Ladner, JA, 1987, Introduction to tomorrow's tomorrow: the black woman, in S Harding, ed, *Feminism and methodology*, Indiana, Indiana University Press

Lawrence, E, 1982, Just plain common sense: the roots of racism, in Centre for Contemporary Cultural Studies, *The Empire Strikes Back*, London, Hutchinson

Lazar, M, 2005, Politicizing gender in discourse: feminist critical discourse analysis as political perspective and praxis, in M Lazar, ed, *Feminist critical discourse analysis: gender, power and ideology in discourse*, Basingstoke and New York, Palgrave Macmillan, 1-28

Lazreg, M, 1994, *The eloquence of silence: Algerian women in question*, New York, Routledge

Lele, J, 1993, Orientalism and the social sciences, in CA Breckenridge and P Van der Veer, eds, *Orientalism and the postcolonial predicament: perspectives on South Asia*, Philadelphia, University of Pennsylvania Press

Letherby, G, 2003, *Feminist research in theory and practice*, Buckingham, Open University Press

Levine, P, ed, 2004, *Gender and empire*, Oxford, Oxford University Press

Lewis, P, 2007, *Young, British and Muslim*, London, Continuum International Publishing Group

Lovenduski, J, Norris, P, 2003, Westminster women: the politics of presence, *Political Studies*, 51, 84–102

Macey, M, 1999, Class, gender and religious influences on changing patterns of Pakistani Muslim male violence in Bradford, *Ethnic and Racial Studies*, 22, 845–66

Macey, M, 2009, *Multiculturalism, religion and women: doing harm by doing good*, Basingstoke, Palgrave MacMillan

Maher, S, Frampton, M, 2009, *Choosing our friends wisely*, London, Policy Exchange

Mahmood, S, 2005, *Politics of piety: the Islamic revival and the feminist subject*, Princeton, Princeton University Press

Malik, K, 2009, *From Fatwa to Jihad: the Rushdie affair and its legacy*, London, Atlantic Books

Mamdani, M, 2005a, *Good Muslim, bad Muslim: America, the Cold War, and the roots of terror*, New York, Three Leaves Press

Mamdani, M, 2005b, Whither political Islam? Understanding the Modern Jihad, *Foreign Affairs*, 84, 1, 148–155

Mamon, S, 2011, Enrolment falls as EMA withdrawn, *Institute of Race Relations* 4 November 2011 http://www.irr.org.uk/news/enrolment-falls-as-ema-withdrawn/

Mani, L, 1998, *Contentious traditions: the debate on colonial Sati in India*, London, University of California Press

Mansbridge, J, 2009. A "Selection Model" of Political Representation* *Journal of Political Philosophy*, 17, 4, 369-398

Marston, G, 2004, *Social policy and discourse analysis: policy change in public housing*, Aldershot, Ashgate

McGhee, D, 2005, Patriots of the future? A critical examination of community cohesion strategies, *Contemporary Britain Sociological Research Online*, 10, 3, www.socresonline.org.uk/10/3/mcghee.html

McGovern, M, 2010, *Countering terror or counter-productive? Comparing Irish and British Muslim experiences of counter-insurgency law and policy*, Liverpool, Edge Hill University

McLintock, A, 1995, *Imperial leather: race, gender and sexuality in the colonial contest*, London, Routledge
McLoughlin, S, Cesari, J, 2005, *European Muslims and the secular state*, Aldershot, Ashgate
McRobbie, A, 2009, *The aftermath of feminism: gender, culture and social change*, London, Sage
Meer, N, Dwyer, C, Modood, T, 2010, Embodying nationhood? Conceptions of British national identity, citizenship, and gender in the veil affair, *The Sociological Review*, 58, 1, 84–111
Meetoo, V, Mirza, H, 2007, There is nothing honourable about honour killings: gender, violence and the limits of multiculturalism, *Womens Studies International Forum*, 30, 187–200
Mercer, K, 1994, *Welcome to the jungle: new positions in black cultural studies*, London, Routledge
Mernissi, F, 1985, *Beyond the veil, Male–female dynamics in modern Muslim society*, London, Al Saqi Books
Miah, S, 2012, School desegregation and the politics of forced integration, *Race and Class*, 54, 2, 26–38
Midgley, C, 2007, *Feminism and empire: women activists in imperial Britain, 1790–1865*, Abingdon, Routledge
Miles, T, 2015, U.N. rights chief calls Hungary callous, xenophobic, anti-Muslim, *Reuters*, 17 September 2015 http://uk.reuters.com/article/uk-europe-migrants-hungary-zeid-idUKKCN0RH21L20150917
Mirza, HS, 1992, *Young, female and black*, London, Routledge
Mirza, H, 2015, Dangerous Muslim girls? Race, gender and Islamophobia in British schools in C Alexander, D Weekes-Bernard, Arday, J, eds, *The Runnymede School Report, Race, Education and Inequality in Contemporary Britain*, London, Runnymede Trust Mirza, M, Senthikumaran, A, Jafar, Z, 2007, *Living together apart: British Muslims and the paradox of multiculturalism*, London, Policy Exchange
Misra, M, 2007, *Vishnu's crowded temple: India since the great rebellion*, London, Penguin
Modood, T, 1992, British Muslims and the Rushdie affair, in J Donald and A Rattansi, eds, *Race, culture and difference*, London, Sage
Modood, T, 2003, Muslims and the politics of difference, *Political Quarterly*, 74, 1, 100–15
Modood, T, 2005, *Multicultural politics, racism, ethnicity and Muslims in Britain*, Edinburgh, Edinburgh University Press
Modood, T, 2007, *Multiculturalism*, Cambridge, Polity Press
Modood, T, 2010, From multiculturalism to multifaithism? A panel debate, *Studies in Ethnicity and Nationalism*, 10, 2, 307

Moghissi, H, 1999, *Feminism and Islamic fundamentalism: the limits of postmodern analysis*, London, Zed Books

Mohanty, CT, 1988, Under Western eyes: feminist scholarship and colonial discourses, *Feminist Review*, 30, 61–88

Mohanty, CT, 2003, *Feminism without borders: Decolonizing Theory, Practicing Solidarity*, London and Durham, Duke University Press

Monshipouri, M, Karbasioun, K, 2003, Shaping cultural politics in the Muslim world: women's empowerment as an alternative to militarism, terror, and war, *International Politics*, 40, 3, 341–64

Morris, N, 2015, David Cameron: Some Muslim communities 'quietly condone' extremist ideology – instead of confronting it, *The Independent,* 18 June 2015 http://www.independent.co.uk/news/uk/politics/david-cameron-some-muslim-communities-quietly-condone-extremist-ideology-instead-of-confronting-it-10330054.html

Nandy, A, 1988, *The intimate enemy: loss and recovery of self under colonialism*, New Delhi and New York, Oxford University Press

Naples, N, 2003, *Feminism and method: ethnography, discourse analysis and activist research*, London, Routledge

Narayan, U, 1997, *Dislocating cultures, identities, traditions, and third-world feminism*, New York, Routledge

Narayan, U, 2000, Essence of culture and a sense of history: a feminist critique of cultural essentialism in U Narayan, S Harding, *Decentering the centre,* Bloomington, Indiana University Press

Nickels, HC, Thomas, L, Hickman, MJ, Silvestri, S, 2009, *A comparative study of the representations of 'suspect' communities in multi-ethnic Britain and of their impact on Irish communities and Muslim Communities: mapping newspaper content*, Institute for the Study of European Transformations, ISET, https://metranet.londonmet.ac.uk/fms/MRSite/Research/iset/WP13%20H%20Nickels%203.pdf

O'Hara, M, 2014, *Austerity bites: a journey to the sharp end of cuts in the UK*, Bristol, Policy Press

O'Toole, T, 2015, *Prevent: from hearts and minds to muscular liberalism*, University of Bristol, www.publicspirit.org.uk/assets/OToole.pdf

Oakley, A, 1981, Interviewing women: a contradiction in terms, in H Roberts, *Doing Feminist Research*, London, Routledge

Okin, S, 1999, Is multiculturalism bad for women? in J Cohen, M Howard, MC Nussbaum, eds, *Is multiculturalism bad for women? Susan Moller Okin with respondents*, Princeton, Princeton University Press

Oliverio, A, Lauderdale, P, 2005, Terrorism as deviance or social control: suggestions for future research, *International Journal of Comparative Sociology*, 46, 1–2, 153–69

Omoniyi, T, Fishman, J, 2010, From multiculturalism to multifaithism? A panel debate, *Studies in Ethnicity and Nationalism*, 10, 2, 315
Orwell, G, 1946, Politics and the English language, *Horizon*, 13, 252-65
Paltridge, B, 2007, *Discourse analysis: an introduction*, London, Continuum International Publishing Group
Parker-Jenkins, M, Hartas, D, Irving, B, Barker, V, 1999, Inclusion, exclusion and cultural awareness: Career services supporting the career aspirations of Muslim girls. In European Conference on Educational Research, Lahti, Finland (Vol. 22, p. 25).
Parmar, P, 1982, Gender, race and class: Asian women in resistance, in Centre for Contemporary Cultural Studies, ed, *The empire strikes back: Race and racism in 70s Britain*, London, Hutchinson
Pascall, G, 1997, *Social policy: a new feminist analysis*, London, Routledge
Patel, P, 2008, Faith in the state? Asian women's struggles for human rights in the UK, *Feminist Legal Studies*, 16, 9–36
Patel, P, Bard, J, 2010, From multiculturalism to multifaithism? A panel debate, *Studies in Ethnicity and Nationalism*, 10, 2, 310–14
Peach, C, ed, 2006, *The Ethnic Minority Populations in Britain*, London, HMSO
Peteet, J, 1997, Icons and militants: mothering in the danger zone, *Signs*, 23, 1, 103–29
Phillips, A, 1995, *The politics of presence*, Oxford, Oxford University Press
Phillips, A, 2004, Identity politics: have we had enough now? in J Andersen, B Siim, eds, *The politics of inclusion and empowerment: gender, class and citizenship*, Basingstoke, Palgrave Macmillan
Phillips, A, 2007, *Multiculturalism without culture*, Princeton, Princeton University Press
Phoenix, A, 2004, Extolling eclecticism: language psychoanalysis and demographic analyses in the study of race and racism, in M Bulmer and J Solomos, eds, *Researching race and racism*, London, Routledge
Pilkington, E, 2015, Donald Trump: ban all Muslims entering US, *The Guardian,* 8 December 2015 http://www.theguardian.com/us-news/2015/dec/07/donald-trump-ban-all-muslims-entering-us-san-bernardino-shooting
Pitkin, HF, 1972, *The Concept of Representation*, Oakland, University of California Press
Poole, E, 2002, *Reporting Islam*, London, IB Tauris
Poole, E, Richardson, JE, eds, 2006, *Muslims and the news media*, London, IB Tauris
Powell, A, Lambert-Hurley, S, eds, 2005, *Rhetoric and reality: gender and the colonial experience in South Asia*, Delhi, Oxford University Press

Press Association, 2015, Hate crimes against Muslims soar in London, *The Guardian,* 7 September 2015 http://www.theguardian.com/world/2015/sep/07/hate-crimes-against-muslims-soar-london-islamophobia

Proudman, CR, 2012, The new Muslim suffragettes, *The Independent,* 18 January 2012 http://muslimwomennews.com/n.php?nid=6600

Pryce, K, 1979, *Endless Pressure*, Harmondsworth, Penguin

Puar, JK, Rai, A, 2002, Monster, terrorist, fag: The war on terrorism and the production of docile patriots, *Social Text*, 20(3), 117-148

Puwar, N, 2001, The racialised somatic norm and the senior civil service, *Sociology*, 35, 651–70

Puwar, N, 2003, Melodramatic postures and constructions, in N Puwar and P Raghuram, eds, *South Asian women in the Diaspora,* New York, Berg

Puwar N, Raghuram P, eds, 2003, *South Asian Women in the Diaspora,* New York, Berg

Raco, M, 2009, From expectations to aspirations: state modernisation, urban policy, and the existential politics of welfare in the UK, *Political Geography*, 28, 7, 436–44

Ramazanoglu, C, 1989, *Feminism and the contradictions of oppression,* London and New York, Routledge

Ramdani, N, 2012, The French minister for women has let down Muslim voters, *The Guardian,* 16 July 2012 http://www.theguardian.com/world/2012/jul/16/french-minister-women-muslims

Ramji, H, 2007, Dynamics of religion and gender amongst young British Muslims, *Sociology*, 41, 6, 1171–89

Rao-Middleton, A, 2015, Private firms are profiting from the collective: punishment and surveillance of Muslims in the UK, Media Diversified, http://mediadiversified.org/2015/06/15/when-counter-extremism-policies-target-children-the-fallout-hurts-us-all/

Rashid, N, 2011, En-gendering Britishness: constructing the Muslim Woman in New Labour's social policy agenda, in C Alexander and M James, eds, *New Directions, New Voices*, London, Runnymede Trust

Rawi, M, 2010, Here come the girls: new female party candidates dress to impress in trendy photoshoot, *The Daily Mail*, 14 April 2010

Razack, S, 2008, *Casting out: the eviction of Muslims from Western law and politics*, Toronto, Toronto University Press

Reeves, F, 1983, *British racial discourse: a study of British political discourse about race and race-related matters*, Cambridge, Cambridge University Press

Reid, J, 2006, Speech to Labour Party Conference, *BBC News*, 28 September 2006 http://news.bbc.co.uk/1/hi/uk_politics/5389542.stm

Rhodes, J, 2010, White backlash: unfairness and justifications of British National Party (BNP) support, *Ethnicities*, 10, 1, 77–99

Richardson, JE, 2004a, *(Mis)representing Islam: the racism and rhetoric of British broadsheet newspapers, Vol 9,* Amsterdam, John Benjamins Publishing Company

Richardson, R, ed, 2004b, *Islamophobia: issues, challenges and action; a report*, Trentham

Richmond, AH, 1973, *Migration and race relations in an English city: a study in Bristol*, Oxford, Oxford University Press

Rowlands, J, 1995, Empowerment examined, *Development in Practice*, 5, 2, 101–7

Rowlands, J, 1997, A word of the times, but what does it mean? Empowerment in the discourse and practice of development, in H Afshar, ed, *Women and empowerment: illustrations from the Third World*, New York, St Martins Press

Ruddick, S, 2009, On maternal thinking, *Womens Studies Quarterly*, 37, 3–4, 3–5

Ruggeri, A, 2011, Italy and the Veil, *The Atlantic,* 3 September 2011 http://www.theatlantic.com/international/archive/2011/09/italy-and-the-veil/244502/

Russell, B, 1950, The superior virtue of the oppressed, in *Unpopular Essays*, London, Unwin Hyman

Ruthven, M, 1997, *Islam: a very short introduction*, Oxford, Oxford University Press

Ryan, L, Koffman E, Banfi, L, 2009, *Muslim youth in Barnet: exploring identity, citizenship and belonging locally and the in the wider context, Research Report*, Middlesex University

Sabl, A, 2002, *Ruling passions, political offices and democratic ethics*, Princeton and Oxford, Princeton University Press

Saggar, S, 2000, *Race and representation: electoral politics and ethnic pluralism in Britain*, Manchester, Manchester University Press

Saggar, S, Geddes, A, 2000, A negative and positive racialization: re-examining ethnic minority political representation in the UK, *Journal of Ethnic and Migration Studies*, 26, 1, 24–44

Sahgal, G, Yuval-Davis, N, 1992, *Refusing holy orders: women and fundamentalism in Britain*, London, Virago Press

Said, E, 1978, *Orientalism*, London, Penguin

Said, E, 1997, *Covering Islam: how the media and the experts determine how we see the rest of the world*, New York, Vintage Books

Said, E, 2001, The clash of ignorance, *The Nation*, 4 October 2001, www.thenation.com/article/clash-ignorance/
Sainsbury, D, ed, 1999, *Gender and welfare state regimes*, Oxford, Oxford University Press
Sales, R, 1997, *Women divided: gender, religion, and politics in Northern Ireland*, London, Routledge
Salgado-Pottier, R, 2008, A modern moral panic: the representation of British Bangladeshi and Pakistani youth in relation to violence and religion, *Anthropology Matters*, 10, 1
Samad, Y, Eade, J, 2003, *Community perceptions of forced marriage*, London, London Community Liaison Unit, Foreign and Commonwealth Office
Sandoval, C, 2000, *Methodology of the Oppressed, Vol 18*, Minneapolis, University of Minnesota Press
Sangari, K, Vaid, S, eds, 1989, *Recasting women: essays in colonial history*, New Delhi, Kali for Women
Sanghera GS, Thapar-Björkert, S, 2008, Methodological dilemmas: gatekeepers and positionality in Bradford, *Ethnic and Racial Studies*, 31, 3, 543–62.
Sassen, S, 1999, Culture beyond gender, in J Cohen, M Howard, MC Nussbaum, eds, *Is multiculturalism bad for women? Susan Moller Okin with respondents*, Princeton, Princeton University Press
Sayyid, S, Vakil, A, eds, , 2010, *Thinking through Islamophobia: global perspectives*, New York, Columbia University Press
Scharff, C, 2011, Disarticulating feminism: individualization, neoliberalism and the othering of Muslim women, *European Journal of Womens Studies*, 18, 2, 119–34
Scott, J.W, 2007, *The politics of the veil*, Princeton, Princeton University Press
Shachar, A, 2001, *Multicultural jurisdictions, cultural differences and womens rights*, Cambridge, University of Cambridge
Shukra, K, 1998, *The changing pattern of black politics in Britain*, London, Pluto Press
Sian, KP, 2010, Don't freak, I'm a Sikh! in S Sayyid and A Vakil, eds, *Thinking through Islamophobia: global perspectives*, New York, Columbia University Press
Sian, KP, 2013, *Unsettling Sikh and Muslim conflict: mistaken identities, forced conversions and postcolonial formations*, Lanham, Lexington
Siddiqui, H, 2003, It was written in her kismet: forced marriage, in R Gupta, ed, *From Homebreakers to Jailbreakers: Southall Black Sisters*, London, Zed Books

Siddiqui, H, 2005, There is no 'honour' in domestic violence, only shame! Women's struggles against 'honour' crimes in the UK, in L Welchman and S Hossain, eds, *Honour, crimes, paradigms, and violence against women*, London, Zed Books

Skeggs, B, 1994, Situating the production of feminist ethnography, in M Maynard and J Purvis, eds, *Researching women's lives from a feminist perspective*, London, Taylor & Francis

Solomos, J, 2003, *Race and racism in Britain*, London, Macmillan

Solomos, J, Back, L, 1995, *Race, politics and social change*, London, Routledge

Spivak, GC, 1988, Can the subaltern speak? in C Nelson and L Grossberg, eds, *Marxism and the interpretation of culture*, London, Macmillan

Stacki, SL, Monkman, K, 2003, Change through empowerment processes: Women's stories from South Asia and Latin America. *Compare* 33, 2, 173-189.

Steuter, E, Wills, D, 2008, *At war with metaphor: media, propaganda, and racism in the war on terror*, Plymouth, Lexington Books

Stroschein, S, 2007, Politics is local: ethnoreligious dynamics under the microscope, *Ethnopolitics*, 6, 2, 173–85.

Suzuki, BH, 2002, Revisiting the model minority stereotype: implications for student affairs practice and higher education, *New Directions for Student Services*, 97, 21–32

Talbot, M, 2005, Choosing to refuse to be a victim: power feminism and the intertextuality of victimhood and choice, in M Lazar, ed, *Feminist critical discourse analysis: gender, power and ideology in discourse*, Basingstoke and New York, Palgrave Macmillan

Thapar-Bjorkert, S, Sanghera, G, 2010, Social capital, educational aspiration and young Pakistani Muslim men and women in Bradford, West Yorkshire, *The Sociological Review*, 58, 2, 244-264

Thornton Dill, B, 1987, The dialectics of black womanhood, in S Harding, ed, *Feminism and Methodology*, Indiana, Indiana University Press

Tomlinson, S, 2005, Race, ethnicity and education under New Labour, *Oxford Review of Education*, 31, 153–71.

Tonkiss, F, 1998, Analysing discourse, in C Seale, ed, *Researching culture and society*, London, Sage

Toynbee, P, 2001, Behind the burka, The Guardian 28 September 2001

Travis, A, 2006, Defiant Reid clashes with Islamist radicals, *The Guardian,* 21 September http://www.theguardian.com/politics/2006/sep/21/terrorism.immigrationpolicy

Travis, A, 2015, Universities told counter-terror bill will not endanger freedom of expression, *The Guardian,* 4 February 2015 http://www.theguardian.com/uk-news/2015/feb/04/universities-counter-terror-bill-freedom-expression

UKHL Mandla (Sewa Singh) v Dowell Lee

Urbinati, N, 2000, Representation as advocacy: a study of democratic deliberation, *Political Theory*, 28, 6, 758–86.

Van Schendel, W, 2009, *A History of Bangladesh*, Cambridge, Cambridge University Press

Van Tijk, TA, 2008, *Discourse and power*, Basingstoke and New York, Palgrave Macmillan

Vertigans, S, 2010, British Muslims and the UK Government's War on Terror within: evidence of a clash of civilizations or emergent de-civilizing processes? *The British Journal of Sociology*, 61, 1, 26–44

Vertovec, S, Peach, C, eds, 1997, *Islam in Europe: the Politics of Religion and Community*, Basingstoke, MacMillan

Volpp, L, 2001, Feminism versus multiculturalism, *Colombia Law Review*, 101, 5, 1181–218

Walker, P, 2008, NHS doctor saved from forced marriage gets court safeguards, *The Guardian,* 19 December 2008 http://www.theguardian.com/world/2008/dec/19/humayra-abedin-forced-marriage

Walker, K, 2010, Jack Straw says sorry over Muslim veil comment sparking accusations of political opportunism, *The Daily Mail,* 27 April 2010 http://www.dailymail.co.uk/news/article-1269055/General-Election-2010-Jack-Straw-says-sorry-Muslim-veil.html

Walter, N, 2010, *Living dolls: the return of sexism*, London, Virago

Webster, C, 2003, Race, space and fear: imagined geographies of racism, crime, violence and disorder in Northern England, *Capital and Class*, 27, 2, 95–122

Welchman, L, Hossain, S, eds, 2005, *Honour, crimes, paradigms and violence against women*, London, Zed Books

Werbner, P, 2007, Veiled interventions in pure space: honour shame and embodied struggles among Muslims in Britain and France, *Theory Culture and Society*, 24, 2, 161–86

Williams, MS, 1998, *Voice, trust, and memory: marginalised groups and the failings of liberal representation*, Princeton, Princeton University Press

Williams, M, 2012, Wisconsin Sikh temple shooting: six killed in act of 'domestic terrorism', *The Guardian*, 5 August 2012 http://www.theguardian.com/world/2012/aug/05/wisconsin-sikh-temple-domestic-terrorism

Williams, A, 2015, Separate and isolated: women and cuts to English language classes, *Open Democracy*, 17 August 2015, www.opendemocracy.net/5050/anna-williams/separate-and-isolated-women-and-cuts-to-english-language-classes

Wilson, A, 2006, *Dreams, struggles, questions*, London, Zed Books

Wilson, K, 2008, Reclaiming agency, reasserting resistance, *IDS Bulletin*, 39, 6, 83-91

Winnett, R, 2008, Muslim women recruited to stop extremists, *The Sunday Telegraph*, 7 January.

WLUML (Women Living Under Muslim Law), 2001, Dossier 23/24 July 2001 http://www.wluml.org/node/389

Worley, C, 2005, It's not about race. It's about the community, New Labour and community cohesion, *Critical Social Policy*, 24 , 4, 483–96.

Young, IM, 2000, *Inclusion and democracy*, Oxford, Oxford University Press

Yuval-Davis, N, Anthias, F, 1989, *Woman, nation, state*, Basingstoke, Macmillan

Yuval-Davis, N, 2009, Interview with Professor Nira Yuval Davis: after gender and nation, *Studies, Ethnicity and Nationalism*, 9, 1, 128–38

Yuval-Davis, N, 2011, *The politics of belonging: intersectional contestations*, London, Sage

Zalewski, M, 2000, *Feminism after postmodernism? Theorising through practice*, London, Routledge

Zayzafoon, L, 2005, *The production of the Muslim woman: negotiating text, history, and ideology*, Lanham, Lexington

Index

S

T

U

V

W

Y